The New
Retirement

The New Retirement

FINANCIAL STRATEGIES FOR LIFE AFTER WORK

Dian Cohen

Doubleday Canada Limited

Canadian Cataloguing in Publication Data

Cohen, Dian
    The new retirement

Includes index.
ISBN 0-385-25746-5

1. Retirement income—Planning. 2. Finance, Personal.
3. Retirees—Finance, Personal. I. Title.

HD7129.C63 1999   332.024'01   C98-932845-7

Jacket design by Sonya Thursby/Opus House
Jacket photograph by Ruth Kaplan
Text design by Kim Monteforte/Heidy Lawrance Associates
Printed and bound in Canada

Published in Canada by
Doubleday Canada Limited
105 Bond Street
Toronto, Ontario
M5B 1Y3

FRI   10   9   8   7   6   5   4   3   2   1

For Lisa, Nina and Tamara,
their partners and children,
with love

Contents

Preface

Bookstores are stocked with retirement books. Do we really need another one? Obviously, I think so; far too many retirement and financial planning books are based on ideas that, if followed, will have the retirees eating cat food. Surprised? A lot of what I've found in the course of putting this book together will probably shock you. It may even make you angry. And so it should: revolutions have been fought over less.

The initial impetus for the book came in 1996, when the finance minister stood in the House of Commons to announce that five years hence, in 2001, the pension system in Canada would be reformed. Bits of the old system would be retained, bits dropped, and the emergent legislation was to be called the Seniors' Benefit. For the last ten years, I've had the privilege of writing a column on pensions for Benefits Canada, a Maclean-Hunter magazine, so I came to the announcement with my own ideas on how the system could be improved. The more I looked at the Seniors' Benefit proposal, the less happy I became about the prospect of saving for retirement in Canada. Gradually, as I stepped back from the detailed, technical elements of the pension system to look at the overall design, the need for a book became clear. For what I found is profoundly shocking, because the proposed reform collides so violently with the ability of Canadians to participate in new wealth creation opportunities around the globe.

Fundamentally, our policy makers have ruptured the social contract that binds together the generations of working Canadians in a common future. No longer is it possible for the ordinary

middle-class Canadian to be assured of a retirement based on private savings. As you'll see, only two groups of Canadians can afford to retire when they want to: those with low incomes whom the government will maintain and those with inflation-protected government pensions. Even those with company pensions who are some years from retirement may find their pensions are not as secure as they may think. Why? Behind the design flaws in the pension plans lies the scourge of a tax system that has lost its economic raison d'être, as well as a list of unfunded government commitments that Canada will never be able to meet. I've concluded that Canada's retirement system is a candidate for Emergency Room treatment.

I've spent the last 30 years studying how economies work. Sometimes I've harangued about particular tax policies or immigration regulations or trade rules that prevent the economy from adapting to new conditions, and that put roadblocks in the way of ordinary Canadians to save and invest for their future. Other times I've concentrated on helping people sort through the economic or financial rules and the political rhetoric so they can see a clear path to their goals. It has been both rewarding and frustrating. The rewarding parts are when people tell me I've helped, or when a particularly noxious policy, like the Seniors' Benefit, bites the dust. What is frustrating are the number of rules, regulations and attitudes that still need to change.

In today's waiting-to-be-discovered pension crisis, there are steps you can take to protect yourself. That's the purpose of this book. Part One provides the perspective you need to share in the incredible wealth that is being created globally. Chapter One provides the overview of changes in how the world works now, and how our governments are reacting to what is happening— to our detriment. Chapters Two, Three and Four are more specific in trying to dispel some of the major retirement myths of our time: the myths of the job, viable universal pensions and universal health care.

Part Two works its way through the process of thinking about

retirement—what it means to you, what your plans to date will likely afford you in retirement, and what you should think about if those plans are not what you expected. In other words, what should you know, what attributes should you examine, and what questions should you ask and answer if there's a gap between too-rosy expectations and the practical realities of today and tomorrow? Part Three is the nuts and bolts of getting from theory to reality.

Thirty years of hanging around financial markets have left me with too many people to thank. First, last and always, to my friend Dr. Guy Stanley, Senior Associate, CETAI, l'École des Hautes Études Commerciales, with whom I've collaborated on two books and many other projects. Guy supplied facts, arguments and text for the parts of this book dealing with international trade and investment and the history of financial services. He is a talented historian and the book is richer for his insights. To the masters of reasoned thinking about pension matters, Malcolm Hamilton, Principal of William M. Mercer Ltd., and Keith Ambachtsheer, President of KPA Advisory Services, thank you for setting me straight on so many issues. Where I've erred, or where you disagree, I absolve you in advance—you laboured long and hard to have me get it right. Lorri Mackay did her usual reliable, timely and good-humoured digging for obscure facts and tables, as well as writing her notes so elegantly that many found their way into the final text. The manuscript was initially edited by Charis Wahl, whose extraordinary vigilance brought order of chaos. She and Kevin Linder made me realize how thankful I am for conscientious editors. Thanks also to Pamela Murray and John Pearce at Doubleday, and to Perry Goldsmith. To Alan Westbrook, Michael Zelding, and many others who have made themselves available for interviews and feedback, merci bien.

Hatley, Quebec
November 1998

....

The "New" Retirement

A great many people think they're thinking when
they're merely rearranging their prejudices.

THE LAST FEW YEARS OF public policy have almost completely undermined the possibility of a conventional middle-class retirement. Apart from those making $150,000 or more a year, there are really only two classes of Canadians who can afford to retire when they want to: the poor and the tax-supported, i.e., public servants. People the government designates as poor can afford to retire because social programs will continue to support them at low income levels. Federal government workers and six-year political veterans can afford to retire—they belong to the richest pension plans in the country. If you're poor or have a permanent government job, you'll receive a guaranteed, inflation-protected minimum income for life of $20,000–$30,000 a year. Many will, of course, do much better than that. The rest of us, unless we make deliberate and extraordinary changes in the way we save and invest, will not accumulate enough to be able to retire when we want to. Moreover, even with aggressive savings strategies, the current tax system will pull the average Canadian saver down to lower income levels mainly to support

the programs for the poor and the pension plans of the bureau-crats and politicians.

Personal taxes are far and away the single biggest spending item in the average family budget, as the government's own measurement service tells us in Chart I–1.

CHART I–1 **The Cost of Living**

	AVERAGE HOUSEHOLD EXPENDITURE ($49,000)
Personal taxes 22%	$10,700
Shelter 17%	$8,500
Transportation 12%	$6,000
Food 12%	$6,000
Recreation 5%	$2,600
Insurance and pension contributions 5%	$2,600
Household operation 5%	$2,300
Clothing 4%	$2,100
Gifts and charitable donations 3%	$1,700
Miscellaneous 3%	$1,400
Household furnishing & equipment 3%	$1,300
Tobacco & alcoholic beverages 2%	$1,150
Health care 2%	$1,000
Personal care 2%	$840
Education 1%	$560
Reading materials 1%	$250

Source: Statistics Canada

Working Canadians now face the Canadian pension paradox: *the retirement system depends on saving, but there's no rationale for saving left in the system.* Chart I–2 shows the amount a Canadian household needs to save as a percentage of its total income: a family with an average income needs to save about 8% of its total income; a family with an above-average income has to save

substantially more. The Canadian Institute of Actuaries cal-
culates that to retire at age 60 and maintain your lifestyle, you
must save 12%–18% of your income from age 30 until retirement.
On average, Canadian families are not saving enough.

CHART I–2 Retirement Savings Needs as a Percentage of Gross Income

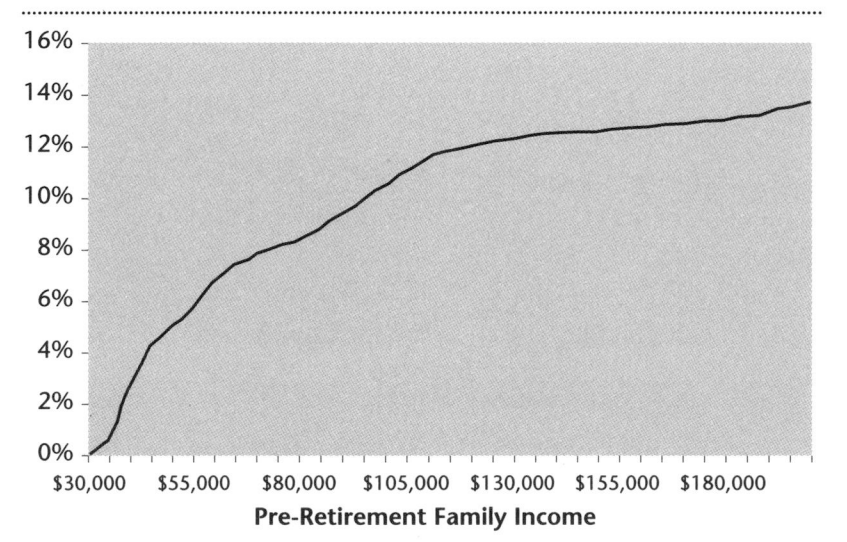

Pre-Retirement Family Income

Source: Malcolm Hamilton, William M. Mercer Ltd.

Unless you're among the top 1% of income earners, any
additional income you receive from your retirement savings will
be taxed back to put you within a few thousand dollars of low to
middle income levels. Worse, when you factor in Canada's deteriorating competitiveness and declining relative living standards
(more about this in Chapter 1), not to mention shaky national
unity, there is no plausible argument for believing that the
money you accumulate in Canada will have enough purchasing
power to make retirement comfortable or enjoyable.

Public policies are supposed to help Canada to become more
productive. But for the last several years those policies—from regulation to education—have been so retrograde that, without

immediate change, our incomes will continue to decline along with the relative number of earners, as the baby boom generation retires. An important example that I often use is the rule that 80% of our tax-sheltered savings have to be invested in designated Canadian assets. This presents a major challenge to any rational diversification of accumulated assets, forces us to accept lower-than-average rates of wealth accumulation, and creates a captive pool of capital that weakens corporate performance because it directs savings to less efficient and less competitive enterprises.

To deliver guaranteed incomes to low-income Canadians, Canada has to be dynamic, productive and competitive in order to attract the investment, the work, and ultimately the tax revenue to pay for them. Yet this country is not responding well to the challenge of globalization and the new ways of staying competitive and creating wealth. Canada has become a disaster zone as far as wealth creation goes: Canadians have become on average 50% poorer than Americans over the last two decades. The number of Canadians born in the "baby bust" years from 1966 to 1986 is 30% smaller than the baby boom generation. Policy makers used to look forward to immigrants taking up the slack and unemployment declining as the much smaller number of people going into the workforce came into great demand. That didn't happen: unemployment has remained near double-digit levels for more than two decades, partly because Canada discourages entrepreneurial activities, partly because we hobble ourselves with interprovincial trade barriers and other wealth-destroying regulations.

If the country is not becoming more productive than its trading partners, is not using technology to become more efficient, and is not adapting its institutional arrangements, taxpayers will not be able to provide enough tax revenue to support social services such as education, pensions, and health and medical care at the levels we're used to. We see it happening: the economy has been growing slowly, real incomes have been falling relative to those in other industrial countries, and living standards

have been stagnant for the last 20 years. Having been handed a country with the second-highest living standard and productivity levels in the world, the current political class has put it all at risk. Our productivity and living standard are now around ninth and eighth respectively in the world and growing relatively worse.

What can you do about this? In the following pages, you'll learn how you can protect yourself and your family against these trends, and how to prepare for a comfortable life after you stop doing what you're doing now. But to do this, you have to think about retirement in new ways and make the system work for you, not the reverse. For example, it is not clear that even the concept of retirement is one we should take for granted. It is, after all, an invention of the industrial age: "retirement" as a societal goal didn't exist in the agricultural era of our grandparents. Most of us no longer live in a world based on heavy physical labour or demanding industrial production. Most of us provide services we could continue to offer for many years after we stop going to the office. Re-examining the concept of "retirement" is part of the *new* retirement.

In rethinking our current approach to retirement and our strategies for living well, I'll be asking some fundamental questions:

Fundamental question no. 1: Where did you get this idea of retirement, anyway? When you knock off work at age 65, you're probably going to live another 10 or 20 years. When the first boomers retire within the next 10 years, we will have created several million more unemployed people, many of them involuntarily so. That's a lot of unemployment. Can this be a good idea? Perhaps it once was, when an old Prussian gentleman named Bismarck seized on universal state pensions as a political tool to use against the German socialists a century ago. But Bismarck was no idealist; he set the retirement age at 65 because the average life expectancy was well below that. When Canada decided Old Age Security would start at age 70, life expectancy was 71. Today you'd have to raise the pension age to 79 to get the same effect. The fastest growing age group in Canada is between 75 and 100.

And with advances in technology, including genetic engineering, it's just going to get bigger. Do we really need to put experienced, accomplished, talented people out to pasture for almost as long as they worked? If we dropped compulsory retirement as a concept and as a goal, a lot of the problems we face—both for financing programs and for individuals—would disappear. Would that slow the next generation's advance? Hardly. Judging from current demographics, there won't be enough replacement workers to fill all the jobs vacated by the boomers. Letting them hang around a bit longer would also smooth the generational transition.

Fundamental question no. 2: Is it ethically acceptable to coerce the young into paying their parents' debts? After all, our children weren't consulted when we ran up the debts. At the very time that workers' obligations to the pension system are growing, so is the dependency rate, that is, the number of nonworkers supported by the paid workforce. The proportion of retired folks and people too young to join the labour force is growing, so unless productivity grows at least as fast as the dependency rate, the GDP will actually decline. When I was a young worker, I remember being told that when I paid my taxes, my contribution went to support one-point-something people who benefited from various social programs. My daughter, now just starting out, pays far more tax than I did at her age because she is supporting almost three people. So far, our politicians continue blithely to assume people will willingly fund retirement plans they would be better off boycotting—and you *can* boycott the system in many legal ways, as I explain throughout.

Fundamental question no. 3: Do made-in-Canada solutions still exist? Besides demographics, there's also globalization to consider. Canada has been and remains dependent on the rest of the world for markets and investment. If anything happens to affect those factors, they will zap back and affect us, too. History has lessons for us. Canada was an oil-exporting country in 1974 when OPEC quadrupled the price of oil. Nothing bad could happen to

us, right? The government told us that the oil-price increase would contribute to inflation, but we had wage-and-price-control policies to deal with that. What no one planned on was a recession. But when people have to pay four times more for energy, they have less to spend on other things. Country after country saw their exports shrink and unemployment rise. Canada wasn't immune. Here's one example of the global merry-go-round. There was a huge transfer of money from the developed (oil-importing) to the developing (oil-exporting) countries. When the price of oil plummeted in the 1980s, the emerging countries such as Mexico and Venezuela were saddled with billions of dollars of debt and nothing to pay it with. Banks collapsed, and money fled the countries until the U.S. developed a plan (the Brady Plan) to allow the workout of the debt. The U.S. jacked up interest rates to curb inflation, but the desired "side" effect was to attract a huge inflow of capital to cover its trade and budget deficits. Canada's public policies fitted right in. In the mid-1980s, Canadian and American financial institutions were caught with billions of dollars of next-to-worthless real estate on their books, the result of continuing to lend after the inflation bubble of the previous decade had burst. The collapse of commodity prices caused the U.S. recession of 1991-92. Canada survived because (1) we could still export oil and (2) we signed the Free Trade Agreement in 1989 which gave us access to an increasingly closed U.S. economy. But we bungled the transition to global competitiveness.

That fiasco took 10 years to wind down. Today, North American businesses are in much better financial shape. But the Japanese banks have still not faced up to their bad loans that originated during the same period. That was the beginning of the Asian flu. Is Canada immune? I wouldn't take bets on it.

Here at home, as many observers have been pointing out for some time, Canadians are saving more individually, but those savings have been more than matched by increases in government dissaving (i.e., running up debt). As a collectivity, we haven't been saving at all. Our total pension and mutual fund assets barely

cover the national debt. The unfunded pension liabilities, if taken as a stock, are equal to the national debt and growing much faster. The pension and medicare liabilities also represent a claim on national savings, even if we do not record them as such. The money to fund them will have to be borrowed. Yet borrowing will be much harder to do, because every country will see its own savings decline when it faces up to its retirement crunch.

If you can't borrow money, or if it's harder to get, the money will have to be earned. Yet that's going to be harder as well, because Canada's productivity is not rising as fast as that of our major trading partners. We'll need more dollars, not fewer, to maintain living standards. However, personal incomes are as likely to decline as rise, because of what is essentially forced retirement.

If this sounds grim, there is some comfort to be taken in the fact that Canada, the U.S. and the U.K. are less in debt than other countries (like France and Italy, for example) whose retirees will have an even harder time. But the main point is that within the countries that make up the Organization for Economic Cooperation and Development (OECD)—that is, the world's industrialized countries whose savers lend us money—Canada is not alone in trying to shore up national pension schemes. In many of these countries, there will be massive public and private borrowing to cover the bills of an aging population. The price of capital worldwide will increase unless these governments simply renege on their social contracts. There is no way Canada can unilaterally protect itself from this, but there are strategies individuals can adopt to defend against these threats.

Then there is the real possibility that the Canadian dollar will not exist when you retire. True, the loonie has a raison d'être: it is the currency of Canadians. The Canadian dollar has historically had an international cachet independent of the needs of residents of Canada. It has long been an alternative for investors who want a safe haven for their funds—and a profitable one, since Canadian interest rates are more often than not higher than

U.S. rates. But that niche has been squeezed in the last several years, as the Canadian dollar has had trouble holding its international value. Now there's another alternative safe haven for international investors: the euro. If the euro reduces the attractiveness of the Canadian dollar as a place to invest, what reason exists for the Canadian dollar? The pressure is already on to create a North American currency.

Fundamental question no. 4: Why not put private savings at the heart of a retirement strategy? Without private savings, no government programs are possible, especially with our demographic profile.

CHART I–3 **Fertility Rates in Canada 1902–1992**

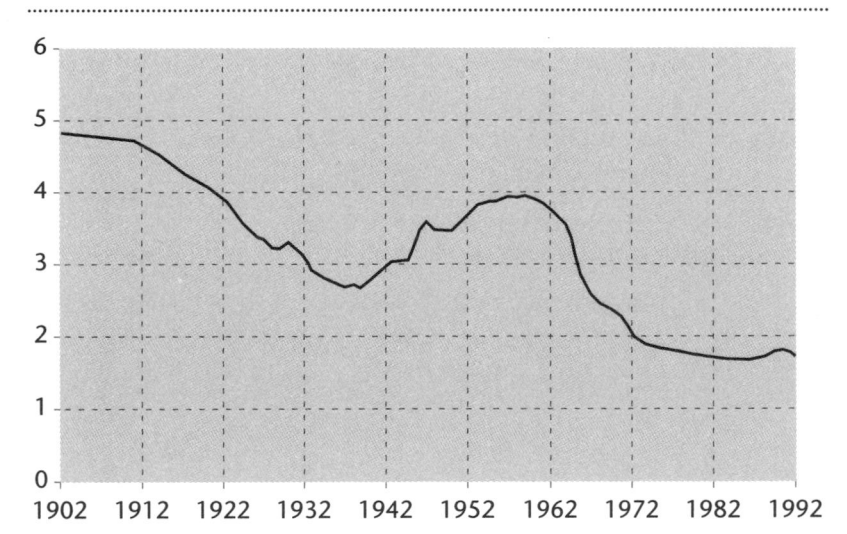

Source: Malcolm Hamilton, Wm. M. Mercer Ltd.

When our government retirement programs were set up, Canada was a net saver, not a borrower. True, we've balanced the budget, but we have a huge public debt to pay down, a debt that's almost equivalent to a year's total production, and a similar amount of unfunded liability in the Canada Pension Plan (CPP) still to cover (see Chapter 4). Government will therefore be a major

borrower for the foreseeable future. This is an opportunity for savers, who can decide whether to invest in the public debt. But there is no way that government can be at the heart of a retirement system when it has to tax back its borrowing costs to cover past and present profligacy. That kills any incentive to invest. Yet that's what's happened to Canada's retirement system. How can we purport to believe that a chronically excessive borrower can effectively design, administer and legislate a retirement savings system? It's like putting the fox in charge of the henhouse.

Today's global capital markets, on the other hand, are about savings and investment for maximum return. They are also broader, deeper and more transparent than any national public sector could ever be. They tap the resources of the world; trillions of dollars' worth of financial assets are traded every day, wealth is constantly created (and occasionally lost), and it's all done in the open, available instantly on everyone's computer screen, or on the nightly news when you get home. Capital markets therefore can provide the basis for a much more positive way forward.

The impact of national borrowing (by the public sector) on retirement programs could be substantially reduced if (1) the national pension schemes changed to some kind of funded basis (i.e., actually having the money they're obligated to pay out) and (2) contributions were moved into an income-earning fund (today, contributions are spent by today's retirees). Above all, we should not be taxing away the return on savings. Instead, the fund should be healthy enough to cover the "defined benefits." There are plenty of ways of doing this without dislocation. We need to think about a mandatory, but individual, retirement plan. Canadians already understand the concept of RRSPs, group RRSPs, and employer-sponsored and administered pension plans.

This is no more than insisting that government pension schemes operate like private sector plans—by putting aside the money in anticipation of the payout and to earn more money. If public sector pensions were run on the same basis as private

sector pensions, we wouldn't be stuck with these gloomy forecasts.

The government, to its credit, is finally moving partway on this: new pension contributions are to be invested in the capital markets, not just used as a source of cheap money for Canadian governments. This is a start, even though for the next few years, funds will only trickle into the new CPP Investment Board, and will be invested only in low-yielding government Treasury bills and bonds. The bigger problem, for reasons already mentioned, is that it will probably not happen as set out in government policy, because the contributions will not materialize once Canadians understand what is being asked of them (more on this in Chapter 4).

A final point illustrates how the foreign investment restriction—a government effort to "help"—is undermining the ability of Canadians to save for their retirement. Canadian equity markets represent less than 3% of global capital markets. It is simply bad investment strategy to concentrate 80% of your assets in 3% of the market! Somehow, we have to educate Canadian politicians so that they eliminate the foreign investment restrictions that now curtail Canadians' ability to diversify their retirement portfolios to minimize risk.

The practical question in all this is not economic but political. Can Canada's quasi-socialist political culture accept a private sector-style national pension system, or do we still believe there's a tooth fairy in Ottawa? So far, the prospects are not good. The political class, and much of the financial institutions industry, benefit too much from this system for them to think about reforming it too fundamentally. They know it could only result in diminishing their role at the policy table.

To review the main points made so far:

- The new retirement is new because much of the old system is broken.
- You can retire when you want to if you're poor or a public servant. The rest of us have to work harder and smarter,

and even then have excessive amounts of our money taxed away.

- Even if we overcome those barriers to retirement, our relative living standards are declining because of Canada's deteriorating competitiveness and the falling value of the dollar.
- Canada is not making the transition to global competitiveness easily or quickly; a myriad of restrictive regulations and obsolete institutions are to blame.
- It is foolhardy to believe that young Canadians will continue to pay more for a retirement system they won't share.
- Even if Canada had the "right" public policies, we are dependent on the rest of the world for investment and markets. Shocks to the system happen; we are not immune, and cannot continue to believe there are made-in-Canada solutions.
- The concept of "retirement" needs to be reconsidered.

So what about you? How should you think about retirement in this new era? Here's a thumbnail sketch of the points I'll make to help you prepare for a realistic retirement.

- Forget the traditional idea of retirement. The conditions underpinning our conventional notions of retirement have changed, so you should abandon the notion of retirement as your mum and dad probably knew it. Plan to do some kind of work until you're carried out face down and feet first. But change jobs often and open a business of your own on the side.
- If you still want a classic retirement, give serious thought to retiring outside Canada, unless the tax system changes drastically. If you want to stay in Canada, you should probably have your assets denominated in other, stronger currencies until national policies change.
- If you're some distance from retirement, don't be beguiled by the familiar: we are living in an era of sudden and discontinuous change. Consider, for example, that Canada

may not exist in its present form 10 years from now. And if it still does, the Canadian dollar may no longer exist.

- Skip the government's game and play your own (unless you're over 50). RRSPs allow you tax-free accumulation, but then you're clobbered when you try to live on the money. Investments made outside Canada with after-tax money may in fact give you a better net return. Otherwise, buy stripped government bonds (see Chapter 9) until you learn enough to build your retirement plan and implement your investment strategy. Property, properly handled, and even insurance, can provide better returns than the plain-vanilla RRSP approach. Certainly, understanding the rules of the government's game will improve your chances of using RRSPs to your best advantage.

- You have the best chance of succeeding if you apply the philosophy of this book when you're 25. Today's capital markets offer some spectacular opportunities. Mutual funds open the best of these to a wider investing public. And tax-free accumulations of gains compound faster than taxed gains. You can still succeed if you're 50, but you may have to rethink your retirement living standard, and you may have to factor in some work to supplement your income from savings.

These and other strategies are discussed step by step in the later chapters of this book. But here's the bottom line: the current Canadian retirement system suffers from fundamental design flaws, so don't count on it to be there when you need it. Nevertheless, despite the government's best efforts to take your money and waste it, there are some powerful strategies you can use to accumulate and safeguard your retirement savings. The purpose of this book is to help you understand and implement those strategies. So read on.

ONE

The Retirement
Paradox

*If, in the last few years, you
haven't discarded a major opinion or
acquired a new one, check your pulse.
You may be dead.*

1

....

Skews and Lags: Ottawa's Model of Retirement

The conventional view serves to protect us from the painful job of thinking.

—John Kenneth Galbraith

FORGET EVERYTHING YOU'VE ever known, thought, believed or heard about retirement. The world has changed. The biggest barrier to sharing what the world has to offer is that we don't really see it the way it is; we see it the way *we* are. If we're to understand the transformation of our society and respond appropriately, we have to change the way we think. We have to give up the economic myths we live by.

We talk about the information revolution, the shift from the industrial to the information age, and globalization, but we still run our lives as though our world were much the same as the world of our parents. It isn't: the networked world of today is as different from the world in which we lived our childhood as the microwave oven is from the wood stove and the Mars probe from the Tiger Moth biplane.

A key question in understanding retirement strategies is this:

How do economies produce wealth? Typically, one's understanding lags behind reality. For example, a generation ago we still believed:

- that the backbone of Canada's labour force opportunities lay in the manufacturing sector, even though more people were working in the service sector since the late 1950s.
- that national governments could manage their domestic economies, although Canada was one of the first countries to pioneer floating exchange rates, in effect admitting that it could no longer control exchange rates.
- that women were only marginally attached to the workforce and that men were the prime income earners and should be treated advantageously, although by the 1970s women made up over half the workforce.
- that if we worked hard, we would climb the "career ladder" and "get ahead." This seemed true at the time, as inflation masked an ongoing degradation in net worth. Between 1971 and 1980, personal income more than doubled (it went up 2.6 times). However, over the same period, the dollar lost half its purchasing power and personal income taxes (in real, non-inflation dollars) doubled. Not surprisingly, consumer debt quadrupled as people borrowed to maintain their lifestyles. Today, without inflation, the nature of work and of careers has changed: one moves from assignment to assignment, perhaps around a network of allied firms, perhaps from company to company. Today, in contrast to a generation ago, you move ahead by moving on.
- that there was an alternative model to free enterprise. Most people thought the Iron Curtain, which separated the First World from the Second, would last forever, and that the planned economies of the communist Second World were based on as robust an ideology as the market-based ideology of the capitalist world. It didn't, and they weren't. The planned economies of the U.S.S.R. and its Eastern European

empire have collapsed. China is experimenting with a market-based planned economy, but today, there is only one dominant ideology: innovation-based free enterprise.

- (encouraged by a generation of New Deal and welfare state economists) that the struggle to maintain economic growth had been won and that economic policy should focus on redistributing wealth. We felt rich enough and sufficiently in control of our destinies that we willingly ceded to governments half our earnings to redistribute to those they decided were most deserving. Not satisfied, governments spent even more, and deficits rose from under 1% of gross domestic product (GDP) to around 5%. Real economic growth rates remained high, powered by rising commodity prices. With the end of the oil-price boom in the mid-1980s, Canada found itself saddled with high debt, high taxes and big safety nets, but without the means to pay for them.

In our more distant past, before the welfare state and Great Depression of the "dirty '30s," Canadians believed that the "new world" would provide them with the opportunity to make a better life for themselves and their children, based on hard work and opportunity—without the poverty and discrimination they or their ancestors experienced in Europe. The Depression changed all this. It was so terrible that it convinced generations of Canadians that market economies were inherently insecure and that ultimately it would be governments, and not markets, that guaranteed their financial security. This was a sea change in Canadian attitudes, and still colours our expectations of government and our views of the state and its role in the economy. These beliefs are an integral part of our national and, in many cases, personal histories.

Our ideas about living, learning, working—and retirement—come from that history. Our ideas were shaped by depression and war, by the shift from a rural society based on working the land to an urban society based on unskilled factory work and

skilled craftsmen, by the horror of experiencing the dog-eat-dog world of failing capitalism, and its result, an acceptance of letting government look after more and more of the things that used to be our individual responsibility.

Now we are adults and the shared experience of history is no longer enough to make us safe and secure. Over the past 30 years, Canadians have become poorer relative to Americans. We have elected governments that have broken every promise to us about the security of our pensions and our health care. Taxes have risen steadily, and for many Canadians, the system now taxes back the Old Age Security benefits that at one time constituted a "sacred trust" between the generations.

Almost no one under 40 believes the Canada Pension Plan will be there for them when they retire. Besides, CPP premiums are rising by 70% over the next few years, so young Canadian workers will have to put far more in than they'll be entitled to get back.

In just the last 10 years, taxes have tripled, federal debt has quintupled and, until coerced by Ottawa, provincial performance was even worse. Politicians told us that these tax increases were necessary because Canadians define themselves in terms of their generous social programs, and to give them up would mean to lose our national identity. So instead of cutting back, we strove to maintain living standards by taking on debt. When economic growth slowed and tax revenues couldn't cover the perks, we borrowed the money abroad (much of it from countries with less per capita income than ours, and yet able to save). The money went straight to paying interest on the debt, or to social programs. The levels of debt and debt service payments slowed our economic growth even more and eroded our international competitiveness as well.

Poor policy made things worse. Continued borrowing raised domestic interest rates to attract foreign investors and kept the exchange rate high as they exchanged their currencies for Canadian dollars to buy Canadian bonds. The high value of the Canadian dollar made our exports too expensive for virtually all

markets except those of the U.S. and, to a much smaller extent, Japan. Paying interest to foreign investors meant less domestic demand to spur economic growth; the whole of Canada's economic growth depended mainly on our ability to increase our exports to the U.S. This meant that Canada's net wealth would continue to come overwhelmingly from resource exports, and that consequently, our relative living standards would continue to go down.

By the mid-1990s, getting rid of the annual deficit became the alternative to an International Monetary Fund (IMF) workout. The high political profile of the balanced budget and the debate about next steps obscured the continuing relative weakness of our economy after a decade of focusing on distribution rather than growth—until the wake-up call in the summer of 1998 when the loonie dipped to 63 cents U.S.

Ten years after the last commodity boom, as the world now enters a period of commodity deflation, Canada is still a commodity producer as far as foreigners are concerned. Now, with no foreign borrowing to put upward pressure on the dollar, and with our second-largest trading partner, Japan, in the midst of its own economic crisis, it's no wonder Canada's dollar promptly followed world commodity prices into the tank. A decade's opportunity to move into higher value-added exports has been wasted. Sure, Canada made some progress, especially in telecommunications, computer equipment, aerospace and biotechnology. But we're a long way from generating net positive earnings in high-technology exports. The low dollar may help exports, but it will not help overcome the growth constraints those industries face: high taxes and difficulty attracting qualified people.

Astonishingly, in light of this failure, the government's post-deficit official line has become, "Now that the deficit is under control, we can afford more of the same mixture of social spending and high (perhaps not quite as high) taxes." Ouch! Wait a minute! What does this mean for retirement? There are some critical issues here about our ability to sustain a top-level living

standard, and especially about our ability to sustain a high level of retirement income.

One issue is the cost of government. The deficit control "victory" is a shell game. The federal government has not spent less; on the contrary, it taxed more. When that became politically dangerous, it pushed many programs and their costs down to provincial governments, who also raised taxes. Provincial governments in turn shovelled them onto municipal governments, who also raised taxes. We are all trying to live with the results: high taxes, and programs that have been streamlined in some respects but have not led to a rethink, redesign and new role for government. The bottom line is that Canada is less and less able to sustain relatively high living standards.

Here's how this can affect you.

A fellow bought a condominium in Florida in 1990 for US$150,000. If he sold it today for exactly what he paid for it—$150,000—he'd make a $28,000 profit. How?

Here's the answer: the exchange rate has changed. In 1990, the Canadian dollar was trading above 86 cents U.S. So US$150,000 would have cost about $174,000 Canadian. In 1998, with a Canadian dollar worth about 65 (or less) American cents, US$150,000 would be exchanged for $202,000. The profit: $28,000. There'd be no profit in American currency—buy at $150,000, sell at $150,000. But everything Canadians want to buy in American dollars is 30%-40% more expensive. Put another way, that's how much poorer Canadians have become in less than a decade (without considering tax). By the way, that "profit" exists on paper only; in real terms, our hero has simply preserved the purchasing power of his original investment by having it elsewhere than Canadian dollars.

Lest you think it's just the Americans who have gotten richer relative to us, here's more food for thought. Most advanced countries have gained in purchasing power relative to us, and the smaller European countries have done particularly well. What's cheaper in Canadian dollars today are the ruble, the baht, the

ringgit and the rupiah (Russia, Thailand, Malaysia and Indonesia). These countries are among our toughest competitors on commodity markets, a further indication that Canadian living standards are likely to go lower unless the country makes some major changes.

Let's review the big changes in the general environment in which we live and hope to retire, so we can see which of the ideas we hold dear are appropriate for the 21st century, and which we should get rid of immediately.

Twenty years ago, when such seers as Peter Drucker and Alvin Toffler tried to forecast the near future, they focused on the broad changes taking place in the economy. They wanted to alert us to change and to help us adapt our thinking about economics and business. The changes they predicted have come to pass. But in Canada our thinking is only just catching up. We are living in a global economy, and it is based on information. In the affluent countries, popular tastes are so similar that there really is a global marketplace and most national consumer differences (pass the Perrier, please) are now just nuances.

And there was more accuracy: national economic models have become less relevant; you have to incorporate a global analysis into your decision making. Employment growth has become unhitched from economic growth; because of new technologies, output can grow without increasing jobs. We didn't prepare for this either. As a result, our long-term unemployment leads the seven largest industrialized countries (G-7). Natural resources have become decoupled from economic growth. More output no longer means more natural resource consumption. New materials and more efficient use of standard materials ensure this.

So what should you bear in mind when contemplating retirement and your need for stable and, if possible, rising income with growing purchasing power? We need some better concepts for figuring things out. The following five propositions are intended

to serve as a checklist and guide to the major forces shaping today's economy.

Proposition 1: Economics is about social arrangements, not just markets. Traditional economics typically focuses on one institution, markets, and ignores others, such as laws, property rights and other social arrangements that affect the way markets work. Today's economists have now departed from that particular piece of naiveté, and have accepted what historians have been saying for some time, namely that markets are one of a family of things called institutions. From an economic perspective, the role of institutions is to make life more predictable. We have institutions that make rules and policies on everything from cultural priorities to politics—the full range of social choices. What this proposition tells us is that underlying issues of material prosperity are social choices that are made outside markets, yet affect how well or efficiently markets work.

For instance, without property rights, and a legal system to defend them and enforce contracts, ordinary transactions won't occur—the uncertainty will outweigh the potential gains. Therefore, without institutions that make transactions worthwhile, economic growth cannot occur. Upon reflection, it's hard to exaggerate the importance of social choices and institutions in producing economic growth. Indeed, development economists have come to recognize that institutions explain why resource-poor Asian economies could develop into middle-income modern economies (and why they're in crisis today) whereas resource-rich Africa has had no similar success, and why Mexico is poor and Texas, just across the Rio Grande, is rich.

Pushing the importance of social arrangements and institutions in explaining economic performance, a new group of economists has emerged to explain economic growth in terms of such arrangements, which they call "endogenous growth factors." These factors include labour laws, educational systems, industry regulation, political systems and more. These economists hold that the keys to wealth and prosperity lie not in natural resources

but in the institutions and social arrangements made in society to permit wealth to be created. In making such arguments, they're reinforcing what classical economists noted over two hundred years ago. The secret to prosperity, wrote Adam Smith in *The Wealth of Nations* back in 1776, lies in the extent of the market and *"division of labour"*—the ability and flexibility to specialize. The question for investors: How many of our institutions promote the ability to specialize and how many are designed to lock in the status quo? What is the likelihood of improvement relative to other countries, and how soon? This line of reasoning is at the heart of discussion about comparative national productivity. Canada, as you might expect, has a mixed record and the jury is out on our ability to get better.

Proposition 2: Its own success kicked the props from under the national welfare state. The economic system set up after World War II fixed exchange rates, liberalized trade in goods, and expected national governments to act as economic stabilizers to ensure full employment and cradle-to-grave social security and health care. There are many explanations for the demise of the welfare state, some more technical than others. Fundamentally, however, what killed these arrangements was their success. The welfare state formula was based mainly on the economic principles of British economist John Maynard Keynes, who saw government as a stabilizer of national markets through taxes and spending, according to the amount of demand in the economy. But once a general level of prosperity had been widely achieved, this formula could no longer deliver jobs and steady growth without inflation.

Here's what happened. Twenty years of full employment and steady growth after World War II, coupled with trade liberalization, generated previously unheard of prosperity for the average citizen, freeing people from the burdens of care about affording medical help and gaining access to post-secondary education. During the mid to late 1960s, the demand pressures this caused began to trigger upward pressure on prices in all advanced

countries. Yet, rather than raise taxes or interest rates, governments increased spending in pursuit of greater social justice (wars on poverty) which, in effect, increased demand even more. The natural disciplinarian of this system, the U.S., was a major offender, trying to run a war on poverty along with a war in Southeast Asia. The increased demand was unable to call forth increased supply at existing price levels because the postwar system was a highly regulated system.

Transportation, telecommunications, financial services, and more, were limited in the number of suppliers and the types and quantity of services they could provide. As a result, prices continued to rise throughout the economies of the West, exchange rates destabilized and gradually the regulatory systems broke down. Elements of the postwar system began to be replaced by freer markets, because only free markets could deliver steady growth and high employment without inflation.

The first thing to go was the system of fixed exchange rates, as the U.S. abandoned the fixed rate of dollars to gold. This effectively obliged all countries who hadn't already, to float their currencies and let markets set exchange rates.

Then domestic regulation was eased, beginning in the transportation sector and continuing through financial services. Meanwhile, monetary expansion was drastically curtailed, sending interest rates (i.e., the price of money) into double digits and provoking a short recession in the early 1980s. This brought so-called "supply-side" governments to power in the U.K. and the U.S., which began the process of liberalizing regulation and privatizing state-owned or state-run enterprises, and eliminating monopolies so that supply could rise to meet demand and competition would keep price levels low. Other countries, including Canada, followed, but without the same overall commitment or enthusiasm. Nevertheless, by the mid-1980s, steady, non-inflationary growth had been achieved by all the major countries.

In the course of these changes, the ability of governments to steer their national economies had been drastically reduced. In

most Western countries, governments were no longer seen as the monopoly suppliers of choice for a great many services, and where they still were, they were expected to be as cost-conscious as business. The main beneficiaries of this process were the privatized companies and their new shareholders, as well as consumers who now could enjoy a greater supply of innovative services more cheaply than before. Almost all the industries most affected were in the services sector, which was not included under the postwar trade rules of the General Agreement on Tariffs and Trade (GATT). So a new round of trade talks began to further liberalize trade, shore up the mechanisms for rules enforcement and, as a top priority, bring services into the trade rules tent.

In concrete terms, one of the outcomes of this is that your long-distance bill has fallen drastically, and will likely fall further. At the same time, many new services have become available because the government-sanctioned monopoly on long-distance phone service has been abolished. On the other hand, you still have twisted copper wire to the house, your TV is not interactive and your computer cruises the Internet relatively slowly because in Canada there is no significant competition for local service. Remember those two secrets of prosperity, flexibility and division of labour. Monopolies don't provide them, competition does. More broadly, the impact of these changes is to sharply reduce the economic role of government. Hence, Proposition #3.

Proposition 3: Globalization has slashed the power of the nation state. The term "globalization" has become shorthand for three revolutions that began in the late 1970s. First, there was a "supply-side" revolution in the management of national economies discussed above. This "supply-side" approach, as its name suggests, contrasts with its Keynesian predecessor, which focused government policy on "the demand side," managing consumer demand through taxing and spending while regulating supply. The supply-side strategy emphasizes competitive markets and so-called "framework" policies. These policies slash red tape so that markets can work better, and encourage the

internationalization of national economies by liberalizing of trade and investment rules. Setting out a framework of transparent and predictable rules, especially for trade in services, helps markets flourish.

Second was the internationalization of the world economy through foreign direct investment (FDI). The careful use of FDI by the world's largest companies enabled the world economy to evolve to the point that roughly 1,000 companies account for almost all the private business conducted among nations. These companies are now huge, with around US$80 billion in annual sales, and they organize production on a global scale, using the computer networks described below. They also have enormous amounts of cash, which they move around world money markets such that about a trillion dollars a day passes through the trading exchanges. So important have these companies become that it makes little sense any longer to discuss economies in terms of national units. Regional groupings—such as the triad of Europe, Asia and the North American Free Trade Agreement (NAFTA) group—are more self-contained than countries.

The third strand in globalization, without which the other two would not be nearly so successful, is the information technology revolution. This revolution—a combination of escalating computer power on the desktop joined with increasingly faster telecommunications—has wired the world into a single, incredible bazaar. In this global bazaar, international networks rather than individual firms have become the heart of value-added production, distribution and payment; direct customer-producer interfaces are replacing intermediaries of all kinds. So powerful is this process that it has obliged even the world's largest firms to eliminate layers of middle managers and mesh themselves into the broader global networks. You can think of today's economy as a global tapestry of glass threads (fibre-optic cable), charged with a fluctuating energy field that covers the planet and shimmers ever so slightly every time anybody anywhere stops at a traffic light, uses a pass card in a subway, makes a phone call,

transmits an e-mail message, or orders something using a debit or credit card. The meshwork's energy flows across not only space but time as well. Its markets include such items as futures contracts, which allow investors to take a buy or sell position in the future to offset a position in the present—like offsetting your bet on red with a bet on black, before the roulette wheel turns and the ball actually lands. It's much harder to lose your stake in a casino like that, which is why the mesh is so much more preferable to the nation-based arrangements that preceded it.

This global meshwork shows how unsustainable, in retrospect, were the postwar ideas of national economies, stabilized by individual governments, with fixed exchange rates and a relatively low volume of international trade in goods, under a set of rules in which states maintained the right of states to act arbitrarily. None of that is true any longer, because the world economy has evolved into an international, computer-coordinated global marketplace in which it makes no sense to have such institutions.

Keynesian formulae could not generate non-inflationary economic growth, as we saw in the 1960s and 1970s. Fixed exchange rates cannot be maintained against international capital movements which, in turn, can discount any national policy. The last of the postwar pillars to fall was the set of postwar trading arrangements. The new ones, whether in NAFTA or the World Trade Organization (WTO), brought services and agriculture under international rules and created new, binding dispute settlement mechanisms that replaced political negotiations of trade disputes with legal, judicial processes. Although the state is still present in these institutions, its operations have been replaced by multilateral panels of lawyers and industry experts.

The next set of propositions explores the consequences of this global meshwork for the conduct of national policy.

Proposition 4: National economic policies won't offset international weaknesses, but markets can. Governments have a number of tools, which they call policy instruments. Of these,

three are paramount for economic policy: the power to tax, the power to spend and the power to add to the money supply by printing money or through the operations of a central bank. These operations involve selling bonds to banks, in order to soak up cash, or buying bonds from banks, thereby injecting cash into the economy. These are known to central bankers as "open-market operations."

Only exceptionally are these policies able to accomplish very much, unless it is to make economic conditions worse. The global economic mesh flows resources (i.e., economic activity) around policies that are relatively less market-enhancing, and flows towards policies that are more market-enhancing. For example, if the Canadian government expects to get money from a tax increase, economic activity slows to nullify it. If the government tries to keep interest rates low to reduce its debt service costs, the value of the bonds drops, so that yields, i.e., the payout in percentage terms, remain unchanged. If governments change policies to increase economic activity, other governments also change policies. To increase their chances of having the desired effect, governments must coordinate their policies and move together —which offsets the temptation to move unexpectedly for some unilateral advantage.

Under these conditions, it takes all the ability governments can muster to ensure steady prices (i.e., no inflation).

A major consequence of this, especially for those with their minds firmly set in 1970s-style industrial policy, is that governments can do nothing much to offset national weaknesses or comparative disadvantages. Markets, however, can. As trade economists have known for decades, liberalized trade enhances both comparative advantages and comparative disadvantages, setting up a flow of investment away from weakness towards strength. But protection and regulation prevent such flows. Countries like Canada with sound infrastructures and educational systems can, if markets are allowed to work, become relative winners in open-market systems. The problem is, you have to understand the

game in order to play it properly. The rules of the game start with your answers to the following questions:

- How stable is the present structure? The case made in this book is that it is not very: this past year's crises (stock market, dollar woes, Asian contagion) alone provide plenty of evidence.
- How safe is the government "protection"? Again, we needn't look further back than a couple of years to see evidence of broken retirement promises (raising CPP contributions, freezing RRSP limits, reducing the age limit for contributing to an RRSP, taxing away Old Age Security benefits). The government's inability to protect individuals extends to the broader environment: raising interest rates in the summer of 1998 (the latest in a string of barren tactics) failed to restore the Canadian dollar to even 70 cents U.S.
- Where can safety be found? Experience suggests that the depth and breadth of the market (and your investment portfolio) are the necessary conditions for safety. The depth of a market means that it is big enough and well-traded enough that it is liquid—you can buy and sell when you want to. The breadth of the market means that investment can take place around the globe, and that value can be found somewhere (for example, when the stock market goes down, the bond market generally goes up). The lesson for wise investors is to hedge their investment portfolios in a broad array of stocks and bonds, either individual or as mutual funds, in a wide array of currencies.
- What is the permanent condition for long-term stability? I think it's Proposition 5.

Proposition 5: Knowledge is the universal substitute, and innovation is its application. I'd love to call this Cohen's Law. When confronted by an entry barrier such as lack of capital, overpriced components, or other problems, firms just innovate

around them. That's how some of today's most successful firms got successful. Take just-in-time delivery. The Japanese figured out that if they could simplify and shorten the steps to making a product, they could eliminate inventories, and so reduce costs without compromising quality. Now everybody's doing it. In the service industries, U.S. financial services are an outstanding example. The entire U.S. banking industry has moved, in the space of 10 years, from deposit-taking to financial risk-management. Mutual funds handle retail deposits, except for day-to-day transactional needs. The rest of the world is now scrambling to keep up, and a new general picture is becoming clear. The banks have become fee-for-service businesses, engineering products to meet the financial needs of their corporate clients. All these products make aggressive use of networks and futures markets.

Besides competition, the most striking features of the new economy are as old as economics itself. Back in 1776, Adam Smith laid down three factors that contribute to the wealth of nations: division of labour, the extent of the market (discussed above), and the skill and dexterity of the workforce. What was true in a materials-based early industrial economy such as the England of Smith's day is even more true in today's electronically meshed information economy.

Why? Because the fastest-growing industries today are products and services based on knowledge—a computer program, say, in a blockbuster game such as Duke Nuke 'Em, or an application such as CorelDraw, or an aircraft simulator such as those made by CAE. Today, computer games and home entertainment devices such as Super Nintendo 64, Sega and Sony Playstation are bigger than Hollywood films. With cheap CD-ROM-printing technology and access to the World Wide Web, any wannabe music group can become big enough to force major distribution companies such as Polygram to take them seriously. With the access to the world that today's home-based technologies provide, making it big just got a whole lot easier. And a whole lot more competitive as well.

What's true for the electronic mesh is also true for the global economy as a whole, which uses the mesh to handle all the back-office stuff while the producer moves material products from its point of origin to you. The bottom line is this: Canada is no longer an isolated country too small to mix it up in the world. Just as capital knows no borders, neither does talent. Living better is a matter of making it relatively easy for talent to succeed.

So what about Canada? We need to sweep away the economic cobwebs left over from the 1970s and join the global economy more aggressively.

How well are we adjusting to globalization? "How many Canadians does it take to screw in a light bulb? Thirty million—one to hold the bulb and 29,999,999 to turn the country around." Or: "Just two—one to hold the bulb and the other to call New York for instructions." While our major trading partners are getting relatively better at international business, we are getting relatively worse. Canada is suffering from the condition Pogo described as being confronted by insurmountable opportunities.

One major challenge confronting the country is that of balancing our traditional reliance on exports of natural resource-based commodities with an increasing export strength in knowledge-based products. Commodity prices have been on a downward trend since the early 1980s. New manufacturing techniques and substitute materials are reducing demand for the metals we produce. As for the forest products side, many factors are keeping prices low: the entry of new suppliers, an aging population that is not into family formation or bigger homes. Yet metals and forest products, including pulp and paper, are still among Canada's biggest exports. Forest product exports to the U.S. bring in only a billion dollars less than automobiles. Metal ores and alloys exports to the U.S. are about the same as auto parts. Oil and natural gas exports south are about the same as truck sales.

In understanding Canada's position, it's important to realize that these natural resource businesses, while still having a lot of

life in them, are essentially businesses of the past. We are a high-cost oil and gas producer; cheaper oil and gas is available. Cheaper lumber is available from non-Canadian suppliers. Our newsprint is coming under attack by environmentalists, and newspaper advertising revenue is in free fall anyway, suggesting either fewer or smaller newspapers in future.

But the news is far from all bad. As in the two-person light bulb story, Canadians have been responding to market signals, and the economy is slowly transforming itself. Nuala Beck has documented that more Canadians are employed in our electronics industry than in our pulp and paper industry; more Canadians are employed in communications and telecommunications than in the mining and petroleum industries. Regionally, too, some major adjustments have taken place: more Quebecers work in health and medical care than in construction, textile, clothing, furniture and mining combined; more Albertans work in financial services than in oil and gas. More people in B.C. work in communications and telecommunications than in forest industries; more Nova Scotians work as teachers and professors than work in fish processing, mining, forestry, pulp and paper and construction combined.

These new knowledge-based industries are soaking up our labour force, but they need to grow much faster and bigger if they are going to generate the exports we need to replace the exports we are losing. They need to develop global strategies and a network of profitable overseas affiliates and partners.

It's instructive to compare our restructuring with that of the U.S. In the U.S., the advanced industries are not only major employers, they're also the economy's major revenue generators. Computers and electronics have greater sales than the automotive industry. (Moreover, new cars use a lot of computing power, so there's some inflation in the automotive proportion.) Medical expenditures (many of them for high-tech services) are bigger than housing expenditures. People spend twice as much on the phone as they do on airline tickets. The top four computer

companies outsold the top four companies in industrial and farm equipment, food, beverages, and forest products.

Twenty years ago, those high-tech businesses—computers, technologically sophisticated medical establishments, complex phone services—barely existed. Now they are among the biggest and fastest growing, and are shaping companies as well as determining the kinds of products and services the economy will be using in the future. Canada is matching these shifts but too slowly. If we can't make these sectors more productive here, we will continue to endure a declining living standard.

So we're moving slowly in the right direction. What's holding us back? Basically, I think Canada is held back by a cherished illusion—that you can deal with challenge by just saying "No." In too many powerful places in our society, we have evolved a culture of refusal. Globalization is a tremendous opportunity for every region of Canada, but our policy makers remain lukewarm; they need to rethink their understanding of the forces at work.

The global economy promises every individual fresh opportunities to display a special genius to the rest of the world, to think big and act boldly, to survive in an unforgiving environment. What could be more Canadian?

The critical question is this: If Canada were a company, would it be on everyone's "buy" list? Don't get me wrong. If you've already decided that Canada, even with its warts, is where you want to live, bring up your children and retire, that's great. Canada undoubtedly has one of the greatest potentials among countries to become heaven on earth. But since the days of Sir John A. Macdonald, we have never taken delivery of the potential. He thought it would happen in the 20th century. It didn't. Yet our proven ability to construct a successful society in demanding conditions proves we can hack it. I think that millions of Canadians understand this, and they will undoubtedly continue to convey their desires every time they go to the polls. But some things are too important to leave to the politicians. Will our potentially sound economy be able to overcome excessive taxation

and regulation, to deliver the promise of comfortable retirement? In a world of global opportunities, will Canada be the preferred place it once was for living, working and investing? Will the Canadian dollar regain sufficient value that middle-income Canadians will again be able to think of travelling abroad? The ability to distinguish between myths and reality—and then to act on the understanding the distinction brings—is a prerequisite to answering "yes" to these questions. The rest of Part One is a road map to reality. Then we will be ideally positioned to evaluate our financial situation today, our opportunities in the future, and what we can do to make ourselves feel comfortable about that future.

2

....

The Myth
of the Job

*Too many people quit looking for work
when they find a job.*

THE INFORMATION REVOLUTION and the accompanying internationalization of every national economy has made the Job as
we know and love (or hate) it obsolete. If you are still thinking
about or planning for a traditional Job, stop. It won't happen.

For the most part, the concept of "national economies" is
obsolete, too. Nations are now elements of one of three economic
regions: North America, including Mexico (the North American
free trade [NAFTA] countries); Europe (the 15 European Union
countries plus those former Soviet Bloc countries that now have
associate status); and the Asia-Pacific region, including Japan,
Southeast Asia and China.

The trading and investment relationships within and between
these areas are based on lowering tariffs, eliminating discrimination of foreign firms and encouraging economic integration
as companies seek to get more of their products to market better, faster and cheaper. Just outside these arrangements stand the
billion and a half people who live in India and Latin America;
they are now attempting to open their markets and join in world

trade. We'll see where they fit in later. But right now, to fully comprehend how completely the nature of the Job is changing, you need to understand the forces that have made the internationalization of the world's national economies irresistible.

New technology and foreign investment are the two overarching forces. New technology lowers transportation costs, and even more important, it lowers the costs of coordinating complex enterprises. What does that mean? Well, think back a few decades to the hassle a French textile manufacturer, for example, must have gone through to sell his wares to a Canadian company. Workers at the company's loading dock would lift bolts of fabric onto a truck, which would head for a port and unload the cargo, bolt by bolt, into a dockside warehouse. When the ship was ready to sail, longshoremen would take the bolts from the warehouse and hoist them into the ship's hold, where other longshoremen were waiting to stow them in place. When the ship reached a Canadian port, the process was reversed, until finally the bolts reached their destination. Just arranging the shipment was a complex task. The repeated cargo handling and storage was expensive. The cloth would sit in the warehouse for weeks, some of it getting damaged or stolen along the way.

Compare that to how it's done today, using new technology like truck containers. That's right, detachable truck containers are new technology. Until about 40 years ago, no one had thought about building a container that could be detached from the truck cab and wheel bed, loaded at the factory, taken to the dock and stacked several high aboard the ship. Once built, however, the cost of shipping fell dramatically, as ships could be loaded and unloaded by a couple of dozen longshoremen instead of hundreds, the need to build protective wooden crates for individual items was eliminated, and theft was much reduced. Then, in the 1970s and '80s, as governments stopped making rules that prevented road and railway carriers from setting up partnerships that would streamline transportation, cargo companies like FedEx and UPS arose which set the standard for intermodal

transport—that is, a combination of planes, ships, railways and trucks to deliver freight fast. And of course, satellite receivers (new technology) in any or all of those carriers keep track of the goods and are responsible for the arrival of "just-in-time" delivery. At every stage of these developments, the Jobs of many people have disappeared or been transformed. In the process, the time it takes to get to market and the cost of goods have been chopped.

But that's only one example of how new technology lowers transportation costs and makes coordination of complex operations and complex organizations easier. Think back again to how the nature of trade has changed. A hundred years ago, international commerce was dominated by raw materials like the stuff we cut, gut and dig. The cost of transporting grain, wood, food and iron ore was high relative to the value of the goods themselves. Today, finished manufactured products dominate the flow of trade, and thanks to new technology—lightweight composites to replace steel and microprocessors to do the job of huge control panels—manufactured goods are lighter and much more valuable relative to the cost of transportation. Think about computer disk drives. Transportation costs are small no matter if they're shipped from Singapore to Alberta or vice versa. When you get to thinking about the information industry, you can see right away that shipping costs are insignificant compared with the value of compact discs or films. And when you consider computer software, shipping costs just about disappear, because the software can be sent over a phone line from one country to another: no ships, no planes, no trains, no trucks.

Foreign investment is the other immense force that is creating a global economy. You can already see that when transport costs decline relative to the value of the goods transported, more trade is going to take place. And in fact, since the end of World War II, trade has risen twice as fast as domestic economic growth. In other words, the global economy has been expanding by about 3% a year, but the volume of trade has been rising by 6% a year.

That certainly explains why, no matter where you are in the world, you're more likely than not to see shop windows filled with imports.

The growth of trade has made the foreign exchange market boom, and has created a lot of different kinds of work. You may have thought that foreign exchange trading was just a bunch of former Nintendo whizzes buying and selling astronomical amounts of currencies to make money on minuscule price movements, but that's not its primary purpose. Obviously, the Canadian fabric importer we just talked about has to pay the French textile maker in francs; first he has to exchange his Canadian dollars for French francs. Those kinds of transactions are happening more frequently and in bigger volumes all the time. In 1973, $15 billion worth of foreign currency was exchanged every day. By 1995, it was up to $1.2 trillion.

But it wasn't just a few more tourists going to Europe or a few more Canadians paying for imported goods that created that kind of growth. The actual way businesses are organized was changing. Businesses stepped up their direct investment in foreign businesses. That may not sound revolutionary, but it is. Instead of a multinational having factories and offices around the world, each making a complete product for its local country market, the branches of the same multinational began competing with each other for the right to produce just one product for the whole world. They did this by searching out other businesses to help them get a competitive edge. A sister company might have a component part. A competitor might be willing to partner in the production of one subcomponent. With the money companies received from selling equity in their business, they reorganized themselves into global entities designed to maximize shareholder value. Shareholder value has never been as important as it is today. A generation or so ago, shareholders were prepared to accept inefficiencies and modest returns because they believed that if profits were plowed back into the company, the company would always be around to pay modest dividends.

Neither consumers nor shareholders will accept that any longer: globalization is obliging companies to match the leaders in economic performance or else disappear.

This new and intense competition is forcing companies to focus on what they do best. For instance, Microsoft is a terrific software marketer but is less good at developing the products it sells. So it lets someone else do a great deal of its product development (and its financial management). Dell is a superbly efficient assembler and direct mail operation, so that's all it does. It has no sales force, no showrooms, no dealer network. Using money that others might spend on a dealer network or increased promotion has made Dell the number two computer vendor in the U.S. That's called "outsourcing." Since its privatization, British Airways has become the most efficient airline in the world. It recently announced that it would outsource ticketing and reservations functions if they could not match an external supplier's cost and efficiency.

Companies everywhere are now buying into other companies to get a competitive edge. They are forming partnerships and alliances—with competitors for one or more components, with suppliers who know the companies' needs as soon as they do, and with customers who will stay loyal only as long as the companies deliver. Thanks to advances in transportation technology, firms can outsource far from home. Thanks to advances in information technology, suppliers, key customers and producers can organize themselves into one global network; everyone in the network can know almost instantaneously what needs to be done. So what used to be done at one plant or office can now be done more efficiently in bits and pieces around the world.

This is a far cry from the way businesses used to operate— vertically, with information coming from the customer to the producer, up through the managerial ranks to the decision maker somewhere in the middle ranks of the firm, then out to the suppliers, until, days, weeks or months later, everything would be assembled and shipped to the customer. And it's very different

from the idea most of us have about trade, that trade takes place when a company buys or sells a final product to a stranger—at arm's length. All our national accounts assume that trade in different products takes place between unrelated companies. In fact, most trade today involves non-arm's-length transfers of components and subcomponents around a global production chain. For example, the U.S. accounts for about 20% of world output, yet an enormous proportion of what gets counted as international trade is U.S. companies moving products from country to country for the design, component manufacture, assembly and packaging. Canada's hefty billion-dollar-a-day trade with the U.S. is dominated by non-arm's-length transactions within multinational firms rather than the classical model of a company performing all its operations in a Canadian location and then transferring a finished product to a foreign customer. It's important, because governments the world over enact bad economic policies based on the erroneous assumption that all trade is arm's-length trade, that if they've bought more from foreigners than they've sold (that is, they have a "trade deficit"), it's bad and "something" has to be done about it. This new way of trading makes a mockery of all national accounts. And it makes a huge difference to the efficiency with which products and services can get to customers. Firms that understand what they do best, and then form close relationships with their customers and suppliers, are the ones that generally will get their products out the door fastest, cheapest and most profitably.

European countries have also developed production and distribution networks outside their home countries, particularly in order to build and sell advanced products. One example is the surge in telecommunications spending by European manufacturing companies. Manufacturers such as Volkswagen and Mercedes Benz outspend banks—and even some phone companies—on telecommunications because they, like their North American counterparts, use a wide array of radio frequency (advanced broad-band) networks to coordinate a complex, multi-country

manufacturing process. As for the Asia-Pacific region, this is where "just-in-time," networked production began.

It may be easier now to understand my earlier reference to India and Latin America poised just outside the triad of economic regions. For decades, these two regions had more or less closed their economies to the outside world with a combination of high tariffs, currency controls, political instability and state central planning. And each had miserably underperformed other developing countries, especially those in Southeast Asia, in terms of industrial output, economic growth, and reduction of poverty, illiteracy and infant mortality. In the last several years, both have repudiated their former visions and are endeavouring to dismantle the systems that have left a billion and a half people far behind in the universal quest for a higher standard of living and a better quality of life. But it is too early to say whether these two giants will join the world in one or another of the trading groups. If they do, then for all the reasons above, they (and we) will profit.

JOBS AS AN INDUSTRIAL ARTIFACT
New technologies and record amounts of direct foreign investment have changed the way business is organized, and have forced companies to compete or die. While global competition has pushed company share values to unprecedented levels (with the expectation of still greater earnings ahead), it has also made the Job merely an artifact of the industrial age. Here's why.

The old "value chain" that made companies profitable, successful and big employers with lots of Jobs was one that allowed them to do everything within their own walls: taking raw materials in (Jobs for unskilled and semi-skilled workers), manufacturing products (Jobs for blue-collar workers), selling them (Jobs for white-collar workers), and providing supporting services such as promotion, service and billing (Jobs for white- and pink-collar workers). No longer. Today's companies outsource or subcontract to designated key suppliers as many links on the value chain as they can, and focus on the operations they do best. The "value

added" to the company's efficiency and ability to beat the competition is in these chain-link networks. And the networks ignore national boundaries. A humble toilet may be designed in Italy, manufactured in Germany and assembled close to the market. Your call to a help line may be handled several thousand miles away, thanks to toll-free phone numbers. A complicated component may cross several borders between design and assembly.

This move to the "networked enterprise" has had a profound impact on work. It has made both skills and wages comparable worldwide. A non-skill job is "worth" only the lowest non-skill wage wherever it is in the world. This means that Canadians who are non-skilled are unlikely to get these unskilled jobs, as they can be done elsewhere at Third World wage rates. Advanced manufacturing jobs can be done anywhere a skilled workforce exists. An engine plant in Mexico may be staffed entirely with college graduates who have mastered statistical quality control and other advanced procedures. They will compete against car plants in Germany and Canada.

The new patterns of production have also eliminated the coordination jobs that middle managers used to perform, hence the relatively new phenomenon of white-collar layoffs and early retirement for executives as part of the reorganization and downsizing to drive down companies' costs. Moreover, continuous technological innovation is generating a similar, but permanent, cycle within the technically skilled workforce. New graduates with the latest knowledge are hired to take the place of older workers—by as little as two to five years—whose skills have not kept up with changes in the industry.

This new world is harsh. As the industrial age matured, people came to cherish the relative stability of the social contract—a Job at which you put in your time productively and then you clocked out and had a life. Nine to five, five days a week, 50 weeks a year for 40 years, for a regular paycheque to feed the kids, buy a house, and a car every few years, no aggravation, and at the end of 40 years, a pension. We learned the skills we needed to deal

with that world. The pace of change was slower. The skills we learned—without a lot of schooling—lasted a lifetime. Now that world is going, going, gone. New skills are required. Today, if you're a technical specialist and retrain continuously to stay ahead of the innovation curve, you will always have work. There's a very serious shortage of highly qualified workers, partly because companies have not upgraded their current staff's training. Instead, they have been relying on the education system to supply the upgraded skills they need. However, this strategy is unsustainable, and companies will have to do more to produce the workforces they need.

While the new engines of work in the information economy are self-employed professionals, entrepreneurs and small businesses, along with the networked transnational companies, services that have to be performed in local neighbourhoods will provide a great deal of traditional work. Nursing, plumbing, catering, electrical, mechanical, restaurant service and other familiar work will all continue to be available, although much of it will be done by self-employed professionals. Many "jobs" will require additional training (for instance, car mechanics now have to understand the microchips that control many automotive functions that used to operate mechanically), but many others will require only the care and attention customers have always demanded of service providers. And new services are showing up every day. It's been 30 years since door-to-door delivery was common. Now it's coming back: dry-cleaning pick-up, milk delivery, and other services such as total household management—people who will do your shopping, walk your dog, tidy the house and take the kids to soccer practice and ballet class.

We are continually prone to underestimating the changes we are experiencing. The nine-to-five job was the product of a century-long interplay between labour markets and technological change. Before industrialization, the link between time and work was seasonal. When workers, newly cleared from their farms, entered the factories in the mid-19th century, the factory owners

tried to make people match the machines in endurance, and started thinking in terms of work hours. Whole families worked around the big textile machines of the day. The Factory Acts at the end of the 19th century put an end to unregulated labour, and productivity rose because shorter hours led owners to look at ways to use their capital more productively.

The efficiency movement, begun by Frederick Taylor in 1870, emerged from an understanding of how to make invested money more productive: it made an economic virtue of precise timing and movement. "Taylorism" (the Total Quality movement of its day), which led to "efficiency experts," the world's first management consultants, set the pattern for the Job as remunerative activity precisely defined by the employer, the supplier of the Job. The Job had a strict task definition, set working hours and a precise position in a hierarchical, compartmentalized and centralized organization. Management styles came and went, but the concept of the Job lasted until today's business revolution rendered it obsolete.

Now, globalization and technology are taking us to a new frontier, and the skills that are valuable on this frontier are not the virtues prized in an earlier era. Today's economy favours entrepreneurial people who treat each job as a freelance assignment, giving maximum value. The best assignments will go to those who have proven they can build and sustain high performance units or organizations. They then design their job to achieve the goals of the client.

Today's prized skills are not those of bureaucrats who oil the wheels of the organizational status quo, but those of entrepreneurs: people who can take a product from lab bench to market, the masters of the risk capital process, those who understand technology transfer, mavens of international regulation. The basics of these skills are taught in business schools, some community colleges, and some executive-training programs, but often they can be learned through involvement in another aspect of the process, using other skills already possessed.

Clearly, if you consider your career to be a series of relatively short-term assignments with a relatively large number of "employers," you can no longer count on a company pension when you reach retirement age. Instead, you may have to coordinate a number of benefits or contribution plans with your personal savings in a personalized retirement strategy. You may want to start today by looking at the pension plan you have at work.

Inflation is less of a problem than it was, thanks to central bankers, but private pension plans have no significant inflation protection. More important, although companies no longer offer lifetime jobs, too often that reality has not percolated down to their pension arrangements. In some 65% of private plans, employees can be fired and not get the employer's contribution to their plan because even after years of employment, they haven't stayed long enough to have the full pension "vested" with them.

As a country, Canada has not adjusted as well as it should have to the revolutions we lump together as "globalization." Free trade and better fiscal management were designed to make us more competitive and raise our standard of living. However, these policies have not been sufficient to overcome the problems created by other government policies. Canada has a very expensive tax structure whose dead weight discourages achievement, innovation and growth. As Chart 2–1 on page 52 shows, among industrialized countries, Canada's tax system is the hardest on average-income families and above-average income earners.

The combined effect of eroding purchasing power and higher taxes has been to depress private savings, as Statistics Canada pointed out at the end of 1997.

Once again in the third quarter of 1997 ... Saving fell below $8 billion in the third quarter compared with $30 billion a year ago, and $57 billion in 1992, its all time high. In relation to disposable income, these saving levels yield a saving rate of 1.5% in the latest quarter, in sharp contrast with 19.7% in the first quarter of 1982.

CHART 2–1 **G-7 Marginal Tax Rates by Income Group**

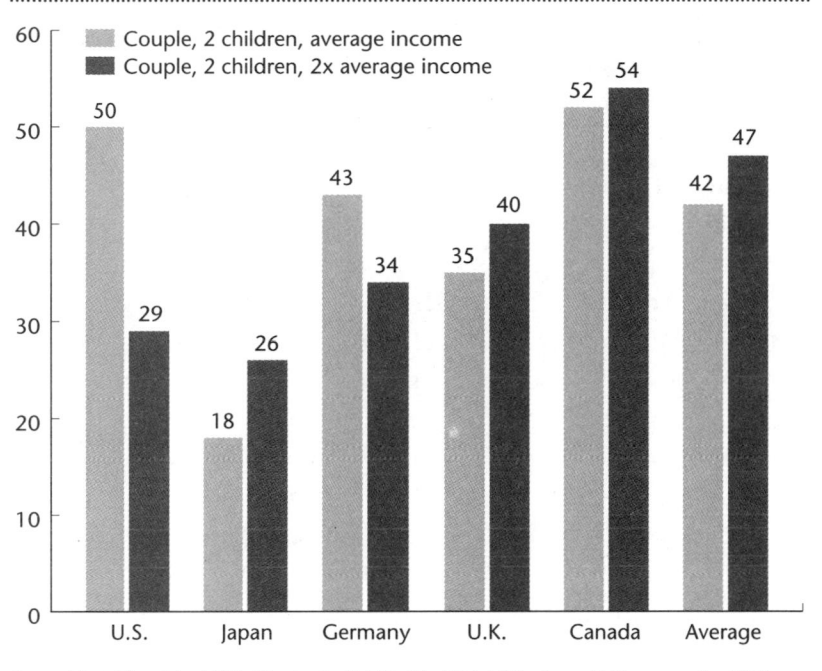

Source: Adapted from School Briefs, "Bearing the Weight of the Market," The Economist Newspaper, Dec. 1997

We support an education system that talks about lifelong learning but effectively preserves the old ways of doing things and is too rigid to provide new skills for people at mid-career. Our uncoordinated and often conflicting provincial, territorial and national regulations make it difficult for innovators to bring new products and processes to market. The result of these policies has been a deterioration in our living standards relative to other countries for the past two decades. Twenty years ago, Canadians had the second-highest living standard in the world, after the United States, measured by GDP per capita. With the exchange rate of the Canadian dollar at an all-time low relative to the American dollar, we now rank eighth, behind such countries as Luxembourg, Switzerland, Norway and Iceland.

Our living standards continue to decline. Educational opportunities to acquire advanced skills and entrepreneurial attitudes

are easier to find elsewhere. Highly skilled professionals are reluctant to come to Canada to work, partly because our immigration regulations make no allowances for working spouses or health-challenged children, but mostly for the same reason that talented Canadians leave: they make and keep more money elsewhere. Unskilled jobs are less available than they used to be, and those that are available (hard, dirty work, with long hours, often outside metropolitan areas) are not attractive to many Canadians.

TABLE 2–2 **Top 10 OECD Countries in GDP per Capita**

	PURCHASING POWER IN US$
Luxembourg	$31,303
U.S.A.	26,438
Switzerland	24,809
Norway	22,672
Iceland	21,938
Japan	21,795
Denmark	21,529
Canada	**21,039**
Austria	20,773
Germany	20,497
France	19,939
OECD Average	19,365

Source: OECD National Accounts, National Aggregates, Vol. 1, March 1997

Part of the erosion of living standards can be traced to weak competitiveness. In terms of national competitiveness, we rank number 10, according to the World Economic Forum annual report, behind such leaders as the U.S., Switzerland and Singapore. Our people and our infrastructure rank near the top; what pulls us back is our management and our government. True, as reported by Statistics Canada, Canada's total productivity has improved during the last 25 years, but so has that of other countries, especially

the U.S. American productivity gains are half again as much as ours in the same time frame.

Moreover, much like our major trading partners, Canada is a high-cost, aging society, and this trend is increasing, that is, our population is increasingly either too old or too young to work. Without significant attention to innovation, we are going to see our national output decline as the baby boomers leave the workforce.

Only increasing our productivity through innovation at the leading edge of technological change will give us the leverage to offset the tremendous drag of these demographic trends. Yet Canada has notably failed to develop such advanced capacity, apart from in the services sector. Canada is the only OECD country that has no significant advanced manufacturing capacity; we are merely a middle-level technological power in manufacturing. This has important implications for our ability to develop the concentrations of next-generation advanced services such as engineering and education that are needed to sustain a leading economy as a whole.

These are very serious failures in the Canadian economy that are not well understood by either economists or policy makers. Clearly, they have to do with our historic dependence on natural resources, whose relative value has been declining since the 1980s. Free trade and deregulation have helped to some degree, but too many sectors are still regulated in economically unsound ways.

For example, our auto-trade regime discourages competition from Europe and Japan. Our wheat and steel shipments (and sales) to the U.S. are curtailed by official and unofficial quota arrangements. Our food, airline and telecommunications networks are protected from foreign suppliers who could substantially reduce prices in Canada. Our financial services are controlled by an oligopoly of six banks that is as much an obstacle as a trampoline for business growth. "From eros to sclerosis" justly describes Canada's economic trajectory from the 1960s to the present and future. Without more creative and harmonious

public policies, Canada will never achieve the improvements in productivity necessary to support a rising standard of living.

An important class of victims of this sclerosis are Canada's unemployed. Canada's policies toward the unemployed have not changed since the days of "relief" during the Great Depression of 1929–39: provide temporary, short-term financial aid until the Job market returns to re-employ them. Our federal and provincial support policies (unemployment insurance and welfare, respectively) have always assumed that the Job market, like the economy, went through cyclical ups and downs, long after it was clear that structural changes in the economy were eliminating whole classes of Jobs permanently. Social programs, intended to "retrain" people whose skills had been rendered obsolete by technological and organizational change, have comprehensively failed because the designers of the programs have underestimated the needs of both the people and the economy. The most creative initiative taken in recent years to "deal" with the unemployment problem has been to rename "Unemployment Insurance" "Employment Insurance."

For several years now, governments have been tightening eligibility requirements for both insurance and welfare, in an effort to pay down their debts. Support payments have never been about employment, only about support. People who take paid work while they are in any publicly supported social program are subject to a 100% tax rate on their income—so they have little incentive to take paid work. It should not be surprising to see the unemployment rate still near double digits, and the burden of taxation on working people as high as it ever was. Aside from the wasted lives embedded in Canada's unemployment and underemployment levels, hundreds of thousands of people unwilling or unable to find productive paid work drag down our GDP per capita and with it our collective living standards.

The panoramic economic picture this paints is this: Canada is an aging, sclerotic country cycling its savings between public and private hands without adding value. The most powerful

economic and political groups are using their position and creativity blindly to make the pace of change accommodate their comfort levels. The middle class pays heavily for an inefficient and ineffective set of social programs, and yet is the prime beneficiary of many of them—education, for example. Politicians are loath to present to the electorate the reality that education is being provided at below-market values for fear of being thrown out of office.

This portrait not only is somewhat depressing, but also has major implications for any Canadian-based retirement strategy. Why? The government retirement programs allow you to tax-shelter up to $13,500 a year. Eighty percent of your tax-sheltered plan must be in deemed Canadian dollars. The Canadian stock market has risen 30% less than the American stock market in the last 20 years. Canadian dollars, which had the same purchasing power as American dollars 23 years ago, now have 40% less purchasing power. The government, which is responsible for maintaining the purchasing power of the dollar, has ostensibly set up the following wager with you: that the tax-free accumulation of your nest egg will be faster than the loss of its purchasing power. Without a 180-degree reversal of the direction of the dollar and the economy, you can't win that bet.

PLANNING FOR 21st-CENTURY RETIREMENT

Whether you take the bet or not, there are general points to learn from what has occurred to Jobs and work as a result of the forces we've been discussing. For one thing, without a major policy change, the Canadian dollar will continue to lose purchasing power as our competitiveness continues to deteriorate. The best of our young people will seek careers outside Canada (as they do now, increasingly) because of lack of opportunity here at home. (This also implies the need for foreign currency to go visit them.)

These same conditions mean that those who have money invested outside the country in foreign currencies will do better

than those who keep their pensions in Canada. (Even U.S. Treasury bills offer higher rates of return than Canadian bonds, and also offer better protection against exchange rate risk.)

These points go to the basic reality that you should organize your life as though you were a freelance consultant—even to your regular job. Our individual chances of organizing a successful retirement would be a lot better if our public policy weren't trying to thwart us at every step by clinging to an outworn picture of the past whenever it seems to suit some short-term advantage. Given the fact that the Job is no longer a reality in the new world of "work that needs to be done," we and we alone are responsible for ourselves—and our retirement. Part Two will show you how to take up the challenge of securing your finances in a world in which instability and insecurity go hand in hand with prosperity.

3

··

The Myth of Universal
Health Care

One of the true tests of leadership is the ability to recognize
a problem before it becomes an emergency.

FACT: THE NUMBER OF Canadians over 65 is expected to more
than double within the next 40 years. Fact: the number of the
very elderly—those over 85—will grow at an even faster rate. Fact:
people over 65 use more than half the hospital days, undergo
about half the surgical procedures, account for about a quarter of
physician billing, and use about 40% of the prescription drugs
in Canada.

In short, our aging population puts huge demands on the
health care system. True, older bodies have more things go wrong
with them and need more attention and monitoring. We also
have large numbers of health care providers who need something
to do, so they are doing more for seniors. And technological
advances allow us to perform more and different procedures.
Whatever the reasons, the fact is that seniors are the single biggest
users of health care services. And this is occurring when health
care budgets have stopped increasing, as Canadian governments
are obliged by their creditors to end new borrowing and get their
debt levels headed downward. With the state of health care and

its funding so precarious, how many of the health care services now provided through medicare may have to be paid for in the future out of retirement income?

Canadians love their health care system. In poll after poll Canadians single it out as a major defining characteristic of the country. When asked in a *Maclean's* and Decima poll what most unites us as a nation, 75% of respondents rated Canada's health system number 1. But during the last five years, pride in our health system has given way to concern, as funding freezes become funding cuts, hospital bed closures lead to hospital closures, and lengthening surgery waiting lists are dealt with privately in for-profit clinics in Canada or the U.S.

At the same time, our expectations for the health care system have fallen. A recent *Maclean's* poll indicated that 81% of Canadians feel a two-tier health system will be in place by 2005. Even respondents who were generally optimistic about the future on other issues foresee a two-tier system by a 3-to-1 margin. And 47% found the emergence of a two-tier system acceptable. They're talking about an official two-tier system. An unofficial one already exists.

Despite their dismay, Canadians' low expectations for health care are closer to reality than are their notions about retirement income or job entitlement. Maybe that's because the unsustainability of the health care system has been evident since its inception. For at least 50 years, Canada's health care system has been shaped by three interrelated tensions:

- federal-provincial wrangling;
- the debate between those who, for ideological reasons, want a public system, and those who, for ideological or economic reasons, want private involvement; and
- funding.

These tensions have pulled in one direction at some points in time and then recombined to pull the other way.

Until recently, Canada's health care system has undergone a gradual movement towards an increasingly uniform, public system. That movement, whether effectively delivering timely health care or not, has slowed, stopped or reversed, depending on your viewpoint. The federal government, the main architect and guardian of a public, uniform system, has given up the financial control that maintained its role in the system; the resulting waiting lists and hospital closures have led to increasing opportunities for private sector solutions.

THE EVOLUTION OF THE SYSTEM

The 1867 British North America Act (and later, the 1982 Canada Constitution Act) explicitly gave provinces jurisdiction over the establishment and management of hospitals. The federal government has responsibility to ensure the safety and quality of drugs and food, and is also responsible for providing health care services to certain populations such as the military, but clearly, jurisdiction over the vast bulk of health care lies with the provinces.

While the provinces wield constitutional jurisdiction, the federal government provides much of the funding for the health system in Canada. Through the use of this federal "spending power," Health Canada has sought to impose its view of health care uniformly across the country. In practice, this has been one of the sources of tension on the system. The federal government's purpose has been to create a near-uniform public system, while provinces have wanted the scope to act in health care as they saw fit. Indeed, this frustrating mix of federal and provincial responsibility first became an issue during the Depression, when the existing network of private, charitable and municipal health care services broke down. Earlier, in the 19th century, Canadians paid doctors, hospitals and other health care providers out of their own pockets. Even after the Depression, until well past the mid-point of the 20th century, Canadians paid for their health care directly. Those who could not pay had to rely on the charity of religious organizations and municipal social assistance,

or they had to band together in cooperative groups to fund medical essentials.

The Depression of the 1930s put stress on all these systems. Fewer people could pay for services, municipalities could no longer provide assistance, and voluntary organizations were overwhelmed by the number of those seeking help. Canadian governments began the slow cobbling together of today's health system.

British Columbia passed a medical insurance act in 1935, but doctors rejected it and the legislation collapsed. The same year, the federal government passed an Employment and Social Insurance Act to help the needy. It was ruled unconstitutional in 1937, on the grounds that it interfered in the jurisdiction of the provinces. In 1940, a constitutional amendment allowed the federal government to pass an unemployment insurance act and to consider other social programs. Saskatchewan was the first jurisdiction to pass successful legislation, with the introduction of public hospital insurance in 1946. Health care had been the main plank of Tommy Douglas's successful CCF election platform, and while the government was not able to do all it wanted to, it started the process. British Columbia and Alberta followed soon after.

The federal government weighed in with National Health Grants in 1948, offering to share costs with the provinces for health planning, training and hospital construction. All provinces opted for this very attractive scheme, perhaps unaware that it was the start of the federal incursion into health care.

The real changes came in the 1950s and '60s with the broadening of public hospital insurance and the introduction of public medical insurance. Until then, many Canadians held private hospital and medical insurance through such organizations as Blue Cross, or doctor-sponsored plans such as the TransCanada Medical Plans. In 1957, the federal government passed the Hospital Insurance and Diagnostic Services Act and offered to share with the provinces, on a roughly 50–50 basis, hospital operating expenses. Provinces like Saskatchewan eagerly accepted the federal offer, which furthered its goal of owning the health

care system and employing the workers in it. Ontario and Alberta were more reluctant to abandon privately financed health care but were seduced by the lure of having to contribute only half the funding. By 1961, all provinces and territories were on board. Quebec subsequently went its own way in 1963, negotiating block grants from the federal government to deliver its own health services as long as those services didn't differ too much from those in other provinces. It organized its health and social services as one unit, using local community services centres staffed by doctors, social workers and community development workers as the entry point.

The jewel in the crown of publicly funded health care was the Medical Care Act of 1966, commonly known as medicare. Saskatchewan had introduced medicare in 1962 and was eager to agree to the federal proposal to share fees. British Columbia and Alberta were also ready to sign the new federal offer when it was made. Within five years, all the provinces had signed on.

All these changes took place amid protest from health care workers, insurance companies and others in favour of a private system. Doctors went on strike when Saskatchewan and Quebec introduced their medicare legislation.

It took less than a decade after the introduction of medicare and other cost-shared programs for the federal government to realize it could not sustain the matching grants it had offered the provinces. In 1977, it introduced the Established Programs Financing Act (EPF), which changed the funding formula from matching grants to block funding in the form of tax transfers and a cash payment based on the rate of change of GNP (gross national product) and changes in provincial populations.

This legislation created general bitterness among the provinces, which felt that the federal government had baited them with attractive cost-shared programs and then, once they were "hooked" for meeting strict criteria, cut the funding. This bitterness grew as the act was amended four more times, reducing the federal government's cash contribution each time. Provinces were

expected to uphold the principles set out by the federal government, but with less money. This is the same bitterness that met the federal government's recent introduction of the Canada Health and Social Transfer Act.

For its part, the federal government had its own suspicions that provinces were not using its health care contributions for health care but for their own priorities, including highway construction (although the federal government could not prove it). In 1979, the Hall Commission warned doctors and hospitals not to "extra bill," that is, charge patients the difference between the agreed billing rates for services and the higher rates that doctors or hospitals wished to charge. These charges, in the commission's view, were creating a two-tier system.

The Canada Health Act replaced the Hospital Insurance and Diagnostic Services Act and the Medical Care Act in 1984. It set out the conditions for federal health care contributions to the provinces: a provincial program must meet five criteria to be eligible for full federal contribution. While these five criteria were originally simply program criteria, they are now treated as the fundamental principles of health care in Canada, and are as follows:

- universality: all residents must be entitled to insured health services;
- portability: services must be available to people temporarily outside their home province and the waiting period for new residents must not exceed three months;
- accessibility: access to services cannot be prevented by charges or other mechanisms;
- comprehensiveness: the provincial program must cover all necessary hospital and medical services; and
- public administration: the program must be administered by a public authority accountable to the provincial government.

To summarize, the Canada Health Act determined the eligibility of provinces for federal health care payments and the EPF determined how much they would get.

The 1996 Canada Health and Social Transfer Act (CHST) was the latest salvo in the health care funding struggle between the provinces and the federal government. It replaced the EPF (which covered not only health but post-secondary education as well) and the Canada Assistance Plan (federal transfers for social assistance). Funding is now provided in the form of cash transfers and tax-point transfers (a reduction of federal tax rates allowing provinces to raise additional revenues without increasing the overall tax burden on Canadians).

The CHST gives the provinces more flexibility to allocate the money as they see fit among health care, post-secondary education, social assistance and social service programs. But Ottawa cut the transfer levels again when it introduced the CHST, so the provinces' happiness with the benefits of the new flexibility was lost in their anger over enduring another cut in federal transfer payments while having to maintain federal standards.

A UNIFORM SYSTEM

Do we have a uniform health system across Canada?

The simple answer is "no." In reality, there is no "system" at all. There is little integration among the various components of health care, from physicians to hospitals and clinics. There are 12 (and soon will be 13) different provincial and territorial delivery systems; each province and territory operates its own health care plan, and spends differing amounts on it. The average spending on health care in 1997 was $1,604 per person, but this figure conceals some wide swings from region to region. For example, in the Northwest Territories, spending was $3,188 per person, in Nova Scotia, $1,414 per person.

What you get for this money is hospital care in a ward, meals, necessary nursing services, provision of surgical, diagnostic, obstetrical, laboratory, x-ray, radiotherapy and anaesthetic supplies and

services, as well as drugs and prostheses doled out in the hospital. You also get outpatient services such as laboratory, radiology and other diagnostic procedures, along with their interpretive services, to help diagnose and treat most minor medical and many surgical complaints. Medical care plans cover medically required services given by a medical practitioner, and usually include some limited dental-surgical procedures, if they are performed in a hospital.

You have to pay for private and semi-private hospital accommodation and special nursing, and for drugs ordered after hospital discharge or prescribed outside a hospital setting. Nor does medicare cover services offered through Workers' Compensation or Veterans Affairs. Cosmetic surgery, sex-change operations, experimental procedures, and a few other things aren't included either. But all provinces and territories provide supplementary benefits to the national program for children, seniors and those on social assistance. Two provinces, British Columbia and Alberta, charge health care premiums: citizens pay for extra coverage, such as for ambulance services. Depending on where you live, you may or may not get dental care, optometry, naturopathic, ambulance or other services. Increasingly popular "alternative" or "complementary" therapies—hypnosis, reflexology, visualization, massage and acupuncture—are generally paid out-of-pocket by individual Canadians. This is one of the fastest-growing areas of health care and is completely in the private sector.

All provinces offer some prescription services, mostly for those 65 and older. New Brunswick offers coverage for those on social assistance, as does Ontario. Manitoba and Saskatchewan offer limited coverage for drugs, and in Alberta, drug costs are covered for those who pay premiums. Quebec has recently introduced a mandatory premium system for seniors and those on social assistance that covers the bulk of prescription costs. British Columbia and the Yukon offer full or partial assistance for all citizens. Few provinces pay for much in the way of home care or extended care services; yet that is one of the directions in which many experts see health care heading.

At latest count, Canada's annual health care spending totalled $80 billion. The universal part, that is, public sector or tax-based spending, accounted for 68%, or $54 billion. Individual Canadians paid the balance. Startling as it may be, Canadians have always paid a significant portion of their own health care costs. In recent years, that share has been growing: back in 1975, public funding accounted for just over 75% of health care spending. So while Canada is in the midst of a debate about "privatizing" health care, we should remember that a great many health care services have always been "privatized." Of the $54 billion paid for out of the general tax pot, the two largest recipients are hospitals (45.5%) and physicians (20%).

Thus, we already pay for about a third of health care expenditures. We buy private health insurance and we pay for prescription drugs, the single biggest category of private health care spending (31%). Individual Canadians pay for their other health professionals—dentists, chiropractors, optometrists, podiatrists, osteopaths, naturopaths, physiotherapists. These make up the second-largest category (26%) of private health care spending. In addition, costs for travel medical insurance, private hospital rooms, hospital-room telephone and television services and private nursing are borne by individuals. We pay for exams and documents for employment, judicial or insurance purposes and, in many provinces, preventive treatment such as flu and pneumonia vaccines and telephone prescription renewals.

THE ULTIMATE MYTH

The federal government is still trying to preserve the myth that Canada has a single-tier, publicly administered, universal health care system. Indeed, the Minister of Health said recently that the government would like to extend publicly insured health care to cover home care and pharmacare. The provinces, intent on deflecting public concerns about deteriorating service, criticize such plans as wishful and accuse the federal government of currying public favour by offering new health programs on top of

programs that are already scarcely affordable. In the meantime, provinces complain about having to uphold the principles of the core system with less money.

What makes the health care battle doubly frustrating and protracted is the two ideologically opposed camps leading the public discussion of health care issues. On one side are those who feel that a publicly funded, uniform and universal health care system is a right of citizenship too important to be left to the market of doctors, patients and hospital providers. On the other side are those who believe that market forces can devise better, more flexible solutions than a health care system dominated by monopolistic government providers. While almost everyone agrees that the health care system needs to be rebuilt, there is very little middle ground between the opposing views on the three major drivers of change in the health system today: funding pressures, the pressure to adapt the system to meet the needs of an aging population and the pressure to cut costs through the application of new technology.

FUNDING ISSUES

Contrary to mythology, overall funding for the health system continued to grow until the mid-1990s (1994). In terms of GDP, that funding has stayed relatively constant for the last few years at slightly under 10% while GDP has continued to rise. Some of the funding changes reflect changing health care practices: for example, we spend less on hospitals and more on drugs, reflecting the power of drugs to shorten hospital stays. We also spend less on physicians (an easy target for the health care bureaucrats) and more on nurses, owing to reskilling and job redesign. Other segments of the system, especially administrators, have continued to receive whopping increases.

This "other" component of the health care system has increased steadily, doubling in less than 10 years—by far the fastest-growing category of health expense. This category now exceeds what we spend on any other component of the system except hospitals.

The new reality of the system reflects this allocation of resources. Real spending has hit a ceiling and administrators rather than health care professionals have increased their control over priorities. Consequently, there are longer waiting lists, shorter hospital stays, more administrators, and more doctors leaving for the United States. In 1997, Quebec mandated forced retirement for hundreds of doctors and nurses as part of its drive to balance the budget by the next election.

There are serious implications for retirement planning. Reality has a way of breaking through even the most cherished of illusions. Eventually, health care legislation will change and the private sector will fill the gaps. If that doesn't happen, those who can pay will buy services outside the visible economy or outside the country. In either case, people who want the services will have to be prepared to pay for them.

Frozen resource levels are at the root of rising privately paid care. When provinces "de-list" health care services, deeming them no longer medically necessary and covered under provincial plans, the private sector steps in to supply the services. Since there is no legal standard in the Canada Health Act to define "medically necessary" services, provinces can define the term any way they like. Annual health checkups, for example, are no longer covered by public insurance in several provinces. Neither are routine circumcisions. Many surgical procedures are now being done on an outpatient basis. Pre-admission outpatient clinics have replaced the one- to three-day hospital stay before surgery. Nursing care and other publicly funded in-hospital services are not covered outside the hospital.

The average stay in hospitals has been shortened by about 25% in the last decade. There's nothing wrong with this; new technological and clinical capabilities allow health care providers to do more to, and for, the average patient. But patients have to recover somewhere. As recovery and convalescence time in hospital decreases, inevitably home care costs rise. Consequently, those who have been discharged early from hospitals or treated

in day-surgery units, and who may still require some care, must pay for it out of their own pocket.

The same trends have led to increased waiting lists for many procedures. In a 1996 Angus Reid survey, 54% of Canadians reported an increase in hospital emergency room waiting times, 53% reported an increase in surgery waiting times, 43% reported longer waiting times for tests such as MRI (magnetic resonance imaging) and 41% reported a decrease in access to specialist services. The College of Family Physicians of Canada surveyed its members on similar points and found higher percentages—in the range of 62%–86% of respondents reporting longer waiting lists. The Fraser Institute, a British Columbia-based research group, regularly publishes a national hospital waiting list survey which suggests that waiting times in most regions are getting longer. Anecdotal evidence suggests this is generally true, unless you know someone in the system. (A call to a doctor one knows well enough to consider a friend can bump that person to the head of the line—part of the two- or three-tier system that already exists.)

Capital spending in the health care system has also levelled off. This means that new, high-tech diagnostic machinery is only slowly being brought into the public system. This is particularly harmful because it means that (1) the quality of health care available to Canadians is slipping and (2) more pressure is building on scarce new resources. The result: more rationing by waiting, or, for those who can't or won't wait, more patients travelling to private clinics to pay for the service. MRI machines, for example, are excellent diagnostic tools, but hugely expensive. With MRI waiting lists more than six months long, many Canadians are pursuing other options—for example, visiting private clinics in Canada, where they pay a facility fee and the rest of the fee is billed to medicare.

But even more telling are those growing figures for administrative costs. While other large organizations are using new technology to slash overheads and turn administration costs around, our health care system is doing the opposite. For example, since

when do we need 13 jurisdictions to handle 33 million potential patients? Four or five would probably be enough, and that would free up additional billions for new labs, diagnostics and surgeries to eliminate waiting lists and improve quality. Trouble is, we can't count on our bureaucrats, who have so much invested in the status quo, to do more than tinker at the margins. Inevitably, then, the system will gradually privatize itself from the sharp end backwards.

Another form of expanding private activity is health insurance. Private health insurance—both employee benefit plans paid for by corporations and those paid for by individuals—is a growing area. Out-of-country medical insurance is the most obvious example of individual insurance, but there are others. For example, some companies now offer dental, drug and medical coverage for those not covered by a group plan—like the self-employed. At least one such company also offers a policy that pays a lump sum to the policy holder upon diagnosis of an "eligible" illness: heart attack, stroke, life-threatening cancer or multiple sclerosis, for example. The policy holder can use that money for living expenses, or for non-insured medical services such as experimental treatments, treatment abroad or private nursing, therapy and other services.

Private companies servicing insurance firms constitute another area of growth in the private system. "Preferred provider network organizations" such as Ontario-based CompreMed Canada Inc. have networks of physicians who provide medical and diagnostic services to insurance companies. (Insurance companies are considered "third parties." If a procedure is requested by a third party, it does not fall under the Canada Health Act and is therefore not a publicly insured service.) Firms also provide "navigation" or "advocacy" services to corporations for their employees, often serving as the primary point of contact with the patient, directing them to the appropriate specialist service in its network, and following the patient from start to finish. According to users, this advocacy dramatically shortens time away from work for recovery, and improves employees' overall health status.

A different sort of private sector firm are organizations that specialize in one procedure or area. For example, the abdominal wall hernia procedure. The patient pays for semi-private accommodation, and the hospital bills the government for all operations according to the prescribed fee. The province may also pay a rental fee to the hospital for use of its facilities. Even after paying both these fees, it is cheaper for the province than to have the operations done in the public system.

THE CHANGING FOCUS OF HEALTH CARE

While funding pressures are forcing big changes in health care in Canada, another set of changes is happening for more positive reasons. The health care model based on healing a disease or illness is gradually changing to one based on keeping people well. While this may seem like a minor force in comparison to funding cuts, it has many consequences. In the current model of health care, determinants of health are defined as "absence of disease." When the focus switches to wellness, determinants of health include a broad range of factors—social, economic, cultural, technological and political—that play a direct or indirect role in the health of both populations and individuals. Housing conditions, nutrition levels, employment, education levels, violence and poverty are a few specific determinants of health.

Clearly, there will always be a need for acute care. But the switch in focus will take pressure off the public system. However, a focus on well-informed, responsible patients means people must take more responsibility for their own health, making lifestyle choices that reduce risks of various illnesses. (For instance, the mortality rate for cardiovascular disease has fallen steadily in the last 25 years, due mainly to healthier lifestyles.) Patients are better informed about their health problems and choices, less deferential to physicians' authority, more likely to seek second opinions and more likely to take responsibility for choosing treatments. As well, there is less reliance on traditional medicine

alone, and more exploration of herbal and other complementary therapies which patients often pay for directly.

This change in focus means that we are moving from autonomous health care services being provided in isolation to an integrated health care delivery system along a network of health care—and in some cases, social services—providers. Prince Edward Island, for example, has established regions that integrate budgets and decision-making for health care institutions, community health services, social services, some justice services and housing.

It is hard to say where all these changes will take Canadians, but there are a few conclusions we can draw.

- There is less scope for federal action. The federal government's role in health care has always existed as a result of its spending. Given the levelling off of health care spending, the federal government has much less authority to mandate national standards and a weaker voice in health care. This is undermining the tenets of accessibility, universality and public payment in the Canada Health Act.
- There is a greater role for the private sector. That is in keeping with both the desires of customers for choice and the capacity of market-based solutions to meet demand.
- The demands on health care delivery will continue. Aging populations put more demands on our health care system, whether public or private. Home care, pharmacare and long-term care are three areas of concern to the highly educated, literate, populous and vocal cohort of seniors that will soon be emerging as the baby boomers age.
- Until then, more health care will be paid for directly.

The upshot? Plan to spend increasing amounts of your own money on medical care throughout retirement. As a rule of thumb, look at your medical bills at age 50 and double them every 10 years until age 105. If you're a boomer, there's a good chance you'll live that long—maybe longer.

4

··

The Myth of Viable Universal Pensions

The world is full of willing people, some willing
to work, the others willing to let them.
—**Robert Frost**

PURSUING OUR LOOK AT the major shifts in the world's economy and their effect on our ability to prepare for a comfortable
retirement, this chapter focuses on what's happened to the whole
strategy of government-led pension systems and why they're no
longer as effective as they once were. The backbone of Canada's
retirement income system is a mix of savings that the government obliges you to make and others that the government,
through its tax system, allows you to accumulate: a combination
of forced and negotiated savings. As a result of the changes discussed earlier, we have come to the point where the assumptions
underlying this kind of approach will no longer deliver the goods.
There must be a fundamental redesign that removes government
as the central pillar and organizer of the system.

The system that has evolved over the last 65 years rests on a
view of the world in which a national Big family member (Daddy,
Mommy or Brother—choose your metaphor) takes charge of your
fate for your own good because it knows more than you, is more

competent than you, and can make better choices than you. Specifically, most Canadians have been encouraged to believe that either government or their employer or both will save for their retirement. Chart 4–1 below sets out a typical situation. A 60-year-old person who has worked for the same company for 30 years and ended her career earning $50,000 a year can expect to have her income replaced as follows:

CHART 4–1 **Income Replacement**

SOURCE OF INCOME	% OF INCOME REPLACED	$
Old Age Security	9	4,500
Canada or Quebec Pension Plan	12	6,000
Pension from work	45	22,500
Personal savings	4	2,000
Total	70	35,000

So what's wrong with this picture? Why is it unlikely to continue?

First, note that almost a third of the retirement income comes from government plans. In the future, government won't have the tax revenue to keep the promises of the pension plans currently in place. Old Age Security and the Canada/Quebec Pension Plan are already being trimmed back and as we've seen in recent budgets, the government is trying to raise contributions to cover these lower payouts.

Second, note that two-thirds of the retirement income comes from pensions from work. This is not likely to continue, either. Pension plans at work are becoming irrelevant to more and more workers, partly because the available jobs during the last decade have mostly been at smaller companies, which are less likely to offer pension plans, and partly because the pension plans offered by big corporations were designed for a time when people worked for a single employer for a long time, if not their entire working

lives. In a world where jobs come and go, either job hoppers do not qualify for a pension or regulations make it hard to get value out of the plan when they leave. Just as important, employers themselves are finding the regulatory world governing pensions increasingly burdensome and costly to administer.

One of the easiest ways to strengthen the system so that people can live a comfortable retirement is therefore to expand the scope for personal saving. Under current arrangements, as the table shows, personal saving typically amounts to only 4% of replaced income. Yet government is in fact making it even more difficult, through higher taxes and restricted contribution levels, for individual saving to shore up the government-supplied portion. Worse, by raising taxes, governments in Canada are also making it less worthwhile for Canadians to save for themselves. So unless the rules change, private savings will play an even smaller role in the future than they do now. Why is this happening?

Governments are still in denial about their changing role in the affairs of citizens. The government-supplied retirement income plans may not disappear, because Canadians want income security, and politicians who want to get or stay in power will fight hard to keep the plans. But to survive and have a meaningful place in retirees' income, these plans need a total redesign that involves a much greater understanding of the way the new world works than politicians have shown to date. Until they catch up, we're left with a system that is antiquated, paternalistic, dysfunctional, and therefore unsustainable. But we have to understand its elements before we can see how to redesign it in our interest.

HOW THE SYSTEM EVOLVED

Canada's retirement income system began as a response to the devastation of the Great Depression of the 1930s and the world war of 1939–45. Ours was a rural, mainly agricultural country in the early part of the 20th century, and pensions were virtually unknown. The vast majority of Canadians worked on the land,

where the "job" was "the work that needs to be done," for which no pensions existed. Neither did they exist for those who moved into the cities to work in factories and stores.

The Depression years saw armies of Canadians unemployed and travelling the land in search of work. For most of them, it took World War II to supply enough jobs and growth to bring the Depression to an end. After so much suffering, sacrifice and despair, it seemed only natural that governments should devise programs to provide minimal income security to everyone. Indeed, the war had shown that governments could play a central and effective role in economic planning. Then, too, Canadians were inspired by the U.S. example of the New Deal and by the cradle-to-grave social programs offered by the new Labour government in Britain.

Moreover, it looked affordable. Canada came out of the war as an industrial nation champing at the bit to grow bigger and richer. The 1950s, even as we were living them, were known as the Fabulous '50s, with growth averaging more than 5% a year. The pent-up demand of consumers who had waited for years for new cars and other goods provided thousands of jobs for anyone who wanted one.

Early in the decade, a universal pension was introduced for all Canadians aged 70 and over who had lived in Canada for at least 10 years. At the time, life expectancy was just under 70 for a man and just over 70 for a woman. The program was therefore not a drain on tax revenues.

Toward the end of the '50s, the government presented working Canadians with the opportunity to save for retirement by registering their savings (up to $3,500) with a trust company and claiming a tax deferment on the money they put into such plans. The idea of investing money that would otherwise go to taxes was brilliant, but there were few takers at the time. Why? The reasons are instructive. Partly it was because income tax rates were relatively low and affordable and, frankly, because so many people in those postwar days were glad of the privilege to pay taxes

to a government of such high quality. (Canada in those days was internationally renowned for the quality of its public service.) So what happened?

The Soaring '60s brought to fruition the hopes and expectations that accompanied nearly 25 years of economic expansion. Canadian public policy was steered by a generation of public servants who shared an ideal of positive government and who were strongly influenced by the economics of John Maynard Keynes. (Keynes is credited with convincing Prime Minister King and U.S. President Roosevelt to "deficit spend"—print or borrow money— to kick-start the economy during the Depression.) By the early 1960s, they had decided that a major responsibility of government was to maintain an economy that worked smoothly. Gradually, the Canadian government came to see its role as twofold. First, it should not, for any length of time, allow the economy to operate below its potential, thereby inflicting unemployment on the workforce. Second, it should not permit excessive inflation, which would erode the value of both incomes and savings.

Flush with tax revenues, and mindful of government's positive economic role, policy makers turned their attention to problems for which they had solutions. One such problem was that older Canadians were not sharing in the wealth that was being created by the postwar economy. Senior citizens were poor. Medical advances meant they were living longer, yet they usually retired at 65. The Depression and the world war had badly curtailed their ability to save. So Canada rolled out social programs: the age threshold for Old Age Security was reduced year by year, to 65 for full benefits and 60 for reduced benefits. A Guaranteed Income Supplement (GIS) for older people with no other resources was tacked on. Medicare and a universally accessible health care system were introduced despite the protests and strikes of medical doctors who feared their loss of freedom to practise medicine as they saw fit. The 1966 Canada/Quebec Pension Plan ensured that all working Canadians would have a basic retirement income upon which to build. In addition, several provinces

began to provide benefits to resident pensioners to supplement the federal OAS and GIS payments.

Income security from the public purse was structured so that employees contributed a small percentage of their incomes (1.6%); employers matched that contribution. The money collected was lent out to the provinces at below-market rates of interest. The only requirement was that they remit the interest payments on time. The common wisdom of the day was that cheap loans would enable the provinces to develop their resources and grow more rapidly; they would then be able to pay back the capital when the loan came due. Loans from the Canada Pension Plan carried no obligation to repay the principal. It was simply "rolled over" on maturity (that is, when a loan came due, the province borrowed the same amount to "repay" it, and perhaps a bit extra for new development).

Money accumulating in the CPP fund was paid out as pensions to Canadians retiring after 1968. This "pay-as-you-go" pension plan was as politically attractive as it was economically seductive. It worked wonderfully when the economy grew faster than the rate of return on invested capital, and when more people were entering the workforce than leaving it. The Canada Pension Plan, and its sister plan for the province of Quebec, promised full benefits (equal to 25% of the average industrial wage) to anyone in the workforce then under 55. So for the first 10 years of the plan, few were eligible, and they received only partial benefits. By 1976, the first generation of participants, who had paid into the plan for only a fraction of their working lives, received full benefits. If the future had unfolded as planned, later generations would have paid the cost of a fully funded plan and no more.

Events, however, unfolded differently. Inflation became a serious problem. The government fought it by raising taxes and interest rates. That had the immediate effect of raising unemployment at home and the value of the Canadian dollar abroad. At home, higher taxes meant consumers had less disposable

income to buy consumer goods; this forced business to produce less. Higher interest rates meant businesses borrowed less. The combination meant people were laid off. Outside Canada, higher interest rates meant foreigners were able to make more if they held Canadian bonds rather than, say, French or U.S. bonds. In order to buy Canadian bonds, they exchanged their currency for Canadian dollars, thus raising the value of the Canadian currency.

Meanwhile, the election promise of 1968 was the creation of the "Just Society." Family allowance payments were increased threefold; the unemployment insurance system was reformed to make it one of the most generous in the world; personal income taxes were indexed to shield taxpayers from the effects of inflation. Government deficits rose, averaging $30 billion annually for more than a decade.

In the later 1960s, before the Canadian "war on inflation," the Canadian dollar was pegged at 92 cents to the U.S. dollar, but in 1970 it started moving up. It was worth slightly more than the U.S. dollar in 1971. That made Canadian goods too expensive to export, causing further unemployment. The Bank of Canada, like central banks all over the world at that time, was concerned more about the exchange rate than about inflation. So it continued to print too much money, fuelling a general price rise.

Then, disastrously, in the mid-1970s, the OPEC nations successfully raised the price of crude oil fourfold, which, coupled with a worldwide food shortage due to bad harvests, sent all commodity prices spiking. The combination of too much money and restricted commodity supplies triggered an inflation psychology throughout the industrial world. A great many economic dislocations occurred between the mid-1970s and the mid-1980s as the world adjusted to a series of "petro-shocks." For example, it was during this period that fixed exchange rates came to an end, pressures began to build for a major liberalization of world trade and the electorates lost patience with Keynes-inspired economic policies. By the early 1980s, voters were turning to the so-called

"supply-side" policies championed by conservative forces symbolized by British Prime Minister Thatcher and U.S. President Reagan. The relevance of this to our pension discussion is that the 1970s was also the origin of Canada's "deficit-debt" problem, one of the elements that is forcing the reform of Canadian social security today, some 25 years later.

The shocks of the 1970s swept away the postwar economic arrangements in favour of greater liberalization, which in turn accelerated the process of globalization of the economy that began after the war. Combined with the computer/telecom revolution of the 1980s, these forces vaporized most of the economic assumptions upon which Canada's public retirement system had been built. (This was discussed in more detail in Chapter 2.) Perhaps an even more important assumption than the economic ones underlying our retirement programs was the demographic one; but then the rapidly growing postwar population became a static, aging population. As Canada urbanized, we stopped having more than two children per family. Quebec, one of the last to urbanize, went from having the highest fertility rate to the lowest in less than a decade.

Here are two other big reversals which trashed the assumptions of our pension-system designers:

- our previously low unemployment rates have become high; and
- our previously rapid economic growth and rising living standards have become slow and stagnant.

These changes make it impossible to have a sustainable pay-as-you-go system in which the present generation of retired persons is supported by taxing the present generation of workers. Without a growing influx of new contributors, the taxes on the present workforce needed to support the system (i.e., compulsory contributions to the system, plus taxes to make up the shortfalls) will drive out private savings. Although "reforms" (read restricted

eligibility, reduced benefits and increased costs) have already been imposed on Canadians (detailed in Chapter 6), the system has not been redesigned to meet the needs of the 21st-century citizen.

The C. D. Howe Institute, a Toronto-based think tank which is highly critical of the Canada Pension Plan, has called it a Ponzi game, a "pyramid scheme in which income for the early investors is provided, not by investment in real assets, but from the capital of later investors." The CPP's designers can be faulted for their assumption that rapid population and productivity growth and low interest rates would continue indefinitely:

> As long as interest rates were lower than economic growth rates, unchanging contribution rates would mean that the present value of each generation's pension entitlement would be greater than the present value of its contributions. But by the time the first recipients of full CPP pensions were receiving their money, this unusual era was drawing to a close.
>
> *Source: William B. P. Robson,* Putting Some Gold in the Golden Years, *C. D. Howe Institute, "Commentary" (Toronto: C. D. Howe Institute, 1996).*

Starting in Expo year, 1967, the number of Canadians under 15 started declining. It was apparent that the labour force growth rate would start to decline several years later. At the same time, the life expectancy of older Canadians was rising, meaning that a smaller number of contributors to the CPP would be supporting a larger number of retirees.

Although the government has continued the myth that the CPP is stable and secure, it has had a more difficult time convincing future participants that they should contribute. A poll commissioned by the Bank of Nova Scotia found that four out of five respondents between 30 and 39 doubted the CPP's ability to provide them with retirement income.

CHART 4–2 **CPP Beneficiaries per 100 Contributors, 1970-2040**

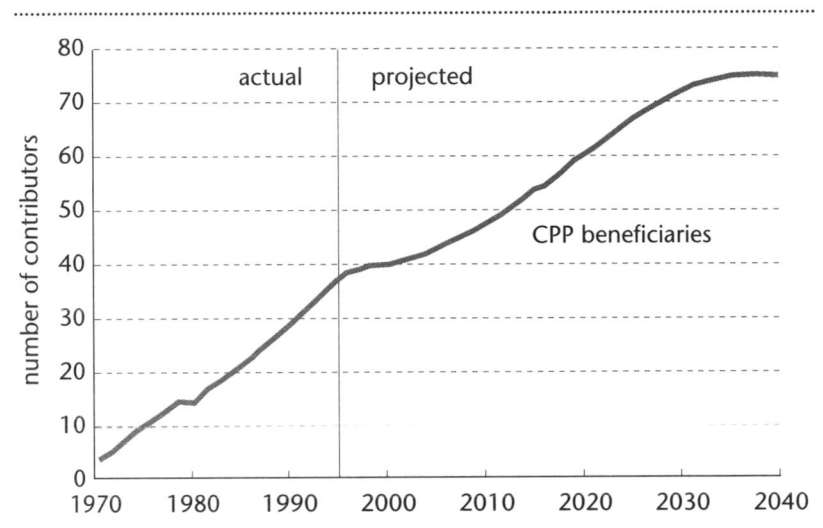

Source: William Robson, C. D. Howe Institute. Data provided by the Chief Actuary.

CHART 4–3 **Return on CPP Participation by Year of Birth, Selected Years 1911-2012**

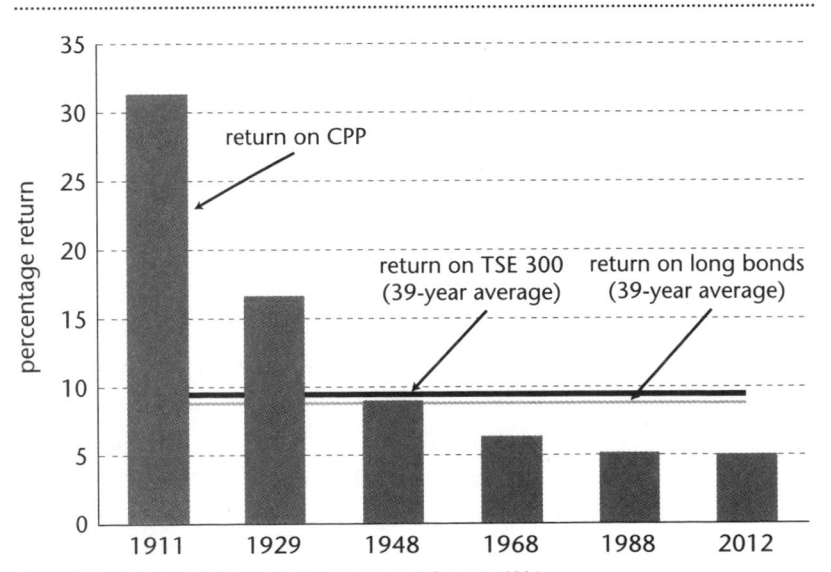

Source: William Robson, C. D. Howe Institute, "Commentary," January 1996.

According to the Howe Institute study, "the thrust of policy in regard to the CPP [has been] to *increase* the growth rate of its unfunded liability ... and because the CPP does nothing to promote growth of the wealth from which future incomes, including those of CPP recipients will come, it is creating overlapping claims on Canada's future resources that threaten to poison the future political environment."

Here's what our collective taxes and wages pay for today.

CHART 4–4 **Government Income Support Programs**

PROGRAM	WHO'S ELIGIBLE	AMT. PAID/YR. (1998)	TAX STATUS
Old Age Security	Everyone 65 and over	$4,900	Taxed back progressively, starting at $53,215 and eliminated at $84,977
Guaranteed Income Supplement	Incomes below $11,568 if single, $15,072 if married to a pensioner and $28,032 if married to a non-pensioner	$5,777 if single or married to a non-pensioner, $3,763 if married to a pensioner	Not taxable
Canada/Quebec Pension Plan	Pay in: everyone between 18 and 70 with "earned income" more than $3,500. Pay out: anyone 60 or more who has made at least one valid C/QPP contribution	Based on lifetime earned income, to a maximum of $8,900 CPP, $9,008 QPP	Taxed as income at highest marginal rate
Disability	Must work and contribute 2 of last 3, or 5 of last 10 years	Max.: $10,597	Taxed as income
Death benefit	Deceased CPP contributor	Max.: $3,859	

PROVINCIAL PROGRAMS

Many provinces offer additional benefits for people over 60, ranging from reduced rate transportation passes to top-ups of CPP benefits to tax credits on property taxes. Ontario, for example, has a Guaranteed Annual Income system, also known as GAINS. The GAINS program provides an automatic monthly payment for eligible Ontario senior citizens. British Columbia offers a guaranteed minimum income to unemployed single adults between 60 and 64 and the opportunity to participate in a Welfare to Work training program. For older residents, B.C. has a Seniors' Benefits program that assures a minimum monthly income. Manitoba has quarterly supplements for eligible residents as young as 55 and for sole-support parents with dependent children. Alberta's Senior's Benefit program targets single seniors with incomes below $13,200 and senior couples with incomes below $17,400 for supplementary cash payments. If a resident qualifies for the Senior's Benefit, health insurance premiums are paid by the province. Extensive regional variations in the support programs offered require people to make inquiries to the provincial or territorial government where they live. Much of the information may be located on each government's website.

RETIREMENT SAVINGS IN THE PRIVATE SECTOR

Canadians who have discretionary money have several opportunities to save for retirement. See Chart 4–5.

Pensions at work, sponsored and administered by employers, became popular after World War II as labour unions realized that they could make pensions in retirement part of the process of bargaining for wages. Unionists looked at pensions as "deferred wages." Today, employer-sponsored pension plans, called Registered Pension Plans (RPPs), cover both unionized and non-unionized employees. More important, employer-sponsored pension plans are now so large that they are major players in capital markets. They are in fact the single largest pool of capital, both in Canada and in the world. Total private sector pension

CHART 4–5 **Retirement Savings Opportunities**

PROGRAM	WHO'S ELIGIBLE	AMT. PAID/YR.	TAX STATUS
RRSP	Everyone between 18 and 69 with earned income	18% of earned income to a maximum of $13,500	Tax sheltered until withdrawn, then taxed as income
RPP	Everyone with an employer-sponsored pension plan at work	Related to income according to terms of RPP	Taxed as income on receipt
*After-tax savings	Everyone	Any amount	Investment income taxed
*Owner-occupied home	Everyone	Any amount	Not taxed

*These are not programs, but strategies for accumulating personal savings that go hand in hand with the programs listed in the chart.

and saving plan assets are more than $500 billion in Canada and over $12 trillion worldwide.

In Canada, these plans are not designed to stand alone. They are integrated into the public sector plans—the Canada and Quebec Pension Plans and the tax-sheltered Registered Retirement Savings Plans. Just about all large and medium-sized companies in Canada offer RPPs to their employees. These plans are sponsored by the company, i.e., the company contributes the money, with or without contributions from the employee, and administers the funds so it can provide a pension to employees when they retire. Contributions are invested to earn more money, and the employer agrees to "make good" any investment losses that would prevent retiring employees from receiving the pensions the company has promised them. The money in the pension funds grows tax-free until retirement, when it is taxed as the retiree's income.

Employer-sponsored pension plans have played an important role in raising the standard of living and quality of life for Canadians in retirement; and will continue to do so for people

who retire in the next few years. However, like the rest of society, RPPs are being reconfigured the better to reflect the realities of the 21st century. With retirement becoming less secure, people who want to retire comfortably will have to understand more about their employer-sponsored plan, and how it meshes with the savings they do on their own.

Funds in pension plans are attracting attention from the companies administering the plans. Surpluses above the amount necessary to honour the employer's financial promises to members are being targeted for withdrawal from the fund, to be put to use elsewhere. Or these surpluses are being cited as justification for the employer to take a break from making contributions to the plan (so-called contribution "holidays"). Legislation is being written to protect both corporate rights to take such contribution holidays and the member's right to get the pension in retirement that was promised when the employee became a member of the plan.

PERSONAL SAVINGS AND ASSETS

In the old days, before governments reduced the benefits of the Canada Pension Plan while raising the contribution rates by 73%, Chart 4–1 was thought to represent a good retirement income. If you added in medicare, it was more than good. Today it is less than good for all but the lowest income earners in the system.

For 21st-century retirees, good pensions will be unaffordable unless productivity improves and investment grows. The Canadian Institute of Actuaries has worked out that without productivity improvements or better investment opportunities that generate higher returns, a 70% pension at age 60 would cost 58% of pay. Even if you can depend on a pension from work of 45% of pre-retirement income, you still need to save an additional 18% of your paycheque yourself. If you are married, you have to assume that one spouse will live an additional five years. Even if the surviving spouse needs only 60% of the retirement income (which

was only 70% of the couple's pre-retirement income), the amount you have to save becomes a prohibitive 65% of pay without an RPP (i.e., if you have to save the whole pension yourself and your surviving spouse) and 20% with the company pension plan.

In light of numbers like these, it becomes important to understand what fuels the engines of publicly funded and privately funded pension plans.

CHART 4–6 **Where the Pension Money Comes From**

VEHICLE	ENGINE
OAS, CPP, QPP	Real growth in the tax base = Working-age population growth + increase in participation rates + real growth in wages
Registered Pension Plans, RRSPs, savings	Real rates of return on investments

Our pension engines are huffing and puffing but don't have the steam to get up the hill. On the public sector side, working-age population growth has slowed dramatically in the last decade and is forecast to remain sluggish for several more. Two-thirds of Canadians over the age of 15 are already in the workforce, so participation rates can't increase much. And real wages have been stagnant for close to 20 years. Thus, our lot for the foreseeable future is rising tax rates to compensate for the smaller than expected tax base, and significant cuts to publicly funded programs over an extended period. As publicly funded programs are cut back, private sector pensions at work and personal savings become more important.

What about the impact of investment on the national economy? The above numbers would be more tolerable if Canada was increasing its share of worldwide foreign investment or delivering above-average returns on Canadian equity compared to those on other major exchanges, or if the value of our exports was

increasing relative to our imports. But in fact, these trends are all running the wrong way as well. We can't make up the weakness in current operations from strengths on the capital account: those strengths are not present.

The implications for viable universal pension income are ominous. Retirement ages in the private and the public sector may have to increase. It may be possible to increase benefits along with contributions in the private sector, depending on the performance of individual companies. But the publicly funded pensions will pay out less and cost more. All of which points to personal saving and investing becoming a whole lot more important.

YOUR PERSONAL SAVINGS OPTIONS

You have a few personal savings options, but most are problematic. Each falls into one of the following groups: tax exempt, tax deferred, tax preferred, and fully taxable. Obviously, the best of the lot is the tax-exempt investment. But as I've cautioned before, don't take anything you know about investing for granted, especially if what you know was true more than 10 years ago. One of the incentives to invest in RRSPs—a tax-deferred option—was that contributions made when earnings and tax rates are high will be withdrawn later, when tax rates are low (because your income will be lower). That incentive has become tenuous.

Contributions for the past generation have been made when tax rates were rising, but they will be withdrawn when tax rates are even higher. In most instances, this will significantly reduce the advantage of tax-free compounding within RRSPs. For those with modest incomes contributing late in life, RRSP contributions actually become harmful. Let me underline this very important point: in tinkering with the retirement system, the finance minister has weakened one of the system's main pillars, namely the incentive for moderate-income Canadian families to save for their own retirement.

In particular, the federal government has moved to restrict the ability of people to save in tax-sheltered retirement plans.

There used to be a certain logic to the retirement system. Some-one must know why the government decided that an income of $86,000 a year was the cut-off point for tax incentives to save, but I do not. Nevertheless, your pension plan at work is calibrated to what you make, originally up to a top income of $86,000, now reduced to $75,000, since the maximum RRSP contribution was frozen at $13,500. The tax system provides assistance for retirement savings of up to 18% of income (18% of $75,000 is $13,500; 18% of $86,000 is $15,500). If you're in a defined benefits plan, there's another roadblock to saving: the Pension Adjustment (PA). The PA reduces the annual RRSP contribution room by the deemed value of a member's benefit entitlement accrued in the year. In making this calculation, the drafters of the legislation assumed that a "typical" pension plan includes very generous ancillary benefits, such as post-retirement indexing and early retirement subsidies. In other words, they modelled the "typical" plan after their own, one of the most generous in the world. Unfortunately, the "typical" plan rarely exists outside the public sector. The result is that the PA significantly reduces RRSP room for their members. Thus, members of defined benefit plans have little opportunity to save inside an RRSP.

In mid-1998, the government bowed to pressure to redress this decade-long inequity by announcing changes to how PAs are calculated. The new rules aren't perfect. First, they apply on a "going forward" basis only—that is, if a person retired between 1990 and the beginning of 1997, their lost RRSP contribution room is lost forever. That could be $20,000, $30,000, or $50,000 of RRSP capital permanently lost. Second, the restoration of con-tribution room is great, but may be unaffordable; that is, if the recalculation says you can put $50,000 into your RRSP, do you have the money to do so? Third, even for the people who can afford to put the capital in their RRSP, the investment income that could have been theirs over the last nine years is lost for-ever. Says Malcom Hamilton, principal of William M. Mercer Ltd., "Perfection in this area is impossible to administer. The

administration of the new rules is inconvenient, the solution is imperfect, but at least it's well-intentioned. That's the best we can hope for." Damned with faint praise, I'd call it.

RRSP limits were scheduled to be $15,500 several years ago. It never happened. The limits have been frozen at $13,500. So hundreds of thousands of people who don't have a pension plan at work are penalized and don't have equal opportunities to save for retirement. Given the savings levels needed to meet the requirements of comfortable retirements, it would make more sense simply to allow individuals to save 65% of their income tax-free and leave the choice (RPP, RRSP, or both) up to them.

CHART 4–7 **Taxation of Retirement Savings**

	CANADA	U.S.	U.K.	NETHERLANDS
Top marginal rate	50%	40–45%	40%	60%
Retirement savings				
Earnings limit	C$86,111	US$160,000	UK£82,000	None
Indexed?	No	Yes	Yes	N/A
Additional tax-sheltered DC Plan	No	Yes	Yes	No
Capital gains				
Rate	38%	22%–33%	40%	0%
Annual exemption	No	No	UK£6,500	N/A
CPI adjusted?	No	No	Yes	N/A
Principal residence				
Taxable gain?	No	Yes	No	No
Deductible interest?	No	Yes	Yes	Yes
Tax-free interest on insurance policy?	No	No	Yes	Yes

Source: Malcolm Hamilton, Wm M. Mercer Ltd.

Take a closer look at who has and has not got inflation-adjusted pensions. Government benefits are fully indexed, but the Income Tax Act is not. Over time the recipients of non-taxable government benefits such as the Guaranteed Income

Supplement will have their benefits inflation-indexed, therefore sheltered from inflation. What about those Canadians who support themselves by working and saving? Forget it—not just tax fodder but inflation fodder, too.

In a nutshell, here's where current government policies have led our retirement system, as stated by the Association of Canadian Pension Management. (The ACPM is the national voice of corporate and public sector pension-plan sponsors in Canada. The association has nearly 1,000 members and represents more than 500 pension plans with assets of $226 billion.) The ACPM characterizes Canada's retirement system as follows:

- generous benefits for
  - those who rely on government;
  - lower-income Canadians with little incentive to save (because government benefits replace most of their income); and
  - other Canadians with little ability to save due to shrinking (in real terms) limits and the inhospitable tax treatment of savings outside tax shelters.
- high taxes for everyone else.

The system as presently constituted has given rise to another obnoxious practice: misinformation paid for by tax dollars. Rather than confronting the retirement system's problems head on and dealing squarely with Canadians about what's happening to their money, the government uses our tax dollars to create a misleading idea about our pension system and how it works. Consider, for example, findings of Statistics Canada studies of the amounts Canadians are contributing to RRSPs. It presents its findings in such a way as to support the patently untrue view that only the rich use RRSPs. Such studies dovetail neatly with the orthodoxy emanating from Finance Canada that the money Canadians put into RRSPs is snatched out of the hands of the government, thereby restricting its ability to redistribute more to less affluent Canadians.

A recent Statistics Canada report stated that in 1995, only 29% of Canadians contributed to RRSPs; 81% of those who did not contribute earned less than $20,000 a year. But Statistics Canada did not compare contributions based on incentives to make such contributions. It could have reported that while only 29% of tax filers contributed to RRSPs in 1995, the participation rate was 77% if you considered only those for whom the RRSP program makes sense!

Canadians under 25 or over 65 are mostly ineligible to participate because they have not yet joined the labour force or are already retired. If they aren't counted (and why should they be?), the number of Canadian tax filers who contributed to RRSPs in 1995 increases to 36%. Then exclude those whose present living standard, while poor, is 100% protected in retirement because they earn under $20,000. Then the economically rational participation rate increases further, to 56%. Add those who could put money into an RRSP but don't because they have a Registered Pension Plan instead and the participation level goes to 77%!

Canadians are also routinely told that the government forgoes a huge amount of tax revenue because of sheltered retirement savings plans. The federal government uses this argument to resist raising RRSP contribution limits, because it would "cost" taxpayers more. Indeed, for years, government has repeatedly said that the cost to Canadians of tax-sheltered retirement savings plans is $15 billion. This figure completely ignores the additional tax revenues that more rapid compounding under tax deferment produces after the revenues are withdrawn. As well, the "forgone" revenue figure assumes that Canadians would save or invest the same amounts whether or not such a tax-sheltered system existed. The government is missing the obvious point that the aim of an incentive to save is to encourage people to save more than they would in the absence of the incentive.

The Canadian Institute of Actuaries says that a more reasonable estimate of the impact on federal and provincial revenues of the RRSP programs is about $5 billion, one-third of the government

estimate. A threefold exaggeration developed at the taxpayers' expense is, in my opinion, going much too far. Canadians need information about the retirement system, not propaganda.

Let's be clear about this. The government wants Canadians to believe things that are not true about the current retirement system: that it is fair when it is divisive, balanced when it privileges the public sector over the private sector, and coherent when its provisions weaken any incentive to participate in the system by those now working and those now earning well above the median income.

The basic problem is that the government has not rethought the system through from first principles. Instead of grasping the opportunity to put together a new plan for the next millennium, with far greater scope for private choice, it has tried to shore up old entitlements by maintaining itself as the central pillar. In the process, it is wrecking the very system that it purports to save.

TWO

Reality

....

Cheque

....

Some see private enterprise as
a predatory target to be shot,
others as a cow to be milked;
but few see it as a sturdy horse
pulling the wagon.
—Winston Churchill

5

Canada's Glass: Half Empty, Half Full

Any fact facing us is not as important as our attitude toward it, for that determines our success or failure.
—Norman Vincent Peale

I WAS BORN IN CANADA; so were my children. I grew up in the west, and have lived in several places in Canada as well as outside it. I always come back, because I love living here. I've found many opportunities to make a good living in Canada, and I've tried to reciprocate by participating in the public policy debates about how to make this an even better place to live. No question, I'm attached to the place. Still, I'm ambivalent about Canada. Sometimes I think I should talk to a psychiatrist about it. I hold two views of the country that together explain why I live here and invest elsewhere.

View One holds that Canadians recognize that a global economy favours the clever and the bold. So Canada has grabbed the globalization ball and run with it. Half our GNP is internationally traded. On balance we export about as much capital (foreign direct investment) as we import. If you divide the size of our tradable sector by the population, the Canadian economy on a per capita basis is among the most open in the world. Canadian

companies are leaders in the high-technology adventures of telecommunications and information technology, civil aviation and biotechnology. Our former branch-plant economy has become one of world-class production platforms integrated into the North American production grid: in most instances at the enterprise level, Canada goes head to head against the best and prospers. The market share of Canadian products in the U.S. has doubled under free trade. Canada–U.S. cross-border business now stands at about a billion dollars a day and is by far the fastest-growing sector of the economy. Canada's unemployment and underemployment rate is quite simply a function of who participates in the global economy (highly educated professionals and highly skilled workers) and who doesn't (those without the skills to hop on board or who have been unable to switch from a public sector situation).

This view, that globalization offers a better chance at prosperity than national mixed economies, began to win general acceptance during the recession of 1981–82. Canadians became less trusting of their institutions. The liberalization of trade policy, combined with the failure of government to restructure its policies to facilitate the changes in just about everything, pushed the skepticism to new heights (or depths). Canadians began to feel cheated by government. And so they should have. For every dollar we pay in taxes, the government is delivering less than 70 cents in services. The rest goes to bondholders, a large portion of whom until recently lived offshore.

People began asking, "Who voted to run up those debts? I don't remember voting for them; in fact, I remember the opposite." Various governments—two headed by Trudeau, one by Turner, and two by Mulroney—promised to control spending, not increase it. They all lied, and we paid. Canadians have a constitutional right to good government but neither the constitution nor anything else saved us from the tax-and-spend crowd. Until Ralph Klein came to Edmonton in the early 1990s. Klein gave the public what it wanted: smaller government budgets. When

the other political leaders saw what he had done and how it helped in the polls, they went right along to echo his performance. Saskatchewan was up against the wall and turned things around. British Columbia, using a little budgetary sleight of hand, did the same thing. Nova Scotia has instituted reforms along those same lines. And after Ontario voters became incensed by Bob Rae, who tried to swim against the tide, they voted in Mike "the Knife" Harris. Harris makes Klein look subtle. According to this picture, eventually Ottawa got some of the message. Finance Minister Paul Martin increased spending in his first budget, based on a promise to slash in the second. He cut some, and built in a lot of spending and taxing. That got the deficit under control, but the overall debt is still a burden of Third World proportions.

But these changes involved no fundamental rethink of government's role and organization. Government has not experienced the radical restructuring the private sector has undergone. So now, with the deficit under control in almost all the provinces and the federal government, spending has again got its advocates. The tax-and-spenders appear to remain firmly entrenched and are once again trying to make government the central provider of programmed services.

The persistence of a big-government vision for Canada gives rise to a second, less optimistic view of its future. View Two holds that while Canada's private economy has generally done well, the public sector still tries to impose its own judgment on the wisdom of market forces. In this view, Canada's politicians succeeded in insulating themselves from change during the bull markets of the 1980s and '90s and still don't understand how they are holding the country back. So, for example, Canada adopted free trade but in a way that shelters most of our biggest companies (outside the auto sector) from the full force of change. Telecommunications regulations still favour the Stentor Alliance; cable TV monopolies are still the vehicle of choice for "defending" Canadian culture. Canadian financial services (despite the findings and recommendations of the MacKay Task Force on Financial

Services) will still be sheltered from significant foreign competition in their home markets. North American airlines will remain organized around an open two-skies (i.e., Canada and U.S. skies) model that protects national carriers, rather than a single open-sky model (for all of North America) that would benefit consumers.

The conclusion, according to this view, is that Canada's political elite is on the ropes, reeling from the rejection of its Keynesian vision which so characterized the postwar years, and repeatedly surprised by the rejection by ordinary Canadians of this self-centred vision. Indeed, so marked is this trend of public rejection of its political elites, that Canada's foremost political writer, Peter Newman, wrote a book about it. He calls it a revolution—from deference to defiance. The rejection of the Charlottetown Accord, he says, showed that Canadians were no longer prepared to take the word of the political elites. The 1995 Quebec referendum—in part a consequence of the rejection of Charlottetown—showed that most French speakers no longer trusted confederation.

Arriving at an assessment of Canada today that integrates these views is difficult. Basically, the problem is that Canadians hold two beliefs simultaneously. On the one hand, they like to believe that Canada has become more competitive and less reliant on government. On the other hand, there's no sign that people are becoming any less willing to believe that government should play a central role as a service provider and mediator of global economic forces. If Canadians had truly moved to embrace self-reliance as a national credo, the call would be unequivocally for lower taxes so individuals could get on with the job of providing for themselves and their families.

The reality is that this schizophrenic vision of a market society protected by big government divides us rather than unites us. Indeed, a powerful thrust in the Parti Québécois arguments against Canada was that the rest of the country was moving away from social democracy. In large measure, the support for the "Yes" side in 1995 was based on continued support for social democracy. That was before Quebec began slashing *its* public spending and

blaming Ottawa for every cut, as Lucien Bouchard (not unlike the other provincial government leaders) always does.

Political scientists have an explanation for this ambivalence. Like so much else, the key is the tax system. The average taxpayer in Canada (i.e., at the income level of $56,000) now pays $27,000 in all taxes combined (including income tax, sales tax, property tax, liquor, tobacco, amusement and other excise taxes, auto, fuel and car licence taxes, and social security, pension, medical and hospital taxes). This average figure hides a regional disparity. The average is made up of three provinces where taxes are above average and seven where they are below average. What's more, when you break the taxes down into the value received, the subsidy to the average taxpayer is considerable. The chart below sets out how the taxes bite.

CHART 5–1 **Taxes on Average Family Income (1996): $56,322**

Income Tax	$10,533.00
Sales Tax	$4,186.00
Property Tax	$1,991.00
Liquor, Tobacco, Amusement, other Excise	$1,362.00
Auto, Fuel and MV Licence	$869.00
Social Security, Pension, Medical and Hospital	$5,197.00
Other (profit, natural resource, duties, other)	$2,909.00
Total Tax Bill on $56,322	**$27,017.00**

Source: Fraser Institute. Ave. family = two or more individuals

This tax bill means that for a relatively trivial outlay (less than 10% of average income) an average family gets substantial medical coverage, for less than another $2,000 a year (property taxes) they get public schooling, police and fire protection, for under $1,000 they get roads to drive on in all weather, and so on. Plus, somehow the total tax bill also ensures that there is post-secondary education available at way below cost for those who want it. It's the federal tax bill that's really agonizing, but a lot of that is

actually paying down debt now held by other Canadians and so gets recycled in Canada, adding to incomes on the roundabouts if not the swings.

This is a consumer-oriented, suburban family-oriented tax system. Only when you try to pursue some economic goals that emphasize growth, like starting a business and making it grow really fast, or accumulating capital for retirement, does the tax system hurt. The assumption—an increasingly erroneous one—behind the tax system is that average individuals don't do these things. Rather, they work in big vertical organizations and don't change jobs, and retire after 40 years of trusted service. Therefore, for most of the life cycle of the average family (especially during the child-raising years), the tax system, while burdensome, still pays out as much benefit as it costs, if not more.

As for the real costs of steadily deteriorating standards of education, research, etc., the loss of productivity in the economy, the failure to adapt rapidly enough to new technologies in so many public sector applications—none of this is readily apparent. For the time being, apart from the income tax, which is onerous and finances far fewer clear benefits than it costs, the Canadian tax system seems like a good deal to most people. The benefits are tangible, the costs diffused across the macroeconomy such that the bills don't come due until much later. That constituency is waning but, shored up by public sector workers (25% of the workforce!), it accounts for the ambivalence about government's role.

Okay, that's the analyst's view of Canada: a political *Titanic* that's had its hull mashed by a fiscal iceberg, the more imaginative voters having started to abandon ship while the rest are still thinking about lunch at the captain's table.

There is a third picture of Canada, one that's much older and goes like this. Canada is a multi-ethnic society spread thinly across a giant territory—the second-largest political jurisdiction in the world. Yet we managed to construct one of the world's most successful societies.

Two elements were crucial to that success. The first was seeing the big picture, especially of ourselves. The vast majesty of Canada is what the world sees when it looks at us, a majesty made accessible using cutting-edge transportation and communications technology. The community is proud because that majesty is ours and because we've built a country here and made it work. The second element flowed from the first, a sense of solidarity based on having accomplished some great things: building the country and making it work despite the obstacles, playing a crucial role in saving trans-Atlantic civilization during two world wars (years before the Americans showed up). More recently, we added a third element: constructing a society based on the belief that a person's human dignity created certain entitlements independent of an ability to pay. In practice, this boiled down to income-maintenance programs for people who couldn't work or couldn't find jobs, and universally accessible medicare. Along the way, we added relatively inexpensive education to the mix. This troika's high point was probably Expo 67 in Montreal, but for almost all the Canadians I know, this image—or something like it—is still what makes them proud to be Canadian.

Despite everything that has happened since the 1980s—from the California tax revolt and Newt Gingrich's "contract on America" to Canada's fiscal crisis—I think the majority of Canadians, including Quebecers, still hold in their heads something like this last model I've described. The problem is, the analyst's vision is also valid and in many ways more in touch with today's demands. And for people who want to get on with the job of looking after themselves and their families, this "vision thing" is a real problem. The analyst's picture of a Canada that's embracing globalization without changing its institutions raises a big question mark over Canada's ability to become a suitable growth platform for the decades ahead. At the same time, we hold our nostalgic vision of Canada as a successful society that conquered the wilderness and still has great things left to do. Yet our practical failure to be bold in adapting to the present is ensuring

that our vision of majestic Canada will decline into folklore as our ambivalence inhibits so drastically our capacity for action.

Planning for our future means coming to terms with the fact that Canada may not overcome its ambivalence, and the declines we've been discussing may therefore continue.

Change is hard, and the changes required now are no less dramatic than the decision of our forebears to leave Europe for the New World in the 1600s and 1700s. When we built Canada, the world ran on natural resources and we had them. The world economy has changed since then, as we know. It now runs on knowledge. In this kind of economy, our leverage is much less and our relative productivity is correspondingly less, so we are relatively less well off. Majestic, yes, but rich? Canada is no longer much richer than many other nations.

Moreover, the failure to integrate Quebec into the political fabric of the nation remains a serious weakness in the ability of the whole country to restructure. There's only one explicit role for Quebec in the traditional picture of Canada I outlined: the chief defender of the French fact in North America. Yet this role is also shared by the federal government of Canada. This "cohabitation" still has to be defined, but our elites are treating it as a game of divide-the-spoils rather than as an opportunity to reassert Canada's uniqueness. This is a profoundly serious issue. Once again, our political elites are failing us; they nearly cost us the country in the Quebec referendum of a few years ago. Putting it coldly, Canada without Quebec is at least 26% poorer. As long as separation remains a possibility, sound retirement planning means having to find ways to hedge against the dislocations caused by any such eventuality.

There is also the persistent question of the Canadian dollar. As Europe adopts a single currency, the pressure will increase for North America (or at least Canada and the U.S.) to move to a monetary union. In practical terms, the recent decline of the Canadian dollar means that Canada has replaced an average tariff on goods of 7% against the U.S. (before the Free Trade Agreement)

with a foreign exchange barrier of 30% or more. The effect of that barrier is the same as of any other protectionist barrier: it rewards the less efficient and the less productive at the expense of the more. For a country that desperately needs to reverse its productivity performance to maintain its accustomed affluence, that sinking loonie (now called the swoonie) is disastrous.

It's tempting to believe that this failure is occurring just because our leaders are inept. But I think we have to look beyond current personalities. We have to understand the cross-pressures. There is agreement that change is needed, but no consensus on where to change. In the absence of leadership, and as the amount of tax money available to governments reaches its limits, reallocation of the revenues, not a broader national project, defines political power.

Suburbanites want to cut social programs at the expense of inner cities. Why? To preserve their own access to below-market-cost health care and education. Many Canadians who want to preserve entitlements at the same time resist the flexibility needed on the job side to sustain productivity. Why? Because they fear losing their own jobs. And throughout senior positions in Canada, whether public or private sector, there is a serious lack of technological understanding. So we are not that great at making correct decisions about the new technologies.

If you look at the current policy mix on the table in Ottawa, its only justification is that our leaders have decided Canadians are not capable of making the changes required to keep Canada on top of the heap. So they've chosen to design a comfortable slide downwards into mediocrity and middle-of-the-pack-ism— just as the British exited from Empire. That policy mix will make it very hard for you to accumulate enough to retire on and, if you do, to enjoy that money when you are no longer working.

Canada will remain a pretty good place to live: it's civilized, cosmopolitan, beautiful, rich, and doesn't like war. But it's not a great place to make or save money and is unlikely to improve (under this scenario).

WHAT DOES THIS MEAN FOR MY RETIREMENT?

Developing and implementing a retirement plan is not compli-cated, but it is time-consuming. The first step is understanding the process. What follows is a framework—the questions to ask yourself and the process to follow; Chapter 8 is a step-by-step elaboration.

START PLANNING EARLY

Most people have to accumulate over a long time to be able to retire. The sooner you develop a retirement plan and start imple-menting a strategy, the better off you'll be in retirement. You'll have lots of time to rethink the plan, especially if you start early. That's the key. If you start at 30 or 35, you'll be able to adjust your plan at least 20 times if you get into the habit of reviewing it once a year. You may even be able to retire in traditional style. At the very least, you'll know where you are financially, and what you need to do to reach your financial goals. If you start at 50, without having thought much about it, you may get a rude shock if you're offered an early retirement package and don't have the savings to top up the company pension. This is one area where wishing won't make it so, but a little planning surely will. Mind you, starting at 50 is better than not starting at all, especially if you're living an upper-middle-class life. Otherwise, you will definitely have to lower your lifestyle expectations.

People can be divided into two groups, no matter what the issue. Either you have a strategy or you don't. Either you visu-alize what you want in your future or you don't. There's lots of evidence showing that the people who end up with more or less what they want are the ones who fall into the first group. So if you're not in that group right now, better shift over right away.

YOU SET THE STANDARD

So far in this book I've talked about the constraints, how the world has changed and so on. Now it's time to change gears and

put the focus on you. The first step in planning a retirement is figuring out what *you* want. You have to start defining some goals.

Having goals to work towards makes for a good life. You absolutely must meet some of the financial goals you set, but you also have to have other goals that aren't financial. You should never think that there's nothing left to do if you meet every goal you ever set. Life is a journey, after all, not a destination. It's the old "reach for the stars" cliché. You just keep growing and setting new goals.

For the last decade or so, I've been working on how I will live and what I will do when I don't do what I do now. I can't really retire in the traditional sense, since I don't have a Job from which to retire. But although, as my friends and family will attest, I have talked about "retiring" for the last 10 years, I doubt that I ever will. Funny that when you start talking to your friends about it, most of them say they want to be carried out with their boots on—even when you know they have more than enough money to retire. Whether you want to be carried out with boots or slippers on, in order to have choices, you need a plan. Developing that plan requires you to be clear about your post-job priorities and goals.

Ask yourself, "When do I want to stop doing what I'm doing today?" The idea of retirement has been the subject of some anxiety over the last decade, but so far, no public authority has suggested that retirement is no longer a relevant notion. You already know that I think the idea of retirement as our parents knew it is obsolete. But there's no question that if you've got a job, at some point, you're going to leave that job. If it's a job with a pension plan, that plan has been structured for you to leave it between age 55 and 65 with an income. If you dream of doing something else, like starting a business, you better start building it into your plan.

Your ideas about retirement age—that is, the point at which you will finally leave the full-time workforce—will likely change as you get older. I had a conversation with an acquaintance

recently, just as I was finishing this book. We talked about retirement in general and agreed that it was really hard to retire. Only after about 10 minutes of conversation did we both understand that we were talking at cross purposes. I was talking about being able financially to retire. He was talking about being able psychologically to retire. That, too, is a consideration. Many people just accept the notion of retirement because no one has ever suggested any other possibility. The majority of Canadian workers are still in a full-time, full-benefit work arrangement. The pension plan your employer has set up is structured to provide you with a pension income at 65 or earlier. But the number of Canadians in this category is declining. Other categories include employment contract with or without defined contribution plans, and self-employment. We should now consider the possibility that retiring at 65 will be what only a minority of people do 20 years from now. Planning is the process of covering all contingencies. It's not going to lock you into anything, and undoubtedly your answers to the questions will change as you get older. The nice thing about having a plan is that you have choices.

Have you thought about doing something else after you retire? Often, the formulae in company pension plans allow people to receive a full pension after 20 years of service. If they began their employment at 25, they could be pensioned off at 45. If you're in this position, you should think about what you will do with the next 30 or 40 years. Forced unemployment doesn't sound like a lot of fun. Do you want another career? What about volunteering? Have you always wanted to go back to school? All these and more, including sitting on the back stoop, are possibilities.

Ultimately, if and when you retire, and what you do in retirement, will depend on what you can afford. What standard of living have you in mind for yourself? How many people will you will have to support? Will you want or need to help your parents? Will you still be putting your children through school?

Determining whether you can afford to retire involves making an estimate of how long you can expect to live. That

determination will be influenced by how long your parents lived, your own lifestyle and health, and whether or not your activities put you more in the path of accidents than the average Canadian. Even if you've never thought about these things before, take a stab at it. It will get easier and more realistic as you revise and refine. If you are doing this for the first time, you'll have to familiarize yourself with a few tables—life expectancy, inflation factors, tax tables, etc.—which will enable you to make some assumptions. You'll find them all in this book, notably in Chapter 8 and Appendix 3.

If all this seems overwhelming, let me take you through a simple decision-making procedure. You can use the process for making any decision, but we'll use it here for making decisions about what to do after full-time work.

THREE QUESTIONS, THREE ANSWERS = DECISION

Where are you going? You know the old saying, "If you don't know where you're going, any path will take you there." A cliché, to be sure, but nothing is truer. So make a decision—and never think it's for ever. Everything you do is a learning experience. Some experiences will teach you not to do them again. Others will go into your database as things to repeat.

How will you get there? There's no one way that's right for everyone. That's why it's so important to indulge in these exercises. It's like dieting. Lots of people with plans to sell will be able to tell what's worked for them and why it may work for you. But let me tell you, as a person who's had to watch her weight for a lifetime, that *all* those programs work. Low-fat, high-carbo, protein, balanced—they all work, and the trick is to decide what's going to work for you. So experiment. You'll eventually find out what works best for you. You may even find out by the time you finish this book. You'll certainly be able to say where your investing comfort level is. And you'll know what you need more information about. I may convince you that traditional advice about wealth building is interesting, and may have value, but needs

SIX STEPS MAKE THE PLAN

1. Set your goals.
2. Develop ideas of how to reach your goals.
3. Identify the negative consequences of each idea.
4. Decide on a basic plan of action.
5. Develop strategies to achieve your action plan.
6. Determine measurable checkpoints.

SIX STEPS IMPLEMENT IT

1. Assign tasks. If you are alone in the plan, you get to do everything. If you have a family or others who share the goal, you have to know who's going to do what. Nothing sabotages a plan faster than one spouse devising goals and plans without communicating them to the partner or children.
2. Define each person's responsibilities and authority.
3. Help set performance goals for each person.
4. Develop a method of reporting to ensure that activities are being carried out on schedule.
5. Measure the results against the checkpoints. If they show that your strategy is on target, go to step 6. If not, revise, rethink and redesign your strategy.
6. Build in a reward system for every person involved in the strategy. Everyone appreciates having a good job recognized and rewarded. Most people perform better the more frequently they have their good work rewarded.

the added value of a perspective on the economic paradigm shift. A bit later on, I'll show you how to factor in the changes I've been talking about. Right now, you have to concentrate on setting out your destination.

How will you know when you've arrived? Clearly, you need a road map and destination points along the way. So you need a measurement or checkpoint system to let you know you've met a goal (or not), and that it's time to go on, or to change direction. Putting all this together is your plan.

This a short chapter, but it will take you some time and some soul-searching to go through the exercise. If the first part of the book depressed you, think again about the dieting analogy. You realize you're an overweight, under-exercised couch potato. You get depressed. You decide to get into shape, which means getting into the right mindset to find the time and follow through. That's where you are now. By the time you finish Part 3, you should be cheered, either because you've decided it's nonsense and you'll take another tack or because it all makes sense and you're committed to it. Either way, you're going to be better off just for making the decision.

6

Banks, Pensions and Mutual Funds

I try to go where the puck will be.
—Wayne Gretzky

RETIREMENT IS, FIRST OF ALL, about living on the income your savings can generate. So let's look at saving and how that's become a whole new ball game.

We used to save our money in the bank so we had it when we stopped working. Today, Canadians still save money in the bank, because they think it's safe, risk-free investing. It may be risk free, but it's not really investing; it's more a safe way of limiting their chances to have choices about what they do when they start thinking about post-job living. Unfortunately, the government and the banks are structured to keep us in ignorance about the full range of available choices—for our money or our lives.

Banks are no longer the pre-eminent place to deposit funds. That place is now the "pooled investments"—mutual funds and pension funds. Mutual funds are pools of traded securities. You may hold some in your RRSP, but they are also bought by others outside an RRSP. Pension funds are the tax-exempt pools of money accumulated from the contributions of employees and/or

employers and invested until employees retire. As of the mid-1990s, in Canada and the U.S., pooled investments have attracted about half of all the assets saved, with pension funds the fastest growing. It wasn't always like this. For our grandfathers' generation, the banks and big companies organized one's retirement. The individual knew only that he was entitled to certain benefits after 50 years on the railroad. Today's pooled investments represent the triumph of markets that make it possible for everyone to save for a later life—better and with more security than did the older system.

HOW THE SYSTEM MADE WAY FOR PENSION AND MUTUAL FUNDS

Mutual funds in themselves constitute an amazing success story. It took banks centuries to become the go-betweens of the nation's savings and investments; it took mutual funds just a generation.

Modern banking began in 1694 when the English monarchs William and Mary got into financial trouble and needed a loan. In exchange for a banking monopoly, the Bank of England took the bonds of the realm at a favourable rate and sold them to intermediaries who re-sold them to the public. The intermediaries were private banks. The British arrangement was thus that of a dominant central bank which controlled a network of (much) smaller private banks and which used the government's power to borrow to discipline the system. It was unique in its day. By the 19th century it had become a model for the planet. By redeeming existing bonds and issuing new ones, the Bank of England was able to link England's sovereign debt to an economy that for the next 200 years led the world in industrialization. It also enabled England to emerge victorious from both the Seven Years' War (1756–63) and the Napoleonic Wars (1790–1815) which left the rest of Europe exhausted and bankrupt.

Europe's recovery, and the economic development of North America, was funded by British savings; the Bank of England just behaved globally as it did domestically. The system lasted until

August 1914. In four years, World War I put an end to that system, as well as the middle-class society that had emerged from it.

The failure to create either a stable peace or a stable international economy after World War I became all too evident when the ramshackle system put in place by the Treaty of Versailles collapsed during the Great Depression. That cataclysmic event brought totalitarianism to Central and Eastern Europe and set the stage for World War II and the subsequent Cold War.

There are many ways one could characterize the Cold War. One of them is as a struggle between two forms of statism: the democratic socialism of the postwar Western welfare states and the tyrannical central planning of the Soviet Union and its empire. The Soviet model failed to survive the 1980s; the social democratic model survives—barely. The symptoms of the disease that ultimately destroyed the state planning models actually appeared first in the postwar Western welfare states, and led to the pooled investments—the mutual and pension funds—of today.

The first clear sign that the postwar economic arrangements were not sustainable was the collapse of the postwar gold-based international system. The post-World War II settlements were based on liberalized trade and currency rates pegged to the U.S. dollar, which was fixed to the price of gold, US$35 an ounce. The postwar system was based on the faith that governments would allow trade to shift if necessary to allow foreign exchange rates to remain fixed. The shifting trade patterns were to be aided by liberalized trade rules enshrined in the General Agreement on Tariffs and Trade (1947), which supposedly made impossible a return to the "beggar-my-neighbour" trade protectionism that (led by the U.S. Smoot–Hawley Tariff) deepened and prolonged the Depression of the 1930s.

However, the system had some destabilizers. One was the role of the U.S. as the prime defender of the West. Permanent U.S. garrisons in Europe created a huge foreign exchange drain, as Americans changed their dollars to buy francs, deutschemarks, lira and pesos. Billions of U.S. dollars circulating in Europe

were a potential claim on American resources. This was tolerable as long as the U.S. sold more abroad than it bought, but by the 1970s, with Europe recovered from the war and coming together to form the Common Market, the U.S. had persistent balance of payment deficits on its trade account—spending more than it earned and adding to the supply of dollars in international circulation.

The other major problem was the ability of politically powerful social democratic institutions to translate their political power into economic rigidity. The GATT was set up to provide a rules-based framework for trade in goods. The idea was to allow trade patterns to shift as countries recovered from the devastation of the war. But the domestic economies of the GATT signatories were controlled by forces that did not want trade patterns to shift, only to grow. Manufacturers in competitively weak sectors allied in a common cause with trade unions, and both pressured conservative and social democratic governments. Every government, out of political, not economic, necessity, had to be concerned that *any* lost trade (even though total trade might be increasing) meant lost jobs. So they put in place subsidies and non-tariff barriers to ensure that trade wouldn't shift. (Non-tariff barriers to trade are regulations designed to keep foreign goods out of one's country: licensing requirements, unreasonable standards for product quality and safety, or simply red tape in customs procedures. Subsidies are payments to domestic producers that reduce the prices of their products so they can compete internationally.) But these policies cost money and weaken a country's capacity to earn money abroad. Gradually, the currencies of those countries weakened, devaluing against the rates fixed against the U.S. dollar. (France was an exception to these policies. Like all countries, France accumulates foreign reserves made up of U.S. dollars, gold and other currencies. Anticipating the devaluation of the dollar against the price of gold, the French government, under Charles de Gaulle, began selling dollars and accumulating gold. This accelerated the inevitable disconnect of the U.S. dollar

from gold, but France failed to understand that the new system would be one of floating, not realigned, exchange rates.)

Devaluations made European goods more competitive in the U.S., making it harder for the U.S. to maintain its fixed rate against gold. Finally, in 1971, the U.S. went off the gold standard and the Western world shifted to floating exchange rates. (Ironically, France now found itself with an overvalued currency, facing not only a far more competitive U.S. trading partner but a German one as well.)

The impact on banking was profound. Once U.S. dollars could fluctuate against other currencies without the fear of panic that used to happen when fixed exchange rates broke, baskets of currencies (pools) could be offered as short-term investments. This opened the way for pooled investment funds to begin to replace banks as the custodians of national savings. Mutual funds could replace bank accounts because they provided better returns through superior investment management. But getting there meant breaking down bank monopolies and other restrictive structures.

FROM MONEY MARKETS TO EQUITY POOLS: THE LONG MARCH

Step One: Money Market Accounts

The first step in the long march was the introduction of money market accounts. Unknown before 1972, these accounts linked short-term deposits and capital markets, those huge flows of funds (now up to a trillion dollars a day, then a mere few billion) roiling around the planet in search of a slightly better price. Suddenly, anyone who made a deposit in a money market account in effect was buying a little piece of what governments and large businesses injected directly into capital markets.

Investors in money market funds got "units" of a fund organized to invest in short-term (under a year) fixed-rate government or corporate "paper" ("notes" are fixed-rate corporate investments under one year, "bills" are fixed-rate government investments under one year, "bonds" are fixed-rate investments over

one year). Investors saw their investment rise or fall according to the value of the fund. The value of the fund was determined by a combination of the price of the paper and the interest rate. Say a person invested $1,000 in a money market fund when the interest rate was 5%. The interest income was $50 (5% x $1,000). Suppose the price of the paper dropped to $625 because of an increased supply of Treasury bills. The $50 "fixed" income would represent a yield of 8% to a new buyer ($50/$625 = 8%). Fixed-income investment prices (short-term notes, bonds) always move inversely to interest rates. If the price of the paper went up, then the interest on the units owned went down. The rapid turnover in short-term paper (the underlying instruments) meant that funds would always be offering close to the most current rate of return.

Bank interest rates, on the other hand, were fixed not by the market but by the central banks. But central banks were generally less independent from government politics than now: the level of domestic interest rates was influenced as much by political considerations as by the need to ensure stable prices. The government-appointed central banks were beholden to politically elected cabinets, so were unable to raise domestic rates enough to forestall additional government indebtedness. The result was that the traditional banking system denied depositors the spread they could get in mutual funds, and so deposits shifted to the pooled investments. When banks began to sell their own mutual funds, savvy depositors shifted their money even faster. And that's when it became really interesting.

Step Two: Securitization
Until the 1970s, a bank's ability to lend was constrained by its ability to attract deposits. Banks were, after 300 years, still intermediaries, attracting deposits with the promise of interest, and lending the money out at a higher rate. However, with money market accounts, banks were no longer dependent on the link between depositors and borrowers. They discovered another way to get the money they needed to lend out: "securitization." For

example, say they had a million dollars' worth of residential mortgages. They could bundle those mortgages, slice up the bundle into $10,000 units, and sell the units to retail investors like you and me. They could then take that new cash and lend it out as new mortgages, which in turn would enable them to create yet another instrument for securitization. Investors in capital markets became the key to bank growth, and many of those investors were not individuals at all, but money market funds.

Step Three: Index Futures

The banks used to make money another way: they had a monopoly on government deposits. When a country's central bank printed money, it was deposited in banks. And when the government borrowed money in world capital markets, the money was deposited in banks. Then it was lent out. Governments were very big borrowers, and they used their dominant position in capital markets to reduce the cost of borrowing. They did this by "arbitraging"—buying in one market and selling in another. For example, say the British pound was selling in London at $1.5945 and in New York at $1.5950. Buying pounds in London and selling them in New York gave a guaranteed yield of 0.05 cents on every pound. For every $1-million order, the profit was $285.06 (less transaction costs).

Governments reduced the cost of borrowing by arbitraging in time as well as space. Different prices for government bonds in different geographic markets create one kind of arbitraging opportunity. The difference between short- and long-term interest rates offers another. Long-term interest rates are traditionally higher because lenders have to wait longer to use their money. So the governments bought in the short-term market and sold in the long-term market. Until the mid-1970s, only governments and huge companies that issued investment-grade corporate bonds could do this. Then, in 1975, the Chicago Board of Trade introduced the world's first interest rate futures contracts, and in 1982 the Chicago Mercantile, North America's largest commodity

exchange, started trading the first stock futures contracts based on the Standard and Poor's 500 Index. Now individual investors could do what previously only governments and General Motors-type enterprises could do. How? The exchanges act as clearing houses, just as the Mercantile does in commodity markets. When a farmer wants to sell a crop before it's planted, he does not have to look for a buyer, nor worry about getting paid. The exchange monitors the credit of buyers and sellers and provides a place where they can trade without knowing each other. Just as news of a drought may reduce the wheat harvest and future supplies, so news of an interest rate increase or a presidential scandal may cause stock-index futures prices to fall as investors react to the possibility of difficult times ahead.

Because futures contracts offer assurance of future prices and availability of assets traded, they provide stability in a volatile business environment. Futures have long been associated with agricultural commodities such as coffee, cocoa and pork bellies (bacon); now they are as likely to be used by bankers and computer makers as farmers. By the end of the 1980s, financial futures accounted for three-quarters of all futures volume. The ability to hedge against financial instability had wide appeal: exporting companies could protect themselves against currency fluctuations by trading currency futures contracts. Investors could protect the value of their investments by trading interest rate, bond- and stock-index futures contracts. Suddenly, the difference between short- and long-term instruments disappeared; long and short were now explicitly parts of the same whole.

Stock-index futures also provided a spectacular opportunity for pooled investment funds, because they could now offer individual investors a form of management that otherwise would be available only to the extremely rich. A further change favouring the pension funds was the change in tax rules that disallowed the so-called year-end "straddle." This was a ploy whereby investors sold their losing investments at year-end to capture the losses in the old year, where they could be deducted from other income,

while moving gains into the following year. By outlawing the straddle the tax authorities were ensuring that most investment money would flow into the pension funds, where incomes were tax sheltered until withdrawal.

Result: Pillar-less Financial Services

By the mid-1980s, less than 15 years after the introduction of floating exchange rates, the whole financial services industry had been revolutionized and, in effect, homogenized. The old distinctions between the so-called "pillars"—banks, trust companies, investment firms and insurance companies—were for all practical purposes obliterated. What remained were simply different forms of investment in capital markets. Add to this the technology of credit cards and bank cards, which essentially provided unsecured loans and instantaneous chequing to anybody. Britain and Canada changed their regulations to allow banks to offer all these financial services (except certain types of insurance). The U.S. achieved similar results through reciprocal banking arrangements between states (agreements by states to allow banking activities by deposit-taking institutions from other states that have similar agreements respecting banks based in those states). Nevertheless, a persistent characteristic of the U.S. banking system is the official separation of deposit-taking institutions (banks) from investment dealers. The sole exceptions to this rule are mutual funds.

The Winners: Mutual Funds and Small, Knowledge-Driven Companies

In this environment, mutual funds took off. They cost less to operate than a bank, and could offer superior returns and investor service. In Canada, banks still had a monopoly over the country's payments-settlement system, so every mutual fund payout had to pass through a bank. This, together with their extensive branching system in Canada, gave banks an edge in the mutual fund business, one which they increased by buying the top securities dealers.

Mutual funds emerged as the real winners from these changes, as the Chart 6–1 below attests.

CHART 6–1 **Mutual Fund Growth in Canada**

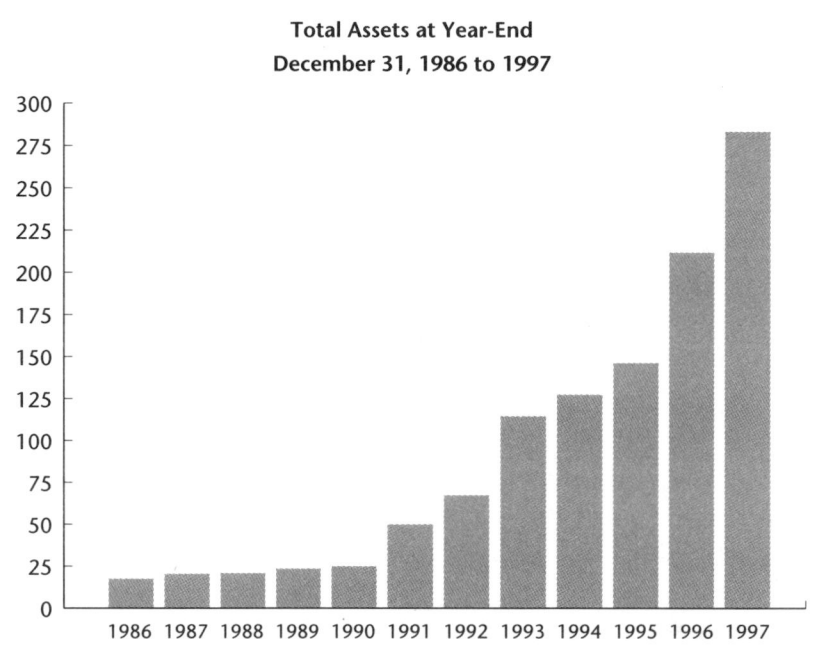

Total Assets at Year-End
December 31, 1986 to 1997

Source: *Investment Funds Institute of Canada*

Other winners were start-up computer companies (like Microsoft), able to get bank credit now that banks had to be more aggressive in seeking loans in order to securitize in the market.

Until the mid-1980s, small and medium-sized business were low on the banks' priority lending list; big business and governments, domestic and foreign, looked like better bets. But then, faced with serious competition for the first time, some U.S. banks actually failed, while those in Canada experienced shrinking profits and diminishing market share.

The causes of the banks' problems were threefold:

1. Corporations discovered they could get a better deal by bypassing the banks and going directly to the capital markets. Canadian banks got a lot of this business back when they acquired the top securities firms. American banks did not.
2. The public sector in Canada and blue-chip companies in the U.S. found they could get loans at better terms from offshore financial institutions than at domestic ones.
3. Banks invested more in relatively riskier assets such as commercial mortgages. This was especially marked in the U.S. but was not infrequent in Canada (as the fallout from the collapse of real-estate values, such as the bankruptcy of Confederation Life, showed). The other area of increased investment by banks in the wake of more competition was loans to small businesses.

The end of the transition period saw the banks considerably weakened. (Their current profitability reflects the huge write-downs they took in recent years on the poor-quality, formerly "preferred" loans.)

The main points in all this are simple. First, capital markets are now a single industry. Second, the banks now have to compete for their traditional business. Third, pension and mutual funds have done a lot better than the banks and are now the main intermediaries between Canada's savings and business credit.

THE REGULATORS

You wouldn't find out any of this, though, by chatting with the regulators of our financial system. Equity markets are provincially regulated; therefore, so are pension and mutual funds. Ottawa concentrates on the banks and near-banks, and on the international competition. In a manner reminiscent of those old stereotype jokes about the men making the big decisions while the women decide what to spend, Ottawa makes the big decisions about bank structure and monetary policy, while markets decide

what financial services will be able to do. Meanwhile, the provinces pretend they're not in the banking business at all, while the pensions of provincial public servants, the biggest pension funds in the country, enjoy a level of economic intervention that Lenin could only dream about.

So why have you slogged through all this banking history when all you want to do is find a way to retire or semi-retire with comfort and dignity? The answer is that a misaligned system such as ours clearly imposes some costs. You can't write a cheque directly to a mutual fund without it passing through an account in a bank. That's an additional cost, both in time and in unnecessary bank services. But more important is the effect on the central bank's ability to set and implement monetary policy.

The central bank buys and sells securities in the market in an attempt to control the amount of currency, paper money and current-account money in the economy. The bank believes that it can control inflation, the pace of economic growth and interest rates. If the economic growth is lagging, for example, the central bank buys securities, paying for them in cash. The cash goes into banks, more cash is in the system, interest rates decline, and people borrow more. Or, if prices are rising, the central bank sells securities, people pay for them in cash, and the cash goes into the central bank and stops being circulated. The money supply is reduced, interest rates go up and people are discouraged from borrowing.

Well, maybe that's the way it used to be. Now, the central bank can talk the talk but do very little else to control liquidity. ("Liquid" funds are cashable immediately; currency and paper money in circulation are cash, as are demand deposits such as current accounts, which are payable "on demand.") Why? One reason is that when half the nation's savings are in mutual funds, the distinctions between long-term and short-term money are no longer relevant to ordinary people: their savings may be in term investments such as Treasury bills and bonds, yet they can treat those savings as though they were cash. In fact, many small

and medium-sized businesses use money market accounts to manage their cash flows. It's cheaper than hiring a person specifically to be responsible for the business's cash.

So how *do* governments control the amount of liquidity in the economy? In theory, they try to keep interest rates under control, by either buying or selling short-term financial instruments such as T-bills or gold or short-term bonds. This has some impact on economic activity, but little on liquidity. Rate changes affect savings, but people who have their savings in mutual funds can slosh them from equities to bonds and back again, depending on the direction of rates, without changing the individual's liquidity. Also, most firms have switched to just-in-time inventories; the firm and its raw-materials suppliers share the financing of the new arrangements. So rates have much less effect than they once did on business activity. Large capital projects use other techniques to work around interest rate fluctuations. For example, say a company has borrowed $10 million for 10 years at a fixed interest rate of 8%. Two years into the project, interest rates drop to 6%. The firm can sell its fixed-rate debt to someone who wants to lock in a fixed rate, and buy a lower, "floating-rate" debt, thus neutralizing the interest rate change.

The upshot of this is that governments don't set monetary policy any longer by manipulating interest rates. It's a big change from regulating bank credit.

One more thing: the 1990s are a period of retrenchment of government borrowing. This further reduces the state's role as intermediary between long- and short-term credit, and the role of the banks as underwriters of government-backed securities. Henceforth, an increasing proportion of capital financing will be done by the private sector, which was crowded out in the preceding decades. The demand can be filled either by banks or by pension and mutual funds. If the 1980s are any guide, the better-quality assets (i.e., projects with a high probability of success) will increasingly be financed through equity and corporate paper, rather than bank debt.

THE PRICE OF MISUNDERSTANDING: POOR ASSET ALLOCATION

A far greater issue arises from these reflections. We are living at a time in which the national financial systems (in many countries) fail to acknowledge their own reality. The effect of this is to impose upon all such countries a whopping price for misunderstanding—in the form of a misallocation of savings.

The current pattern, in which half the nation's savings are in bank accounts and the other half in mutual funds, essentially mimics an overly prudent investment strategy of matching risk and reward. Bank savings are risk free when covered by deposit insurance and have low real rates of return; mutual funds, which can lose money and are not insured, offer at least double the bank's rate of return. That is, insured savings today offer between 1% and 5%, while mutual funds returns are still in double digits. Assuming that stocks have an equal chance of going up or down, an equity mutual fund that offers twice the bank's rate of return is offering an equivalent investment to that of a bank account because you have a 50% chance of losing money, but you get twice as much when you gain. In fact, mutual funds have offered four or five times the bank's rate of return, so on a risk-reward basis, Canadians still overinvest in bank accounts. If you factor in risk of inflation, which could erode your bank savings (you're locked into a term investment which may not fully reflect the effect of inflation on purchasing power, but is reflected almost immediately in the stock market), then the misalignment is even greater. Then there's moral hazard—the possibility of loss because of the actions of the person sustaining the loss. Say asset quality, such as the value of a real-estate portfolio, is deteriorating. If your bank account and term deposits in the institution are insured, as they are by deposit insurance, you will not necessarily take your money to a safer haven. If you are uncomfortable about an uninsured equity investment, you will sell it and transfer the funds to another asset. Even more reason to be prudent about keeping your money in a bank.

The upshot is that after any typical period, Canadian savers

are less well off than they otherwise would be—by quite a large margin. Suppose you have $100,000 divided equally between a bank account and a mutual fund. Say the fund pays four times the bank's rate of return. It would be sensible to have twice the allocation in mutual funds as in the bank, i.e., $33,000 in the bank and $67,000 in the funds, instead of $50,000 in each, for the two investments to have equivalent expected value.

The failure of the current system to make this explicit results in a greater number of Canadians who will be that much more dependent on the state after they retire. This may be politics as usual, but it is good public policy only if you believe that the federal government should protect the banks instead of taxpayers and savers.

GETTING RID OF THE CANADA AND QUEBEC PENSION PLANS WOULD HELP

Young people who recently joined the workforce would each be about $400,000 ahead at retirement if they could take their mandatory contribution to the Canada or Quebec Pension Plan and invest it privately. William Robson, senior policy analyst at the C. D. Howe Institute, projected the financial benefits of a 24-year-old who started working in 1995 and stayed employed until 65. Putting the equivalent of the CPP contributions into investments earning a modest 4% a year (after adjusting for a 3.5% inflation rate) would produce a nest egg of $1.1 million. The comparable CPP benefit package earned over the same period would be worth $667,000, to be paid out over the average life of a retired Canadian, including a death benefit to a surviving spouse. And a real 4% is not exactly a spectacular investment.

C/QPP is at a disadvantage relative to market investments for a couple of reasons. First, it supports disability pensions. Second, it has collected contributions far too low to fund the benefits owed to retiring workers. The burden on young participants is eased, but not eliminated, by the increase in contribution rates to 9.9% by 2003. All the increase in contribution rates (i.e.,

taxes) does is build the CPP reserve fund and eliminate the need for even steeper hikes as the baby boom generation retires. Two groups take the brunt of the hit: the young and the self-employed, the two groups that, quite frankly, are the most innovative and the most mobile. This is exactly the formula we need if we want our children and grandchildren to work in Florida, California, Australia or Ireland—in fact, anywhere but Canada.

The basic premise of the CPP is that the way to maintain people's incomes after they stop working is to tap the earnings of future workers, rather than require each generation to save for their own retirement. So it shouldn't be surprising that after 30 years of operation, the CPP fund has only a few years' worth of payouts in it; that's how it was designed. The gap between the pension promises and the amount in the fund is bigger than the national debt—in the $800-billion range. In fact, even if you can imagine that some day the public debt will start to decline, now that the deficit seems to be under control, the burden on future workers to fund the C/QPP continues to grow. It takes a great leap of faith to believe that tomorrow's young workers are going to bear such a burden once they realize that they aren't going to share the wealth. The lure of the C/QPP was that in exchange for small contributions today you'd get large benefits tomorrow. Try instead the appeal of high contributions today for low benefits tomorrow.

The increase in the contribution rate enacted in 1997 has been billed as the final one which would put the CPP on a stable footing. Not true. It was necessary in order to prevent the fund from running dry—in 2015, by the Chief Actuary's estimate. (Since then, the Chief Actuary continued to argue with the Department of Finance about the assumptions on which the CPP funding projections are based. In late 1998, Chief Actuary Dusseault was relieved of his position.) What everyone (not just youngsters) must understand is that the design of the plan is fundamentally flawed. That understanding will come as, inevitably, the age of eligibility rises and broad categories of benefits are reduced or dropped.

The solution is to phase out the C/QPP and phase in a universal private system, a mandatory, but individual, retirement plan. This would be fairly easy, as Canadians already understand the concept of RRSPs, group RRSPs, and employer-sponsored and administered pension plans. I'll discuss these plans more in subsequent chapters.

For all this reform to happen without waiting for a crisis to force stop-gap responses, a carefully orchestrated plan has to be implemented over several years. In 1996, the Howe Institute suggested staging a transition to a universal private system by (1) immediately starting a publicity campaign to inform all Canadians about the dire state of the CPP, (2) raising contribution rates in 1997, (3) separating the disability programs currently included in the C/QPP into a stand-alone plan, (4) phasing in, from 1998 to 2018, an increase in retirement age to 70, and (5) scaling back to 60% all benefits accruing from 1998 onward. So far, the government has done (2). In defending the present system, it is maintaining that there is no need to further link retirement to markets (other than to set up a CPP Investment Board to invest future contributions in Treasury paper and index funds). The point, however, is that the present pension system, even with an increase in contribution rates, doesn't mean the CPP sickness will cure itself.

Let's review:

- Banks used to be where we saved our money. Over the last 25 years, pension and mutual funds have caught up with the banks as the preferred depository for savings because these funds provide better returns through superior investment management.
- Communications and information technology have opened the world of investment—previously available only to governments and huge firms—to ordinary investors. The four "pillars" of financial services (banks, trusts, investment houses and insurance companies) have become parts of one capital market.

- Regulators are "playing catch-up" in the fast-moving real world. Since the world economy is still in transition, the people and institutions with vested interests in keeping the old rules are imposing costs on the evolving new system.
- One important cost for people concerned about saving for retirement is that the rewards of risk-free investment look more attractive than they should, and the task of managing the risk of much higher returns looks much more difficult than it should.
- The present retirement system is skewed towards an unsustainable public pension system.
- The key to financial independence is understanding how to invest in global capital markets.

The next chapter introduces you to your custom-tailored strategy.

7

Your Age Is
Your Strategy

The time to repair a roof is when the sun is shining.
—John F. Kennedy

RETIREMENT IS A FAMILIAR idea. We've grown up with it. Industrial employers have built it into the way employees are compensated. It's part of the fabric of Canadian society, so it's not going to disappear overnight. But it is endangered. Employers welcome employee demands for more say in pension asset allocation; defined benefit plans are less relevant for workers who have four or five different jobs in their working life than for those who had one. Even without such demands, more employers are changing their pension structures to "money purchase" plans in which employees take responsibility for investment decisions. Besides, the high level of merger and acquisition activity means that another wave of employees will be cut loose with lump sums of money for which investment decisions have to be made.

I have known only one young couple who didn't laugh their heads off when I suggested that they should be thinking about saving before anything else (they were 18 and 23).

I'm sure there are others, but they're a rare breed. Yet this is the generation who know that Old Age Security and the Canada

Pension Plan will not be there when they get to retirement age. What they need (and even that may not do it) is a rationale that makes sense.

Yes, you can retire, but ... you need to define your retirement, plan early (and often), understand what you have to understand, and keep abreast of the big items that will squash you if you don't keep your eye on them.

Let's start with understanding what you have to understand. Competition, for one thing, is vastly more intense than it ever was, and it's not going away. Businesses, big and small, are jockeying to find markets globally or locally. The investments needed to acquire, build and maintain physical and intellectual assets are huge. That's one reason we're seeing record merger and acquisition activity as well as spinoffs and business start-ups. Every business decision may make or break the company. Thus there are big winners and big losers.

Whether we like it or not, the information and communications revolution is transforming our world beyond recognition. The biggest winners are firms and individuals who assume this new perspective as though it were a new skin. In this novel world, anyone can find out more or less whatever they have to know: networking ability is instantaneous and immediate; you can join a network just by dialling up a bulletin board. Such a society favours small producers and entrepreneurs who are very specialized and can react quickly.

Learning has become a lifelong undertaking, and is available at home, on the job, and in between, as convenient as turning on a tap. Schools still serve a purpose, of course, but when the world's best teachers and so-called great books are available on interactive CDs, and current knowledge is available on databases, the organization of schools has to change—a lot. Books are not going to disappear; far from it. They're a lot more portable and a lot more fun to read than a computer screen. Still, the book-computer thing is at the heart of the challenge of an information-based world. When the Greeks started writing things down for

posterity, people no longer had to memorize important ideas; books destroyed the need for memory as the main engine of knowledge accumulation. With books came libraries (unknown in the preliterate world), institutions where a non-expert could consult the world's knowledge bank and add his own reflections, that is, create new knowledge. This launched what ultimately became a kind of world brain, a self-organizing organ for accumulating and disseminating knowledge.

But books are expensive, slow to produce, and cumbersome to copy, store and transport. So the information in them is migrating to cyberspace—where the banks keep your money, in William Gibson's telling definition.

In the distant past, an educated person was someone who had memorized those things that were deemed important by the dominant social group. Later on, an educated person was someone who had consulted the books deemed important by the dominant social group. That definition has broken down in our own lifetime; the discussion of what is now an educated person has settled on core sets of competencies or skills. Big change: we are moving from knowing *what* to knowing *how*, a very important shift, in my opinion. It parallels a couple of other dramatic changes, such as the rise of the global economy and the revolution in manufacturing, the adoption of zero-defect quality standards in our economic life, all of which are made possible by wiring computers into the world information flow.

One can and should use a computer to help understand, say, Shakespeare's plays. But will the computer, even if it can generate a cyberplayer's version of Shakespeare, ever be a satisfactory substitute for human performance? I suspect not, for the very real reason that great theatre and great literature in general are about *human* experience, not really about moving characters in space. The trouble is, as our machines grow more sophisticated, we become less and less certain of what is uniquely human. If you're a science-fiction fan and follow the literature on robotics, you know that if the machines respect Asimov's laws of robotics,

they can and will encounter tragic situations leading to their own destruction. (If you don't read sci-fi, the first law is to "do no harm to humans.") The real question posed by Hal in *2001* is, how do we distinguish between machine and man? Or, even more poignantly in *Blade Runner*, between replicant and human in a world of genetic engineering? If machines are conscious of their tragedy, does that make them more human? The point is, wiring up challenges us to think about these things. There's more to this than "hit the lights and watch the bytes." Knowing *how* does not free us from exploring the biggest of all *what* questions: What does it mean to be human? It will no longer be possible for anyone to keep a monopoly or define what "correct" knowledge is. To be sure, there'll be standards, but no standardization.

Dr. Roger Selbert, publisher of a futurist newsletter, writes that

[as] a metaphor for the new economy, the entertainment industry serves well …. The growth of entertainment— TV, video, movies, music, publishing, theater, spectator sports, theme parks and more—is both a driving force behind, as well as a defining result of, a growing popula- tion with more time, money and inclination to be enter- tained. But while more entertainment gets produced and more consumers spend more money to access, acquire and enjoy it, companies in the industry operate in an extremely tough profit climate …. And the future looks even tougher: more competitors producing more products, offering more choices for an audience that is fragmenting into a myriad of market segments that in most cases prevent economies of scale from being realized.

The entertainment industry is our world in microcosm: a massive pillar of activity with no guarantee of success.

The one choice we do not have is whether to be in this world, living in this economic paradigm. We therefore have to learn about our new world, see it with new eyes. And we have to ask new

questions of our advisors, when we think about education for our kids and ourselves, the kind of career we have had or may want, and what we will do when we are finished doing the job we got five, 10 or 20 years ago. And when we think about our new retirement.

Making money is about to get a lot easier. First, the largest-ever transfer of accumulated capital is underway: the savings of the World War II generation are being transferred to the postwar baby boomers. Second, the boomers are entering their big savings years, and the RRSP money or equivalents they're putting aside are driving up the price of stocks worldwide. The glitch in the markets that began in the summer of 1998 doesn't negate this statement. The transfers and wealth accumulation will continue for another 15 years in the West, followed by another 25 years in the Asia-Pacific region (which began its wealth accumulation a quarter-century later). All that capital needs to find opportunities to invest in.

Now, it so happens that, out there eagerly seeking to be invested in, are a whole lot of opportunities. We've had 10 years of explosive growth of information technology-based industries. As competition breaks into the local telephone loop, the price of communicating is going to go into freefall. Already, computer memory is virtually costless. Sure, we've seen computers move onto our desktops and shrink, as they hook up to each other via the Internet, but the next wave of change is about to hit: virtually every economic transaction will happen on a network. What's more, the current generation of managers—the next generation of senior suits—actually understand this capability and will have no trouble figuring out neat things to do with it.

And there's more. Biotechnology is just about to hit in search of investment dollars as well. Up to now, biotech stocks have taken from eight to 10 years before showing any signs of paying off, and much of that payoff has been buried in clinical trials. That era is rapidly reaching its close. Just as microprocessing power has been doubling every two years for the last two decades, biotech is developing a doubling process that will slash product

development times to those approximating software. Key to this is genomics. Genomes are the genetic programming every living creature—human, plant and animal—carries around like a personal computer program just waiting for the right machine to read it. (And there's much less difference between us, plants and animals than you might think.) Information technology has vastly increased our capacity to understand genomes, especially the way proteins and polymers work in living things. Already, most of the world's agriculture has been revolutionized by biotech, and the technology is now in the pipeline to revolutionize manufacturing as well.

These revolutions are going to transform most of the basic economic processes we live by, and will inevitably affect our social processes for the better. Perhaps the main effect will be that the human species will tread upon the planet with a much lighter foot. Using biological plants to manufacture things through photosynthesis leaves no industrial waste. When you don't need chemicals for dyes or pesticides or fertilizers, you've eliminated many of the substances that harm the environment.

The demand for experienced, thoughtful people to participate in and facilitate these changes is going to shoot upwards. So forget rocking on the front porch until you die. Face it, active engagement in this exciting new world is going to be hard to avoid.

This means that you're unlikely to retire as if you were never going to earn another cent. A more realistic approach would be to see your retirement as the launch of a small business—and that business is you. Your "retirement plan," which most books suggest should be a packet of passive-investment instruments, should instead be a powerful business plan that will put you in the driver's seat of a significant value-creating entity. If you've got a family, they should be included, too.

Some Canadians are way ahead of most of us: we all know, or know of, people who have always been go-getters, who have piled up a nice little nest egg, thanks to riding the waves of change mentioned earlier in this book. These people may "retire"

much as we will, but they're already planning future projects, and they're comfortable that they'll always have the money they need to live the way they always have. Not all of us enjoy spending our time (or getting our identity from) making money, but understanding their attitudes towards the future is what we need in order to think our way through the new retirement.

IN YOUR 20s

Here are the most sensible things I could do if I were 18 or 23, or even 30. If I were earning minimum wage as my full-time activity, I would forget about saving. I would take the chance that there would be a government program for me throughout my working and non-working life. But as soon as I began earning more than minimum wage—even $10 an hour qualifies—I would immediately tell myself that I was earning 10% less. That 10% would go into savings.

As soon as you have what is called "discretionary" income, you have choices. Among the choices: to use or not to use credit. Your best bet in disinflationary and deflationary times is to qualify for a credit card but use it only for the two big-ticket items you will ever need it for, a car and a house. (In inflationary times, borrowing is a good strategy, as I explain in Chapter 9.) I'm not suggesting that you can buy a house on Visa, but to buy a house you need a credit rating. Without a credit rating, you don't exist in the financial system. So get a card, save some money, then use the card and pay it off as soon as you get the bill. Now you have a credit rating. (Do the same with borrowing. Go to a financial institution, borrow a small amount, and then pay it off with money you have on hand. Now you have a borrowing history.)

The only sensible way to use a credit card is to get more out of it than it costs you. That means being able to pay it off before interest is charged, and/or having an "affinity" card which gives you a rebate on purchases you make, or buying something on sale when you don't have the cash on you—but only if you have the money saved. In other words, a credit card should be a

convenience card; otherwise, it's an expense. One of the best rules to take from the business community is, "Maximize your profit centres, minimize your cost centres." No matter how prosperous things may seem, and no matter how many politicians tell you the economy is strong, these are (and will continue to be) uncertain times; and the last thing you need when you're knocked off your feet is debt.

When you are just getting used to being out on your own, there are a lot of these "cost centres": all the things you have or want to buy, and the services, such as insurance. There are lots of budgeting books around, and it's a good idea to read at least one of them. Get some perspective on how much things really cost. (You bought a great outfit on sale for $179.95? Terrific. With taxes, that's around $207, right? In order to have the $207 to fork over, you had to earn how much? Here's a little chart to tell you.

CHART 7–1 **The Pre-Tax Cost of After-Tax Purchases**

SINGLE TAXPAYER, ASSUMING BASIC PERSONAL TAX CREDIT, 1998

If Your Weekly Take-Home Pay Is	Your Marginal Tax Rate Is About	Pre-Tax Earnings to Earn About	After-Tax Purchase
$400	18.5%	$255	$207
$600	41%	$350	$207
$1,200	45%	$380	$207
$1,800	51%	$420	$207

Once you get into the habit of thinking about your spending on a pre-tax basis, you will find that your priorities change. This is particularly true of big purchases. Let's say you decide to get a car or a computer. Inform yourself about the options. For example, consider leasing. Figure out the difference between the two. Assess the cost differences versus the flexibility that comes with a lease. (For example, with a lease, you are renting for a couple of years. You will continue to hold on to the money you would otherwise have to hand over to own the car or computer. Can you put that money to work to make a profit?)

Spend some time thinking about your profit centres, too—investing in yourself so you can both earn more and gain the skills that, more than anything else, will ensure you are never involuntarily without work. It's also a good time to formalize the "what if" dreaming that all of us do: "What if I save $1,000 a year and make 10% a year on it? How long will it take to accumulate $1 million if I can make 8% on the $200 a month I save? What if I make 12%? 15%?" There are a number of software programs that let you plug in your own numbers. As you indulge in the "what if" game, it will become apparent pretty quickly that there are only a couple of simple, long-term strategies virtually guaranteed to bring you security: owning the roof over your head, and owning profitable businesses. (There are lots of investments that will make you money, but they are more complicated, and you will need time to learn about them; see Chapter 9.)

Certainly, with many years stretching before you, attitude is critically important to developing and achieving your objectives. It's the time to take the new economic paradigm seriously and throw out all but long-term advice. In other words, if you *are* making minimum wage, ask yourself why. Is that all you aspire to? How important is it that you live comfortably? What are your prospects for getting ahead? What keeps you from commanding more income?

If part of the answer is that you need more education, get it. You no longer have to like school or even be good at absorbing mass education. If you don't have an overriding passion for some particular occupation, consult a vocational counsellor and find out what you're good at. Then you can design your own course of study and learn at your own pace. Even if you need a diploma or certificate, you can still develop your own schedule.

IN YOUR 30s

Once the "basics" have become second nature to you, it's time to move on to the bigger picture. You've probably figured out that the assumptions above were that you were not just young, but without dependents. Lots of people are "unencumbered" for

their entire lives, as the birth rate falls and Canadians support themselves throughout their lives. But lots of others live in families—tended, blended, mended, and extended. Children, siblings, parents, grandparents, friends; the age groupings are arbitrary, but the things you should be thinking about are added to things you've already mastered. You will regularly revise your focus as you accomplish some goals and aspire to others.

The next big question is, "Where is the best place to invest my free cash?" Whether to buy a home is your first decision. There are great advantages to doing this, in Canada and elsewhere. In Canada, this is a tax-free investment. As we enter the new millennium, real estate is still 20% or more lower than it was a dozen years ago, and interest rates are lower. In the U.S. an owner-occupied home has a tax-preferred status, and your mortgage interest is deductible from earned income. (Of course, you have to have American earned income, but that's another decision.) A fundamental rule of investing is, "Never do it just for the tax break." But if you like the lifestyle, and you don't succumb to the idea that your property will make you rich (which it probably won't), it's a tax-free roof over your head.

Whether you "lock in" to a multi-year mortgage is a matter of comfort. Countless people choose three- or five-year terms because "we can afford it," even though the interest rate is one or two percentage points higher, but such thinking is obsolete. Interest rates are not moving up as they were throughout the 1970s and part of the '80s. (You will know that, if you keep abreast of the global financial events I touched on earlier.) At the very least, calculate how much the lowest interest rate mortgage saves you over one year, and how much rates have to rise, and for how long, before you'll be paying more than the "locked-in" rate. Real estate as an investment for "cash flow" (not for capital appreciation) is another strategy for people who are handy at home repairs and are thinking of retirement income (more about this in Chapter 9).

The second decision you have to make is where, geographically, to invest your free cash. Canadians have been conditioned

to think only about investing in Canada. This has been a great strategy for perhaps 10 of the last 40 years; Canadian equity markets represent less than 3% of the equity in the world, and Canada is not the fastest-growing economy. True, we need Canadian funds to spend, because we live in Canada, but the steady decline in the value of the Canadian dollar relative to most other currencies means that most of the capital gains made have been swallowed up in the currency devaluation.

It is no more difficult to open an American bank or investment house account than it is to open a Canadian one. Nor is it difficult to buy American stocks or mutual funds. Clearly, you can also open a US$ account in Canada. That's okay as long as you believe there will never be exchange controls. In view of the fact that several countries imposed controls on capital flowing into and out of their countries during the currency upheavals of 1998, this is a big leap of faith. If you decide to do your international investing in Canada, it is wise to open a US$ account for no other reason than that brokerage houses charge exorbitantly for exchanging Canadian dollars for U.S. The spread between buying and selling is customarily 5%, which may mean that your broker makes more on your trade than you do. With a US$ account, you can settle your account at the prevailing exchange rate, or wait until you liquidate a US$ investment.

The timing of this next decision is hard to pinpoint, but somewhere between your mid-20s and mid-30s, you should begin estate planning. You've probably acquired a partner and perhaps children, although, if you're typical, you'll have little in the way of substantial assets. Now is the time to act to protect your dependents should you or your partner die or become incapacitated. That means looking at life and disability insurance.

IN YOUR 40s

It's okay to read in the newspapers or see on TV that the stock markets are toppy or sloppy, i.e., that they are volatile or overpriced or about to have a correction. But the only way to invest

is for the long term, and in the long term, there's almost nowhere else to make significant amounts of money.

Obviously, money isn't everything, but it is surely the only reason you are reading this book. Don't wait any longer to take control of your investment education, because unless you plan to stay in the under-$30,000-a-year category, your financial comfort in retirement depends on it. You can do this in your spare time, either on-line, by correspondence, or at a local community centre or investment house. If you engage a financial planner in your 40s, you still have 15-25 years to grow a nest egg.

From your 40s to your early 50s, you may be enjoying a higher income. It's not likely that you will have huge amounts of money to invest, because if you have children and a mortgage, they will take up a large part of your disposable income. Nevertheless, it's a good time to complete an investor profile in anticipation of the day when your mortgage will be paid off and your children launched. Any investment house will be happy to send you a sample profile.

IN YOUR 50s

By this time, you're established. You know how to earn an income, and maybe you have a partner. If you aren't divorced, and you decided earlier to buy a home, you've just about paid off your mortgage. And you're probably within sight of your kids being more or less on their own. If you are divorced, you're being squeezed by having to help support two households, or you're struggling with bringing up the kids yourself on a smaller income or juggling home and work responsibilities. Either way, you have to worry about outliving your work; business is still restructuring, and your job may be on the line. So in your 50s, there may be a lot of issues to deal with: how to get the skills you need, if you are a divorced, stay-at-home parent; how to upgrade your skills; how to make more money; what asset mix to consider for your portfolio; whether to take early retirement; how to develop a business plan for your start-up company. If you still have young

children, they're the best reason to make a strategic review of your life.

This is the stage of life when you may also have to be increasingly involved with your parents, who will likely be in their 70s or 80s. If they are anything like my parents, they are "of the old school" and not inclined to discuss their financial affairs with "the children." But you need to be particularly alert, to catch wind of any assistance they may need. If they don't need your financial assistance, they may need help in other aspects of their lives, and be unwilling or unable to ask directly.

Even if your life is on an even keel, you probably need to consider all these things once or twice a year, if only because we are living in such uncertain times. These are also the years when you begin to save seriously for your later years. And if you've been making a good living, it's amazing how rapidly money can accumulate if you have a business plan and a strategy. Now is the time to think about tax planning, how much you want to be able to help your kids, and how best to allocate your assets. It's also time to review your physical well-being and your lifestyle.

IN YOUR 60s

It's time to pay attention to your estate plan. There's still some time to put your financial house in order, but not a lot of time for delay. Asset allocation, some consideration of ensuring a steady income stream in retirement, looking at tax-liability insurance needs, and involving your family in your financial affairs are priority items. It's a good time to set aside some money for health care not covered by the public service. If you have a mind to, it may also be a good time to buy your cemetery plot and/or make your final arrangements.

You may want to "practise" living on the amount of income you have designated for your retirement years. This takes a little doing; you'll have to keep track of your spending in more detail than you're used to. Nevertheless, it's a good idea, because if you find after a year that you need more money to live as you would

like, you still have time to make the needed adjustments. (At worst, you'll have time to reduce your expectations.)

IN YOUR 70s

If you haven't yet experienced chronic illness, you're in a select but growing segment of the population. People are growing older without experiencing serious illness, but after 70, the likelihood that you will use medical services begins rising sharply. Now's the time to ensure that you have access to rehabilitation and convalescent services that are outside the purview of the public health care system. You should review your powers of attorney, and be comfortable with the decisions you've made regarding your finances and how you want to be treated should you not be able to speak for yourself. (More on this in Chapter 12.)

I find it useful and satisfying to make "to do" lists. I do it almost every day, and there's (for me) nothing as satisfying as crossing off things that have been accomplished. There's nothing as comforting as transferring to the next day things that haven't been done yet. The checklist below is more a lifetime philosophy than a list of what you have to do today. You can undoubtedly do better for yourself, but its purpose is to start you thinking along a trajectory that will get you to a comfortable retirement. The earlier you put the sentiments into practice, the more likely you will reach your goals.

Checklist

THINGS TO DO	FIRST DEVELOPED (DATE)	REVISION #1 (DATE)	REVISION #2 (DATE)
Develop a savings goal			
Make a budget			
Think "aftertax"			
Pay cash			
Establish a credit rating			
Have an emergency fund			
Start regular reading about the economy			
Organize your receipts			
Re-evaluate your budget and financial plan once a year			
Get a good tax preparer			
Buy a home			
Buy insurance as needed			
Learn about investment choices			
Understand the equity market			
Invest for the long term			
Start serious tax planning			
Check the pension plans outside your control—defined benefit, C/QPP			
Make a will			
Review all financial aspects of your life once a year			

THREE

PLAN, PLAN, PLAN

*What distinguishes us one from
another is our dreams ... and what
we do to make them come about.*
—Joseph Epstein

8

Developing
Your Plan

Anyone can wish for riches, and most people do;
but only a few know that a definite plan and a
burning desire are the only dependable means
of accumulating wealth.

YOUR BASIC AFTER-WORK NEEDS

Once you've spent some time thinking about your goals and priorities (as discussed in Chapter 5), the next step is to develop your own plan. When you first start doing this, you probably have only an intuitive idea of whether your ideal is going to be possible. Studies have found that most Canadians want to retire about 10 years before they can afford to. According to a recent survey, only one-third of Canadians have even bothered to calculate how much they'll need to live on when they decide not to work. Not surprising, then, that most people grossly overestimate how early they can retire—a rude awakening for those who discover that fact only when they reach their chosen retirement age.

Much better to know what it's going to take to make retirement a reality. That's what the following exercises are about. The beauty of them is that you alter them as your circumstances change. If you use a computer, one of the budget/planning software programs

CHART 8–1 **The Investment Process**

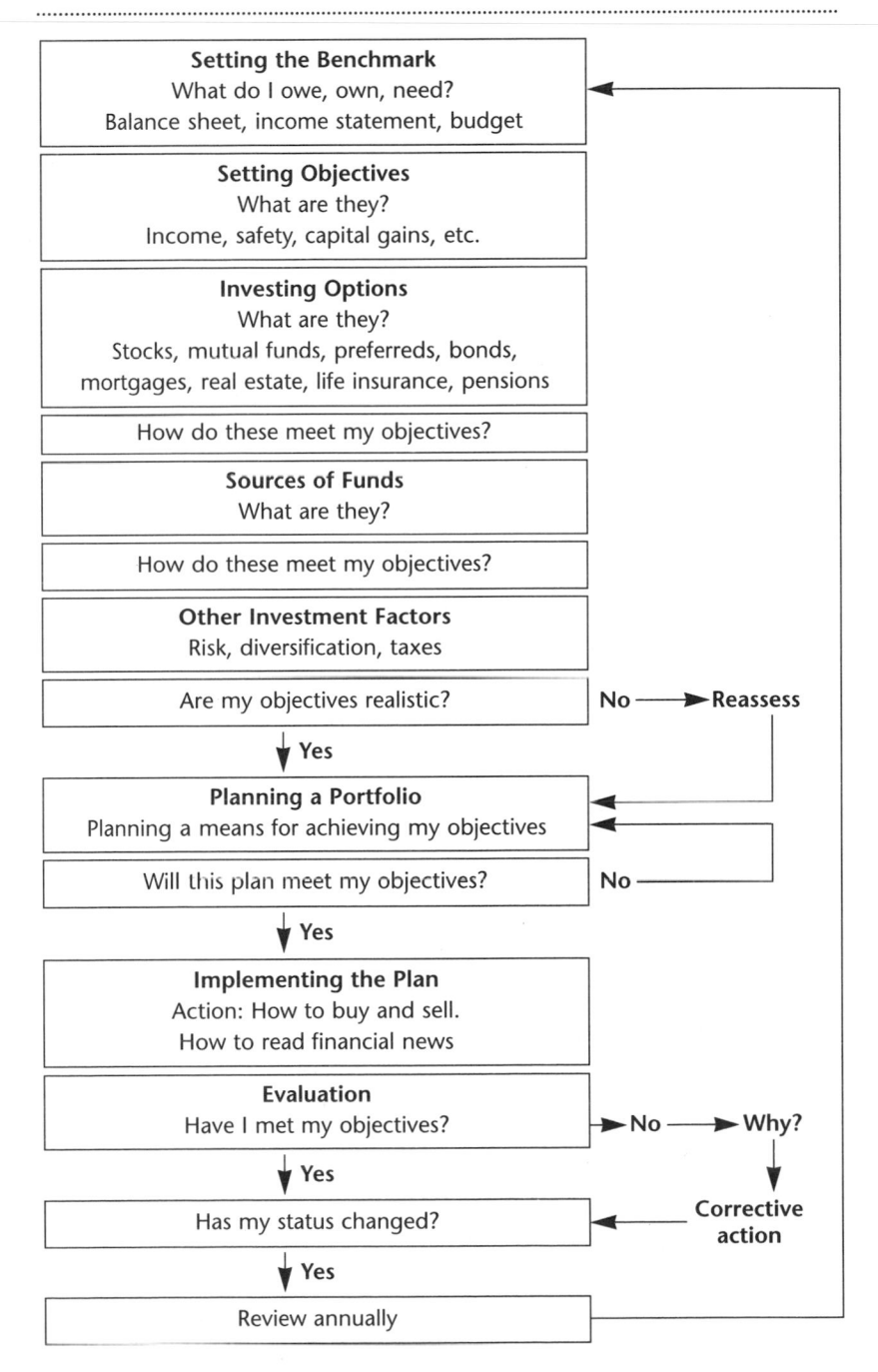

Setting the Benchmark What do I owe, own, need? Balance sheet, income statement, budget	
Setting Objectives What are they? Income, safety, capital gains, etc.	
Investing Options What are they? Stocks, mutual funds, preferreds, bonds, mortgages, real estate, life insurance, pensions	
How do these meet my objectives?	
Sources of Funds What are they?	
How do these meet my objectives?	
Other Investment Factors Risk, diversification, taxes	
Are my objectives realistic?	No ⟶ Reassess

↓ Yes

Planning a Portfolio Planning a means for achieving my objectives	
Will this plan meet my objectives?	No

↓ Yes

Implementing the Plan Action: How to buy and sell. How to read financial news	
Evaluation Have I met my objectives?	⟶ No ⟶ Why?

↓ Yes

Has my status changed?	Corrective action

↓ Yes

Review annually

makes it really simple: enter just about any assumption and experiment with lots of "what if" scenarios. There is a sample worksheet in this chapter and more in Appendix 2. If you have a partner, you may want to complete the exercises together.

See Chart 8–1 on page 148 for a quick fix on the investment process.

SETTING A BENCHMARK

We're not going to do the complete budgeting exercise here that you'd be wise to do (or have done since your 20s). You can do it now using the worksheets in Appendix 2. And if you're some distance from retirement, your first priority is to get out of debt, live 10%–15% below your means, and invest the rest. Our goal here is retirement planning, so we'll set the benchmark for pre-retirement planning, not life planning.

The starting point is to figure out what you spend today, so you can figure out what your spending might be in retirement. Use the worksheets in Appendix 2 to do an income statement (Worksheet 1), budget (Worksheet 2) and balance sheet (Worksheet 3), if you haven't started this process yourself. If you don't budget, this exercise will have the added advantage of giving you some idea about how you might streamline your current spending. It shouldn't be too hard to plug in your expenses, as long as you hold on to the receipts that come with just about all of them. As for your income statement, your payroll cheque stubs should allow you to complete it easily.

We begin with Worksheet 4, which uses the information you organized when you completed Worksheets 1, 2 and 3.

WORKSHEET 4 **Pre-Retirement Planning**

CURRENT EXPENSES	WORKING	ESTIMATED AT RETIREMENT
Mortgage/rent		
Property taxes		
Utilities—heat, light, phone, cable		

Maintenance	
Property insurance	
Food	
Clothing	
Personal (hair, dry cleaning, etc.)	
Car registration, licence	
Car payments	
Car operating costs	
Car insurance	
Public transit costs	
Life insurance	
Disability insurance	
Loan payments	
Credit card payments	
Education	
Medical, dental	
Gifts—birthday, Christmas, etc.	
Contributions to charity, political parties, etc.	
Entertainment/recreation	
Vacation travel	
Income taxes	
Savings	
Alimony, child support	
Other	
Lump-sum payments for vacation home, etc.	
Financial assistance to others	
Inheritance	
TOTAL	

Once you've done this, you can estimate which expenses might fall in retirement and which ones you think will rise. For example, if you own a home, your mortgage payments will likely end before you retire. Then your choices are to continue to live in your home and pay only taxes, insurance and maintenance,

or to sell it. If you sell, you also have choices: you can rent and invest the proceeds of the sale of your home. You can buy a smaller accommodation; if it's a condo, you have to slot in condo fees and expenses. You might want to move to a warmer climate for part of the year. What expenses would this entail? Will you buy there, or rent?

If you've been working at a job to which you have to commute, your transportation expenses in retirement will be lower. Possibly your clothing expenses will go down, too. You may stop paying life insurance premiums, unless you have a desire to leave behind an inheritance. (Life insurance has long been thought of as an "instant estate": money to replace your earnings should you die before you've built up your own estate. Life insurance can play an important role in your retirement and estate plans. These possibilities are examined in depth in Chapter 10, Tax Planning, and Chapter 9, Savings Strategies and Investment Options.)

Some expenses may rise in retirement. If you plan to buy a retirement home, you may have lump-sum expenses—big outlays such as the down payment or the full amount of the house. If you plan to travel, your entertainment/recreation/travel expenses will rise. The likelihood is that your health care/medical expenses will rise, partly because of increased fees for services but mostly because of changes to health care in Canada. You may want to help your children buy a home or finish their education.

You may need to help your parents financially. You may want to leave an inheritance.

If you have a partner, you will have to take into account the fact that women live five or six years longer than men, on average. This is important for your calculation of how long your money needs to last. If you are a single woman, you will need to plan even more carefully, both because you will probably live longer in retirement and because you may well not be earning as much now as a man in the same job. If you have children and/or stepchildren, you'll want to consider them in your plan.

In doing this exercise, think of all the possibilities for the future, and put them into your plan.

Case Study: Priscilla and Tom Gregory

PRESENT AGE	PRESENT INCOME	RETIREMENT AGE GOAL
Priscilla—53	$42,000	62
Tom—53	$39,500	62

WORKSHEET 4

CURRENT EXPENSES	WORKING	ESTIMATED AT RETIREMENT
Mortgage/rent	$12,300	$0
Property taxes	2,300	2,300
Utilities—heat, light, phone, cable	2,400	2,400
Maintenance	2,400	2,400
Property insurance	700	1,050
Food	7,000	4,500
Clothing	5,000	3,600
Personal (hair, dry cleaning, etc.)	1,200	800
Car registration, license	400	400
Car payments	3,000	0
Car operating costs	3,000	2,000
Car insurance	600	450
Other transportation	300	300
Life insurance	7,200	0
Disability insurance	0	0
Loan payments	0	0
Credit card payments	0	0
Education	0	1,000
Medical, dental	1,200	2,000
Gifts—birthday, Christmas, etc. Contributions to charity, political parties, etc.	1,500	1,500
Vacation travel	2,000	9,500
Entertainment	2,000	2,500
Income taxes	23,000	23,000

Savings	3,000	0
Alimony, child support	0	0
Assistance to others	1,000	0
Lump-sum payments for vacation home, etc.	0	0
TOTAL	$81,500	$62,100

SETTING OBJECTIVES

The next step is to figure out how much money you'll need each year in retirement, and for how many years you'll need an income. Here's step one:

CHART 8–2 **Number of Years in Retirement**

1. Your present age   _____
2. Your retirement age   _____
3. Years to retirement   _____   (#2 minus #1)
4. Life expectancy (Table 8–1) _____
5. Years in retirement   _____   (#4 minus #3)

TABLE 8–1 **LIFE EXPECTANCY**

AGE (YEARS)	FEMALE	MALE	AGE (YEARS)	FEMALE	MALE
45	36.5	31.5	57	26	21
46	35.5	30.5	58	25	20.5
47	34.5	30	59	24	20
48	33.5	29	60	23	19
49	33	28	61	22	18
50	32	27	62	21.5	17.5
51	31	26	63	21	17
52	30	25.5	64	20	16
53	29	24.5	65	19	15
54	28	24	66	18	14.5
55	27	23	67	17	14
56	26.5	22	68	16.5	13

69	16	12	76	11.5	8.5
70	15.5	11.5	77	11	8
71	15	11	78	10	7.5
72	14.5	10.5	79	9.5	7
73	14	10	80	9	6
74	13	9.5	85	6.5	5
75	12	9			

Tom and Priscilla Gregory's CHART 8–2

1. Your present age   _____53_____
2. Your retirement age   _____62_____
3. Years to retirement   _____9_____ (#2 minus #1)
4. Life expectancy (Table 8–1)   _24.5 & 29_
5. Years in retirement (approx.) _15.5 & 20_ (#4 minus #3)

Step two in determining how much you need for how long is to consider inflation. Recently inflation has been steady and low, after almost two decades of steadily rising prices. In fact, the rate has been less than 3% since the early 1990s. Moreover, many prices, such as those for electronic equipment, furniture and real estate, have been declining sharply for several years. Many people still believe inflation is a big threat, though I must confess to not sharing that belief. Indeed, were I to worry about price levels, I would be more concerned about the possibility of steadily *falling* prices. Your money would go farther, but you might have less of it, since interest rates would be lower.

Nevertheless, you may want to cover all the bases by considering the effect of inflation on your income. Table 8–2 shows you how many more dollars you'll need for selected incomes.

Now you're ready to project your estimated retirement income into the future, depending on what you think the inflation rate might be throughout the years you'll need income. Using the inflation factor table on page 156, multiply your estimated expenses in retirement by the inflation factor you think is appropriate.

TABLE 8-2 The Effect of Inflation on Income

	2% 10 YRS	4% 10 YRS	6% 10 YRS	2% 20 YRS	4% 20 YRS	6% 20 YRS	2% 30 YRS	4% 30 YRS	6% 30 YRS
$40,000	48,760	59,208	71,632	59,436	87,644	128,284	72,456	129,736	229,740
50,000	60,950	74,010	89,540	74,295	109,555	160,355	90,570	162,170	287,175
60,000	73,140	88,812	107,448	89,154	131,466	192,426	108,684	194,604	344,610
70,000	85,330	103,614	125,356	104,013	153,377	244,497	126,798	227,038	402,045
80,000	97,520	118,416	143,264	118,872	175,288	256,568	144,912	259,472	459,480
90,000	109,710	133,218	161,172	133,731	197,199	288,639	163,026	291,906	516,915
100,000	121,900	148,020	179,080	148,590	219,110	320,710	181,140	324,340	574,350

TABLE 8–3 **Inflation Factors**

YEARS TO RETIREMENT	2%	4%	6%
1	1.02	1.04	1.06
2	1.04	1.08	1.12
3	1.03	1.12	1.19
4	1.08	1.17	1.26
5	1.10	1.22	1.33
6	1.13	1.27	1.42
7	1.15	1.32	1.50
8	1.17	1.37	1.59
9	1.20	1.42	1.69
10	1.22	1.48	1.79
11	1.24	1.54	1.90
12	1.27	1.60	2.01
13	1.29	1.67	2.13
14	1.32	1.73	2.28
15	1.35	1.80	2.40
16	1.37	1.87	2.45
17	1.40	1.95	2.69
18	1.43	2.03	2.85
19	1.46	2.11	3.03
20	1.49	2.19	3.21
21	1.51	2.28	3.40
22	1.55	2.37	3.60
23	1.58	2.46	3.82
24	1.61	2.56	4.05
25	1.64	2.67	4.29
26	1.67	2.77	4.55
27	1.71	2.88	4.82
28	1.74	3.00	5.11
29	1.78	3.12	5.42
30	1.81	3.24	5.74

WORKSHEET 5 **Future Value of Retirement Expenses**

Estimated expenses in retirement (from Worksheet 4) _____

Multiplied by inflation factor (from Table 8–3) _____

Equals the future value of your retirement expenses _____

Tom and Priscilla Gregory's WORKSHEET 5

The Gregorys think inflation will continue to be low, around 2%, for the nine years they will work before retirement.

Estimated expenses in retirement (from Worksheet 4) _____$62,100

Multiplied by inflation factor (from Table 8–3) _____1.20

Equals the future value of your retirement expenses _____$73,500

SOURCE OF FUNDS

Now you have an idea of how much you need a year in order to live the retirement lifestyle you'd like. Where will that money come from? Let's start with what part of our tax dollars our government sees fit to give back to us. The 1998 maximums for Old Age Security, Guaranteed Income Supplement and Canada/Quebec Pension Plan are as follows:

CHART 8–3 **Maximum Social Program Payments**

MAXIMUM CPP	BASIC OAS	GIS MAX. SINGLE	GIS MAX. MARRIED	SPOUSE'S ALLOWANCE	WIDOW/ WIDOWER
$8,900	$4,900	$4,906	$3,782	$8,668	$9,569

The maximum pensionable earnings that would give you the maximum C/QPP is $36,900 in 1998. It is indexed to the Consumer Price Index. Your maximum pensionable earnings show up both on your tax return and on your pay stub. You can also request an estimate of your entitlements from the nearest Canada or Quebec Pension Plan office. It goes without saying that if you're

eligible for the maximum C/QPP benefit, you will not get a Guaranteed Income Supplement and your Old Age Security will be taxed at your highest marginal tax rate.*

If you have a pension plan at work, you will have received regular notices from your company of how much you can expect when you retire. What you need to plug in here is what benefits you can expect from your company plan when you retire. If you can't find your file, check with your company's human-resources officer or the administrator of your pension plan. Many of these plans are now on-line, and you can review your entitlements from your home computer.

DEFINED BENEFIT PLANS

Most company pension plans are "defined benefit" plans, the benefit being determined according to a formula based on earnings and length of service. Often, the pension benefit is a percentage of earnings, say 2%, multiplied by the number of years you've worked. The earnings may be the average of your total years, or the average of the last three or five years. There are many variations in these plans, contingent on the trust agreement that governs the benefits paid out. These include the length of time you have to work in order to be guaranteed the benefits (vesting), whether there are spousal benefits should the member or retiree die, the ease with which you can transfer your benefits to another plan should you leave your place of employ, etc. Most have a menu of options from which to choose, such as health benefits, disability insurance, etc.

There is an annual limit on the amount of pension income paid in retirement: $60,000. That's about half what it is in the U.S., and points out why highly paid employees need supplementary plans at work if they are to achieve the same percentage of their pre-retirement income as do people who make less

---

*Phone CPP at 800-277-9914 (Eng.); 800-277-9915 (Fr.); 800-255-4786 (hard of hearing). Phone QPP at 800-463-5185; 873-2433 (Montreal); 643-5185 (Quebec City).

than $60,000. According to pension consultants at Watson Wyatt Canada, at least one in eight salaried Canadians is going to be unpleasantly surprised about the final value of their company pension plan because the law does not permit them to contribute enough to either their company pension or their own RRSP, as discussed earlier.

Under defined benefit plans, the employer is the plan sponsor and is responsible for making the contributions to the plan. The employer is also responsible for administering the plan, for writing the investment policy and goals, for hiring the money managers to invest the assets in the pension fund, and ultimately for covering any losses that reduce promised benefits.

You may not be a member of a defined benefit plan at work. There's been a trend for the past decade for companies to move to "defined contribution" plans. The characteristics of those plans are spelled out below. If this is what you have, you need to know the balance of the plan and its rate of return in order to estimate what it might yield in income when you retire. The administrator of this plan can help you out if you don't know.

DEFINED CONTRIBUTION PLANS

The trend towards defined contribution plans is the result of several changes in the economy. First, administering defined benefit plans has become increasingly burdensome in terms of accounting and other financial and regulatory obligations. Second, defined contribution plans are better suited to the needs of the 21st-century workforce, who are unlikely to stay with the same company for their entire working life.

The defined contribution plan provides a pension based on the amount of money in the plan when the person retires. The pool of money comes from the contributions of both the employer and the employee. The recipient of the proceeds (the employee) has some choice over how the pool of money is invested. At retirement, the money is used to purchase an annuity, or is rolled over into an eligible retirement plan such as a Registered Retirement

Income Fund, a Life Income Fund or, if the retiree is under 69, a locked-in RRSP.

Defined contribution plans, also called "money-purchase" plans, being flexible and portable, are uniquely suited to people who change jobs frequently. They are also more responsive to the demands of the beneficiaries of the plans who take more responsibility for the choice of investments in their plan.

There are several types of defined contribution plans. Money-purchase, in which the employer and employee contribute a specific amount of money, based on the formula agreed to in the plan document, is the most popular. There are also "profit-sharing" plans, in which the employer deposits a proportion of the company profits, "stock bonus" plans, in which a portion of the employer's contribution is in the form of corporate shares, and "employee stock ownership plans" (ESOPs). These last are plans that regularly set aside shares in the company during an employee's employment, according to the terms of the plan; at retirement, the shares are given to the employee.

There are several things to consider if you have the choice of defined benefit or defined contribution plans. Defined benefit plans are beneficial for older people who have been with their company for many years, provided that the company is solvent. Employees have no say in the investment decisions, but pension benefits are clearly defined and related to the employee's earnings, not to the performance of the investments. The amount that is your entitlement is spelled out in the vesting arrangements, and the financial strength of the company. "Vesting" refers to the time it takes for you to own the employer's contribution to the pension plan—which doesn't necessarily happen when you are admitted to the plan. Also, the fortunes of the company can affect the employees' retirement income. Moreover, what goes into your defined benefits plan must be subtracted from the total you are allowed to put aside each year in tax-sheltered retirement benefits. (This is the pension adjustment [PA] that has to be calculated on your income tax return each year.)

Invariably, these plans leave little room for members to put money into an RRSP, although in 1998 the government issued new rules that allow employers, on termination, to restore part of their contribution room. If you have left a job recently, but not retired, you should ask your former employer about the pension adjustment reversal (PAR). You may be able to put more money into your RRSP.

Defined contribution plans, on the other hand, are not unlike group RRSPs or mutual funds. They are administered by the plan sponsor, but the member has input into the investment decisions. These plans are generally advantageous for younger employees, who are more likely to change jobs frequently. They are registered in the member's name, and are easily portable. The amount of the pension benefit is based on how long the employee is in the plan and on the employer and employee contributions to the plan. The amount of money in the plan at any moment is known, but the amount of the pension at retirement is dependent on the performance of invested funds.

EMPLOYER-SPONSORED HEALTH AND MEDICAL BENEFITS

Before the 1960s, the idea of health care benefits as part of one's retirement package was almost unknown. But with a booming economy and the introduction of tax-financed, universal medicare and hospital access, many businesses, encouraged by their unions, began supplementing the universal plans in areas where the publicly funded plans were deficient. In addition to dental plans, group disability insurance, and payment for prescribed drugs, other benefits such as critical-care insurance are being rolled out regularly. It's important that you find out what you're eligible for, as it will affect your health-expenditure budget as you get older.

DEFERRED PROFIT-SHARING PLANS

Some employees have the opportunity to share in the profits of the company they work for. Contributions to the plan are recorded

in your name and are not taxable as part of your current income. Paying the tax is deferred until you retire.

YOUR HOME

Most Canadians have the biggest chunk of their savings in their home. For the last generation of savers, home ownership was a great investment: the value of a home purchased before the early 1980s rose almost exponentially. If you are one of the lucky ones, factor in the value of your home, even if you don't intend to sell it at the moment. The value of your home—that is, what you can get for it minus the mortgage—goes into the list of assets. It's there to remind you that it has a cash value if and when you decide on a different lifestyle or decide to liberate the cash for income. Do the same for the family cottage; you may have paid "almost nothing" for it, but if it was bought 25 years ago, it's probably valuable enough for the kids to fight over.

REGISTERED RETIREMENT SAVINGS PLANS

Registered Retirement Savings Plans are the only type of investment eligible for tax-deferred status. This money can be invested in a variety of government-approved investments until age 69, at which time it must be used for one or more government-approved investments that will provide an income for retirement or beyond. The tax deferred during the years the money has been in an RRSP is collected when you take it out as income. If you have an RRSP, you need to know the balance, the rate of return on your investments, and how much you can contribute each year. Revenue Canada will send you, when it acknowledges receipt of your income tax return, the maximum amount you can contribute each year. (If you don't have an RRSP, read Chapter 9 for reasons to begin one—or not.)

TAX-PREFERRED INVESTMENTS

If you hold tax-preferred investments, such as stocks or preferred shares, outside an RRSP, you need to keep track of them to know

when to sell, and to ensure that you pay no more capital-gains tax than necessary. So keep your brokerage receipts, which list your purchase price, as it might have been years ago.

TAXABLE INVESTMENTS

Rental income, interest on your savings account, money market funds and so on, all are taxable. If you've inherited money, or someone has given you a gift of money, any money which that money earns is taxable. You need to keep track of these investments as well. If you don't have files that allow you to put your finger on the numbers almost immediately, you need to get organized. (Use the forms provided in the appendices.)

Canada's baby boomers are gearing up to receive a collective $1 trillion inheritance. About 40% of them have already received it or expect to in the next 10 years. This is the greatest intergenerational transfer of wealth in North American history. If you are, or expect to be, a recipient of an inheritance, estimate how much it is likely to be, and put it on your list.

Here's your worksheet to add up what you will have available to you annually in retirement.

WORKSHEET 6 **Sources of Retirement Income**

SOURCE	AMOUNT	GROWTH RATE	AMOUNT AT RETIREMENT
OAS		CPI index	
GIS		CPI index	
C/QPP		CPI index	
Pension from work		Estimate from work	
RRSP			
Other savings			
Earnings from work			
TOTAL			
Assets			
Gifts/inheritances			
Home			

Tom and Priscilla Gregory's 1998 WORKSHEET 6

SOURCE	AMOUNT	GROWTH RATE	INCOME AT RETIREMENT
OAS	$4,900	CPI index	$0 - clawed back
GIS	3,782	CPI index	0 - (ineligible)
C/QPP (x2)	17,800	CPI index	17,800
Pension from work (x2)	32,400	Estimate from work	40,000
RRSP/RRIF	40,000 (total)		3,500
Other savings	0		0
Earnings from work	?		?
TOTAL			$61,300
Assets			
Gifts/inheritances			30,000 (total)
Home			150,000 (total)

Once your sources in retirement have been calculated, you can figure out how they will continue to grow even as you withdraw some of the capital regularly. The only assumptions we can make about the public pensions is that, if we're lucky, they will stay as they are. If you're conservative, you'll consider not relying on them unless you are in a low-income group. Whichever decision you take, plug in the numbers. Similarly, your pension from your place of employment is likely to remain the same, or possibly be indexed to inflation. If you have a defined contribution plan, or if you're self-employed and have saved both inside and outside an RRSP, then make an assumption about your savings rate of return over your retirement. After all this is done, you'll be ready to calculate whether the total amount of money will be enough to cover your retirement income needs. The rough and ready way to do this is simply to take the amount of money you think you need each year (taking inflation into account) and multiply it by the number of years you think you'll be in retirement.

Now that you've estimated your retirement income needs and your projected resources, a simple subtraction of your required

income from your estimated resources will tell you how much additional capital you need in order to satisfy your retirement income needs. A software program will do all the calculations for you, but here's how you can do it manually.

WORKSHEET 7 **Retirement Balance Sheet**

Estimated future value of retirement expenses (from Worksheet 5)	_____
OAS/GIS/C/QPP (from Worksheet 6)	– _____
Employment pension payments (annual)	– _____
Amount needed from savings each year	_____

If your income is bigger than your estimated future expenses, congratulations! You have estimated more income than outgo. If it's not, you will have to figure out how to close the gap.

Tom and Priscilla Gregory's WORKSHEET 7

Estimated future value of retirement expenses (from Worksheet 5)	$73,500	
OAS/GIS/C/QPP (from Worksheet 6)	–	17,800
RRIF (from Worksheet 5)	–	3,500
Employment pension payments (annual)	–	40,000
Total income		61,300
Amount needed from savings each year	$12,200	

The Gregorys are going to have to save sufficient money to generate $12,200 a year.

DEVELOP A STRATEGY TO FILL THE GAP

There are only two ways to close an income gap. Either you decide to need less income, or to increase your resources. We'll deal with savings and investment strategies in the next chapter, if you decide you need to increase your resources. Otherwise, redo the worksheets with more modest expectations. (The real

value of a software program is that changing assumptions is so simple!)

Because they have started planning nine years before they want to retire, the Gregorys have many choices. The $30,000 they expect to inherit can be invested to provide between $1,500 and $3,000 a year. They can invest their RRSP portfolio more aggressively to allow the capital to grow more rapidly. If they invested to earn an average of 8% a year, their $40,000 would be $80,000 in nine years' time. But they will still be short. They can postpone their retirement by one year, which will give them an additional year's income and the accompanying slightly higher pension. They can trim back their estimated expenses, or investigate a reverse mortgage. They can consider part-time work. Or they can try to save another $200,000.

IMPLEMENT THE STRATEGY

If you are intent on growing your assets, you have to have at least five years before you embark on your life after work. (Better to have more time, of course.) You can concentrate on growing your financial assets and working for pay longer than you had planned, or you can plan on working for pay for a protracted period. All of these need time to mature. Work is always available, but requires time, research and possibly skills-upgrading. (You can learn a bit more about growing your financial assets, beginning with the chapters subsequent to this one.)

REVIEW AND ADJUST

Once you're into this exercise, it becomes addictive. I have been into it for a couple of years now and find it reassuring. (I wish I'd started earlier.) Even in a couple of years, I've changed my views, about whether it's more gratifying to work for pay or work in the volunteer sector, and about not working at all. Ten years ago, I was convinced that I didn't want to work at all. Then I changed the mix of what was occupying my time and discovered I was just tired of what I was doing before. Knowing you're

responsible for and in control of your life, as much as any person can be, is exciting.

Here's how the Gregorys revise their plan:

1. Sell the house ($150,000), buy a condo ($100,000); net proceeds $50,000.
2. Invest the RRSP to grow more aggressively to $75,000.

The Gregorys calculate that, even invested conservatively, the additional capital will give them another $7,000 a year in income. They are still short $5,000 a year, so they go back and revise their Worksheets 4 and 5.

Tom and Priscilla Gregory's WORKSHEET 4

CURRENT EXPENSES	WORKING	ESTIMATED AT RETIREMENT	FIRST REVISION
Mortgage/rent	$12,300	$0	
Property taxes	2,300	2,300	$1,600
Utilities—heat, light, phone, cable	2,400	2,400	1,500
Maintenance	2,400	2,400	1,800
Property insurance	700	1,050	
Food	7,000	4,500	
Clothing	5,000	3,600	
Personal (hair, dry cleaning, etc.)	1,200	800	
Car registration, licence	400	400	
Car payments	3,000	0	
Car operating costs	3,000	2,000	
Car insurance	600	450	
Other transportation	300	300	
Life insurance	7,200	0	
Disability insurance	0	0	
Loan payments	0	0	
Credit card payments	0	0	
Education	0	1,000	
Medical, dental	1,200	2,000	

Gifts—birthday, Christmas, etc. Contributions to charity, political parties, etc.	1,500	1,500	
Vacation travel	2,000	9,500	
Entertainment	2,000	2,500	
Income taxes	23,000	23,000	
Savings	3,000	0	
Alimony, child support	0	0	
Assistance to others	1,000	0	
Lump-sum payments for vacation home, etc.	0	0	
TOTAL	$81,500	$62,100	$59,900

Tom and Priscilla Gregory's WORKSHEET 5

The Gregorys think inflation will continue to be low, around 2%, for the nine years they will work before retirement.

		FIRST REVISION
Estimated expenses in retirement (from Worksheet 4)	$62,100	$59,900
Multiplied by inflation factor (from Table 8–3)	1.20	1.20
Equals the value of their retirement expenses nine years hence	$73,500	$71,900

Their revised expenses cut $2,200 from their budget, and even after the inflation factor over 20 years, cuts $1,600 from the future value of their 1998 expenses.

They decide to monitor their plan and decide in the next four or five years whether to delay retirement. They have not factored in the income from their expected inheritance and are open to the possibility of part-time work.

IMPLEMENTING THE PLAN

Financial planning is a complex business that involves not just your assets but your aspirations, securities investing, accounting,

insurance, tax and estate planning, and the legal aspect of all these disciplines. And in Canada, financial planning is pretty much unregulated. Anyone can hang out a shingle and start practising. The *Financial Post*'s Jon Chevreau has put together a list he calls the Alphabet Soup of financial planners. All these designations involve training. But the fact that there is no standard in Canada is a warning to be cautious.

JON CHEVREAU'S ALPHABET SOUP OF FINANCIAL PLANNERS

DESIGNATION	CONFERRED BY
CFP—Certified Financial Planner	Financial Planners Standards Council
RFP—Registered Financial Planner	Canadian Association of Financial Planners
CHFC—Chartered Financial Consultant	Canadian Association of Insurance and Financial Advisors
CLU—Chartered Life Underwriter	Canadian Association of Insurance and Financial Advisors
PFP—Personal Financial Planner	Institute of Canadian Bankers
SFC—Specialist in Financial Counselling	Institute of Canadian Bankers
CIM—Certified Investment Manager	Institute of Canadian Bankers
CFA—Chartered Financial Analyst	Association of Investment Management and Research

This doesn't mean that there aren't some darned good advisors out there, but it does mean that you have to find them, and interview the heck out of them, as you do with your doctor, lawyer, accountant, etc. Probably the best way to find someone good is by word of mouth and personal interview. If you don't know anyone who has a financial planner, ask for references from the planner you think you might want, at your first meeting. And phone the references. Even if you go this route, you should know the basics of investing. That begins in the next chapter. What you're taking from the current chapter is this: planning your retirement in your head is great, but putting it down on paper is a better way to make it happen.

Developing your plan is where the rubber hits the road: taking responsibility for your life is emotionally difficult and time-consuming. Once done, however, it needs to be updated only once a year, or if something big happens in your life. And you have the satisfaction of knowing you will almost certainly join a select group of Canadians who will be able to do something else after work, and when you do so is your choice.

9

....

Savings Strategies and Investment Options

There's no security in life, only opportunity.
—Douglas McArthur

THE RULES OF INVESTING are very simple: start early, diversify, and stay invested. Of the three, starting early is the most important. The miracle of compounding really is within the power of everyone to activate, as Table 9–1 shows. Save $1,000 a year when you're 25—that's less than $20 a week—at a 6% rate of return, and at 55 you'll have saved more than $80,000. If you can make 8% on your money, which is still doable, your savings at 55 will be $113,000. Save $50 a week and at 55 your nest egg will be more than $250,000. Do a little homework and average 10% or 12% with your $50 a week, and you'll come close to, or top, $500,000. Obviously, the more you can put away, the better.

TABLE 9–1 **Future Value of Saving $1,000 a Year**

....

NUMBER OF YEARS	RATE OF RETURN				
	5%	6%	8%	10%	12%
10	$12,578	$13,181	$14,487	$15,937	$17,549
20	33,066	33,786	45,762	67,275	72,052
30	66,439	79,058	113,283	164,494	241,333
40	120,800	154,762	259,057	442,593	767,091

Use the following table to figure out how much you have to save to reach your goal.

Table 9–2 **Future Value of $1 Invested Today**

NUMBER OF YEARS	5%	6%	RATE OF RETURN 8%	10%	14%
10	1.63	1.79	2.15	2.59	3.70
20	2.55	3.20	4.06	8.73	13.74
30	4.32	5.74	10.06	17.45	50.95

Example: $1,000 invested today at 8%, compounded annually for 20 years, would accumulate to (4.06 x $1,000) = $40,600.

HOW MUCH AND FOR HOW LONG

The numbers in the tables above do not include the effects of taxation. If your annual return of 8% is subject to tax, your savings will be considerably less. Hence the popularity of RRSP tax-deferred savings. Yes, it does make a difference if you pay tax on the money 30 years from now rather than every year. The longer you save in a tax-deferred vehicle, the more valuable the tax deferral is—up to a point. It used to be that there was no qualifier to the last sentence. But it also used to be that we believed our tax rates in retirement would be lower than in our working years.

Taxes have been rising steadily for the last decade, and governments have a hard time remembering that the money you make is yours. Until that mindset demonstrably changes, you have to experiment with how long you should shelter money in an RRSP. Luckily, there's software to help you do it. What If Software Inc., a Markham, Ontario–based company, has a package that will calculate when you should stop contributing to an RRSP and start saving in an unregistered plan. Here's an example taken from a *Financial Post* interview with What If Software's president, Joel Hoffman. The assumptions are, in the first case, that an Ontario-based investor 25 years from retirement contributed $13,500 every year to his RRSP, and, in the second case,

that he contributed $13,500 to his RRSP for only 11 years and then forwent tax deductions for 14 years and invested $13,500 outside an RRSP. In both cases, the investments are assumed to make 8% a year. If you live in a higher or lower tax regime, the numbers in the example will change slightly.

CHART 9–1 **When to Stop RRSPs**

	RRSP/RRIF ONLY	SAVING INSIDE AND OUTSIDE RRSP/RRIF
Value of plan at retirement	$1,086,885	$1,050,776
Annual RRIF withdrawals	74,755	49,874
CPP/OAS income	13,800	13,800
Draw from non-RRIF funds		24,700
Total income	88,377	88, 374
20 years' retirement income	1,767,540	1,767,480
Tax due on RRIF income	909,540	555,455
Tax due during working years	—	133,812
Tax due on non-RRIF income	—	95,509
Total tax due	909,540	784,776
Net disposable income	858,000	982,704

Source: Jonathan Chevreau, Financial Post

In this example, the added benefit is that investing outside an RRSP is not ruled by the 20% foreign content limitation that the RRSP/RRIF is. Over the last 25 years, U.S. markets (and others) have returned higher profits than Canadian ones.

How much you need to invest and for how long is essentially what you figured out in Chapter 8. Your pension income has to continue from the day you retire until the last of your dependants no longer needs your support. If you plan to retire at 65, you need to secure an income for at least 22 years. If your partner is younger than you, or you had or intend to have children late in life, or you plan to retire earlier than 65, you may need to secure an income for some years longer. One of the great

disappointments of many people is that they cannot afford to retire when they want to. That's why it's important to develop a mindset that includes securing part of the income you need in retirement by part-time work.

Knowing what strategies not to follow is as important as knowing what strategies work. First and foremost, don't start investing without a concrete investment plan. The worksheets in Appendix 2 will put you on the path to accumulating the amount you decide you need to live comfortably for the rest of your life.

Second, don't delude yourself into thinking that your investment plan is going to activate itself without you. Following through with an investment plan is like following through with a fitness program. It's the follow-through that brings success.

Third, keep records. After all, you have to know whether you have a capital loss to offset your capital gain, whether you have balance in your asset allocation. Even if you don't want to make all your investment decisions yourself, even if you're working with a financial planner or broker, it's your money and your retirement. I can't tell you how many people tell me they're comfortable with their savings progress and the advice they're getting from their professionals, but don't know what they're invested in, or whether their professionals make their money by commission or fee, and don't know the management fees charged on their mutual funds. If you don't know these things, you have no basis for measuring whether you could do better in another kind of investment. If you can't measure it, you can't manage it, and if you can't manage it, you can't count on being where you want to be when you want to be there.

Fourth, don't take advice you don't understand. Don't ignore the professionals' advice; just make them explain it in a way you understand. Managing your money makes you the chairman of the board, the president, and the chief executive officer of the business. No one cares about your wealth accumulation more than you do. There are lots of people who would like you to pay

them, but if you don't care enough to know what you've got and to buy investment vehicles rather than have them sold to you, you have no one to blame but yourself if your plans don't work out. (You won't even know if you have a claim against a professional's bad advice.)

So you need an advisory board: an accountant, lawyer, financial or estate planner, and insurance and real-estate broker. You won't need them all at once and maybe you won't need them often, but their advice will be valuable from time to time. You will have someone to answer your questions and help you improve your knowledge and financial skills. If you already have substantial assets, a group session with your lawyer, accountant and financial planner will likely result in the more efficient use of your resources, either by saving on taxes or increasing your investment returns.

Fifth, don't put all your eggs in one basket. You'd be surprised at the number of people who think the company pension or the OAS/CPP/QPP will ease them into a comfortable retirement. It *may*, but when you're 63, you won't have many options if it doesn't. An astute financial planner once said, "The national flower of the sensible investor is the hedge." And we're not talking just about balancing stocks, bonds, real estate and precious metals.

There are many kinds of financial risk against which you must protect yourself, and you have to know what they are in order to discover your own tolerance of risk.

1. Inflation and deflation From the late 1960s until the late 1980s, inflation was always in the environment in which we invested. Early on, people had very little comprehension of the effects of inflation on their savings—that it ate up purchasing power, and that a strategy of saving up before one bought anything was a surefire way to lose in the game of asset accumulation. Eventually, the winners learned that borrowing to invest was a good strategy, because the investments you made grew with inflation, and

the money you paid back was paid with dollars that were cheaper than when you borrowed them.

By the end of the 1970s and beginning of the '80s, it was time to shift strategy. A sea change in the economy was already evident: downsizing had become a mainstream word; many of the assumptions about steady work and career ladders had been shattered; taxes had gone up faster than food, shelter and clothing expenses combined; interest rates had become sufficiently high and economic growth sufficiently low that the risk of having to pay back borrowed money at high rates of interest was growing rapidly. Those who understood this paid off their loans and locked in high interest rates. Those who didn't may still be having a hard time.

During the last several years, inflation has not been a problem. Interest rates have returned to the levels of the late '60s, levels at which no one will be able to accumulate enough money to retire. Although many people believe that inflation is still a threat, an equal number believe that deflation is a bigger threat. (Canadians have not experienced deflation—generally falling prices—for close to 70 years.) Today, we're experiencing disinflation—prices increasing by less than they did the year before (close to zero)—and price levels are decreasing in other parts of the world. Deflation is not considered a serious threat to North America among mainstream economists, although some acknowledge that markets driven by innovation (which ours are) can be tipped into widespread recession if not depression. But deflation is happening in many parts of the world, and it is imprudent not to understand its implications on our investment decisions.

Deflation means that, measured by general price indexes, the prices of more things fall than rise. We can see some things getting cheaper today: house prices have fallen 20% in the last decade; interest rates have fallen; the prices of electronics have plummeted in the last decade; commodity prices have fallen. And, for some people, wage rates have fallen. (This has been happening more generally in Asia throughout the '90s. In Japan, in

particular, the prices of many industrial products have been falling for seven or eight years. Japan has been in a recession for that long because as wages fall, people have less money to buy goods, and demand shrinks.)

For strategic purposes, deflation is a continuous fall in the prices of real estate, commodities and industrial products which may or may not spread to consumer prices. For us, deflation is still only a hypothetical possibility, but one whose probability rises as global financial instability continues to be mishandled by governments. The important thing is to be cognizant of what's happening in the global economy in order to know how and when to shift one's investments. The upside for investors is that deflation always leads to lower interest rates. (Japanese bond rates seven years ago were about 8%; today they are under 2%.)

In deflation, the most prized asset is guaranteed long-term cash flow. That's what government bonds provide. Deflation raises the value of debt to equity, so government bonds, and the bonds of corporations that have very little debt, are the most profitable places to be. It follows that if you are in debt, you should get out of it as quickly as possible. There is nothing more catastrophic than owing money at 6% or 7% when interest rates are falling to 2%. That's exactly what has happened to Asia, Russia and parts of Latin America.

If the American economy starts slowing down, Asian style, you'd be shifting to long-term government bonds. Government, because it will be last to renege on its debt. Long-term bonds, because if interest rates continue to drop, the face value of the bonds will rise. (As long as interest rates are positive, they can go lower.) Holders of those bonds therefore will make a capital gain. Other strategies include investing only in companies that are free of debt. (Repaying debt taken on when interest rates were higher will be difficult to do when product or service prices are falling.)

2. Boom and bust The regular but unpredictable ups and downs of business activity are another background noise you should be familiar with. There's nothing you can do about it, of

course, but you can do something about your investment strategy. Falling inflation, robust growth and an eight-year-old bull market have developed an equity cult in the U.S. I think equities are the place to be in the long term, but the signs are lighting up that the market is going from boom to bust. The U.S. stock market is selling at 20 times average corporate earnings even as earnings are falling. The *Global Investment Strategist*, an international investment service, published an interesting chart, reproduced here, showing that low inflation or deflation changes the historic relationship between equity and bond returns. Historically, when stock returns go up, bond returns go down. At some point, as we saw in August 1998, falling interest rates are bad for equity markets. Canadians have a slightly wider window since Canadian interest rates are higher than those in the U.S. and the spread is widening.

CHART 9–2 **U.S. Bonds and the G7 Business Cycle**

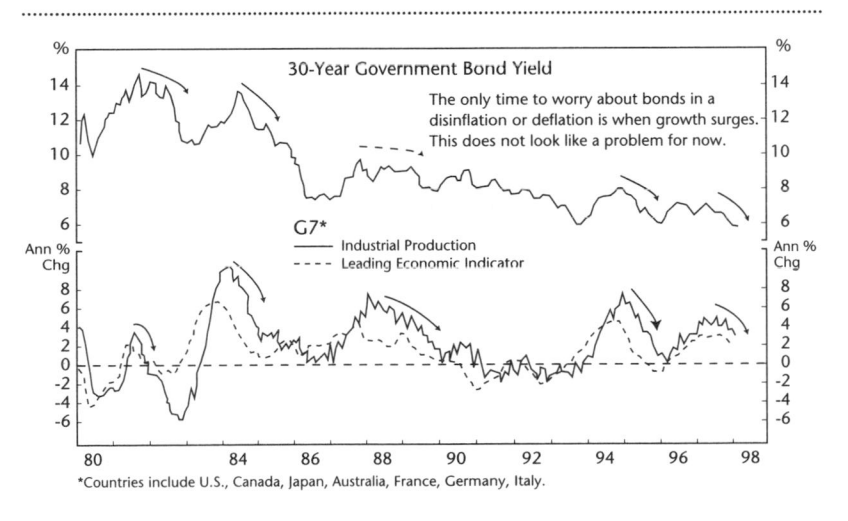

*Countries include U.S., Canada, Japan, Australia, France, Germany, Italy.

3. Market risk relates to the overall volatility of the markets for different kinds of assets. It is measurable, although not in advance and not precisely. What is important to you is the volatility risk in your own portfolio. Different categories of assets have

probabilities of risk that can be measured relative to each other. Chart 9–3 on the next page is typical.

4. Business risk refers to the change in fortunes of individual companies. For example, the misfortune of Corel Systems competing with Microsoft in the computer software business drove Corel's share price from $10.95 to $2.30 in 1997. Speedy Muffler King went from $11 to $2 (and its president went on to other activities outside the company). On the other hand, Ballard Power Systems, with an experimental fuel cell that eliminates carbon dioxide emissions from cars and buses, moved from $27 to $109, with a brief stop at $117 before it split 5-for-1. As an ordinary investor, you can't usually know these things in time to buy them at their lowest price, but you can read professional analyses and understand what areas are growing fastest.

5. Political risk refers to the stability of governments. It's important to keep track of, in a global economy where investment in countries far from home can be done on your home computer.

6. Currency risk refers to changes in the value of your home currency relative to another in which you may have investments. If you invest abroad, you have to be interested not just in the foreign real estate, stocks, bonds, or mutual funds, but in the value of the currency vis-à-vis the Canadian dollar. (For the last 15 years, investing outside Canada has been accompanied by currency gains as the Canadian dollar has depreciated against many major currencies.)

Ten years ago I created the chart on the following page to help people determine their risk profile. At that time, insured savings accounts were paying 6%. Today, with insured savings accounts paying less than 2%, you may need to take more risks to reach your wealth accumulation goals. Go ahead, bite those nails.

WHAT KIND OF INVESTMENTS
If you know next to nothing (or not much) about investing and the fundamentals of investment, then hire an advisor.

CHART 9-3 The Fingernail Scale of Major Investment Choices

THE STATE OF YOUR NAILS	TYPE OF ASSET	EXPECTED RATE OF RETURN (1998) (BEFORE TAXES)	INVESTMENT TIME	WHAT YOU STAND TO LOSE
Exquisite	Savings account, money market fund	2%	No specific investment period required	No risk of losing your capital. Deposits up to $60,000 insured by CDIC. An almost sure loser for growing assets
Beautifully manicured	Term deposits, GICs, Canada Savings Bonds	3–5%	Money must be left for entire term to take advantage of higher rate	Early withdrawals subject to penalty
Evenly trimmed	Government bonds	5–6%	Money must be left till maturity to get full yield, between four and 20 years	Very little if held to maturity. Possible capital loss or gain if sold prior to maturity
Looked after at home	Corporate bonds	6–7%	Money must be held till maturity to get full yield	Company must be carefully chosen to ensure solvency and continued ability to pay
A little ragged	Diversified portfolio of blue-chip and growth stocks Real-estate mutual funds Commodities and collectibles	8–25%	No specific investment periods required, and all may be sold at any time. The average 12% expected return assumes a five-year hold and is only a rough guideline	Moderate to substantial, because of market and business risk. With careful management and a relatively long holding period, only moderate
Down to the quick	Anything you don't understand			Everything. Don't do it

Here's the absolute fundamental: there are only two kinds of investment, equity and debt. Equity is something you buy and own. Debt is something you've lent your money to, which you'll get back with interest. A stock or a share is equity, a little piece of a company; you own that bit of the company. If the company does well, it shares its profits with you in the form of dividends and you can sell your shares at a profit. A bond is an IOU. You've lent your money (to a company or a bank or a government) for a specific period of time at a specified rate of interest. You may get your interest every year or at the end of the term, and you'll get back the principal, i.e., the amount that you loaned, at the end of the term.

Although that's all there is, there are dozens of variations, but it's really easy to tell what they are. Just ask yourself, "Is it debt or equity?" Do you own it or have you just lent your money for a set period of time? If you don't know, ask the person who's trying to sell you the investment. If they don't know the answer, which still happens a lot, get a financial advisor immediately. There's no way you're going to develop a portfolio that will help you reach your goals on your own.

TAX-EXEMPT INVESTMENTS: OWNER-OCCUPIED HOMES

Most Canadians aspire to own their own home, and with some qualifiers, it is still a good strategic investment. In postwar Canada, it was a good investment because house prices were low and so were interest rates. After 1960, it became an even better investment. Interest rates were still low, you could lock in a 25-year mortgage, and inflation was beginning to lift the prices of just about everything. In the early 1970s, the combination of inflation and the tax reform that exempted owner-occupied homes from capital-gains tax made owning your own home one of the great investments of the next 15 years.

Both residential and commercial properties benefited from 40 years of more or less inflationary price rises, first in the modestly inflationary '60s, as Canada urbanized rapidly, and then

even more after the tax reform of 1971. Now technology and demographics have combined to reverse those developments.

Real-estate prices almost everywhere in the country have declined by about 20% since their peaks in the mid-'80s. The annual growth of Canadian households has slowed to half the rate of the past three decades. There are at least 200,000 fewer first-time home buyers—traditionally people between 25 and 34 —than there were a decade ago. Therefore, total demand for housing is not likely to pick up until the "shadow" baby boom, the kids of boomers, are old enough to be house buyers, sometime around 2013. But with interest rates low and house prices still declining in many parts of the country, home ownership is once again a viable economic investment. The fact that it remains tax exempt makes it an important savings vehicle, both for the soon to be retired and as an estate planning technique for the children of the soon to be or already retired. As well, carefully selected real estate will be a satisfactory investment even if it is not occupied by the owner. (See tax-preferred investments, below.)

Although people who manage to pay off their mortgage understand that they have accumulated significant savings in their homes, being able to use these assets is still problematic. There are several ways of tapping them: the property can be sold and the proceeds used to buy a smaller home or condominium, or the money can be invested and the income used to cover the rent on an apartment. If cash is not needed, the home can continue to be home, and the asset left as part of the estate.

If the retiree wants to continue to live in the home but needs cash, a "reverse mortgage" is available in many provinces. With a reverse mortgage, a person borrows a portion of the equity in the home, and gets it in a lump sum or in a fixed monthly payment for a specific period of time. There are no monthly mortgage payments: the loan repayments, including interest on the loan, are "capitalized"; that is, they are added to the portion that has been borrowed. Upon the death of the home owner, the

home is sold and the loan repaid. This is a recent alternative for people over 63. Here's an example of how it works:

Say you are 70 and live in a home that has been valued at $250,000. A "reverse mortgage" seller calculates that you will live for 15 more years. She will lend you up to $100,000 at current rates, because the mortgage payments (not paid), added to the loan, will in 15 years equal $250,000—the value of your home.

TAX-DEFERRED INVESTMENTS

Registered Retirement Savings Plans (RRSPs) are a tax-deferred investment. They should not be confused with Registered Education Savings Plans (RESPs), which are government-approved investment vehicles in which *after-tax* money can grow tax free until withdrawal. So the difference between an RESP and an RRSP is that the money you put into the RESP you have already paid tax on. The advantage is that the money ends up in the hands of your child, who pays the tax, presumably at a lower marginal tax rate than you do.

An RRSP is a government-approved investment vehicle which allows eligible Canadians to shelter from taxes a specified amount of money each year.

Anyone who is 18 and has earned income can have an RRSP. "Earned income" is salary, wages, disability payments, Canada or Quebec Pension Plan, rental income, support payments. Anyone with earned income can also open and contribute to an RRSP for a spouse (or a partner of two or more years), even if the spouse (or partner) does not have earned income.

The amount that can be sheltered each year equals 18% of earned income, to a maximum of $13,500. As I noted earlier, that maximum was supposed to rise to $15,500 in 1996, but the government froze the maximum at $13,500 until 2003, thus ensuring that people who have no employer-sponsored pension plan are unable to save an equivalent amount in a tax-sheltered vehicle. If the income earner wants to contribute to a personal and a spousal RRSP, the combined maximum amount allowed each

year is $13,500. Contributions are supposed to rise in 2003 to $14,500 and in 2004 to $15,500. Don't hold your breath.

TABLE 9–3 **Maximum Annual RRSP Contributions at Various Incomes**

EARNED INCOME	MAXIMUM ANNUAL CONTRIBUTION (18% OF EARNED INCOME)
$25,000	$4,500
30,000	5,400
35,000	6,300
40,000	7,200
45,000	8,100
50,000	9,000
55,000	9,900
60,000	10,800
65,000	11,300
70,000	12,600
75,000	13,500
80,000	13,500
85,000	13,500

Most financial planners will tell you that saving through an RRSP is such a good deal that people should beg, borrow or steal the money each year to do so. However, the present configuration of the tax and social security system suggests that this is not necessarily so. People with earned incomes of below $30,000 will have their incomes almost totally replaced in retirement by benefit programs that amount to a guaranteed annual income, so why bother with an RRSP?

One of the most dangerous delusions is that if you invest inside an RRSP, that's a good thing. Period. To this day, 40 years after the introduction of tax-deferred vehicles, many people, including financial-institution personnel, still don't know the difference between an RRSP, a mutual fund and a GIC. A friend of mine went to her friendly, local banker and borrowed $15,000

to fill up her RRSP. She knows diddly-squat about investing, so when the banker said, "Take a bit of each of the mutual funds in our family of funds," she did, and ended up with about $1,000 in each of 15 funds, including a fixed-income fund paying 2% and three international funds with lousy track records.

An RRSP is just an empty box you can put lots of different stuff into. The banks push their own mutual funds because those make the banks a bundle of money. That's okay if the mutual funds make you a bundle, too, but you can't just leave it to the fund seller (or to commercials). You have to know the basics. There are more mutual funds in Canada than there are stocks, so they are no simpler to pick than stocks; and you have to pay the fund managers and administrative staff, even when the fund is advertised as "no-load." Now that the big stock exchanges have created pools that are miniature mirrors of their indexes, you can buy diversification directly from them. For example, the Toronto Stock Exchange sells an index made up of its top 35 stocks (TIPS), another of its top 100 stocks (TIPS 100). The Standard and Poor's rating agency sells an index of the top 500 U.S. companies (SPIDERS). Buying an index costs the price of the unit, plus a broker commission, but no administration or other costs thereafter.

If the RRSP is for you, be sure you know your limit. Since 1990, you are allowed to carry over from previous years any money to which you were entitled but did not contribute. (Your RRSP contribution room is noted on the back page of the "notice of assessment" form you get from the government after they have reviewed your past year's income tax return. If you don't have that at hand, you can phone Revenue Canada's TIPS line, listed in your phone book, to get your up-to-date contribution room.)

One difficulty of investing through an RRSP is that traditional investments—fixed-yield investments such as bonds and investment certificates—don't grow very fast at low interest rates. Increasingly, it looks as though investment in equities such as stocks and equity mutual funds should be done over a lifetime,

both inside an RRSP and out. This doesn't mean that you should buy them and leave them to sit for years (although there are "buy-and-hold" investors who do just that and do very well; Warren Buffett, chairman of Berkshire Hathaway, whose shares trade around US$60,000 each, is one). However, when income is taken out of the RRSP, it is taxed as income, no matter what form it was invested in, rather than at the lower rate applied to investments that pay dividends or produce capital gains. (Asset allocation is discussed later in this chapter.)

TAX-PREFERRED INVESTMENTS

There are two types of tax-preferred investment vehicles available. One is stocks and preferred shares; the other is any investment that yields a capital gain. Stocks and preferred shares are different ways of owning part of a company and sharing in its fortunes. You have two opportunities to make money. First, the company shares some of its profits each year, in the form of a dividend. Dividend income is eligible for preferred tax treatment (through a complicated formula on your tax form, or that your tax preparer knows). If you are in the highest tax bracket (about 52%), the tax rate on dividend income would be about 36%.

The second opportunity to benefit from owning stock is the possibility of capital gains, which arise when you sell the stock at a price higher than your purchase price. Seventy-five percent of the capital gains are taxed at your top tax rate; the other 25% are tax free. If you are in the top tax bracket, your capital-gains tax rate would be about 40%. Capital gains can be made on many other investments besides corporate stock. Anything that can appreciate in value—real estate, art, collectibles—attracts capital gains, and capital-gains tax.

TAXABLE INVESTMENTS

All investments outside the tax shelters and preferred rates discussed above and that earn income are taxable at your highest tax rate, in the year you earn the money. Thus, rental income,

interest on your savings account, money market funds and so on are all taxable.

Mutual funds are pools of money, just as RRSPs are empty boxes. (Go back and read Chapter 5 if you don't understand that.) Money managers invest the pools of funds according to how they think money can be made. Investment can be in almost any kind of investment vehicle: stock of big or small companies, their bonds, the bonds of governments, mortgages, royalty trusts, etc. You have the initial responsibility of deciding which mutual funds best fit your investment goals. You have the continuing responsibility of monitoring the performance of the funds.

INVESTMENT STYLES

Sure, you need to know the basics about different kinds of assets, but there are also different investment styles. A whole variety of styles work in the hands of good managers. (If all money managers thought the same thing about the same stock at the same time, no trades would occur.) It is important to read the prospectus of funds you may be interested in. Once you've bought into funds, you need to keep up to date on the money manager. If he or she leaves, you need to know the investment style of the replacement manager; it may not mesh with your investment goals.

Kim Shannon, a mutual fund manager with Toronto-based asset managers AMI PARTNERS Inc. has identified several investment styles.

1. *The Guru on the Mountain* (aka Sector Rotators) develops an economic forecast, identifies the industry groups that would do well in the economic scenario forecast, and then buys those industries, at the same time selling industry groups that are likely to be harmed. Clearly, the economic forecast is crucial.
2. *Mad Scientists* (aka Technicians) read price and volume charts looking for arcane patterns (like "head and shoulders"

and "breakouts") that might indicate whether a stock should be bought or sold.

3. *Trend Anticipators* (aka Story Stock Buyers) buy stocks related to a concept. For example, a manager whose concept is that doing business electronically is a growing trend will build a portfolio based on computer stocks.

4. *Party Animals* (aka Momentum Investors) get on the buying bandwagon after there's clear evidence of fast growth, and try to jump off when the growth slows.

5. *Brand-Conscious Shoppers* (aka Growth Managers) are "bottom-up" analysts who look for companies with consistent, above-average historical profitability and growth.

6. *Bargain Basement Shoppers* (aka Value Investors) buy stock in companies that are out of favour in the financial community because they are experiencing financial or operating difficulties. Their stock price is low relative to the book value of the company, that is, the amount originally invested in the firm plus all subsequent earnings after dividends have been paid. Price to book value (P/BV) is a term you hear often when people talk about whether a company stock is "fairly" priced.

7. *Virtuous Valeries* (aka Ethical Investors) buy stock in companies that have a stated position on some social issue —the environment, human rights, tobacco, etc. These companies not only talk the talk, they walk the walk: they don't do business in countries or with governments that have a history of "unethical" behaviour however they define it.

THE COST OF MANAGEMENT

In exchange for researching what investments to buy, implementing a strategy and doing the day-to-day monitoring and trading, the mutual fund charges an "administration" or "management" fee. This has nothing to do with whether the fund is a "load" or a "no-load" fund. Management fees are considerably

higher in Canada than they are in the U.S., typically 2% of the money you invest. These fees are coming down, albeit painfully slowly, as investors realize how burdensome they are when investment returns are moving towards single digits.

Conventional wisdom says that if you are "risk averse," that is, you don't like the possibility of losing any money, you should buy conservative investments—bonds or other fixed-income investments such as GICs, and blue-chip stocks that pay a high dividend. That wisdom is handed regularly to people in their 50s and 60s who are looking forward to retiring and want lots of income from their portfolios. However, they also want their income to grow so that rising consumer prices won't make them poorer. Even with the current modest inflation rate of about 1%, your grocery bill will be up 9% in a decade, and 20% after 20 years. The solution to the twin wishes—available income and growth in income—is to have a significant part of your portfolio in stocks as well as bonds. The bonds give you risk-free income, the stocks offer the potential for capital gains, which you withdraw to supplement your steady stream of income.

ASSET ALLOCATION
Once you've decided on the kinds of investment vehicles to invest in, you need to decide how to divide your assets among them. Your overall asset allocation will take into account how far away you are from retirement, your risk profile, and how much you need to make. Asset allocation is about arranging your portfolio to achieve high returns and low volatility. To do this, you have to understand how the returns on different assets are related. Returns on equities are more volatile than on bonds. Historically, when stocks go up, bonds go down. So a risk-averse investor who leans towards bonds can get a better mix of risk and return by adding stocks to the portfolio. In North America, the optimal ratio of equity to debt for the last 70 years has been 3:1. If you use mutual funds as an investment vehicle outside your RRSP, you might want to look at the taxes you will have to

pay. Some funds attract less tax than others, because the managers manage their investments specifically to minimize taxes. Some investors prefer not to receive dividends, interest or capital gains, because they have to pay tax on them. A manager who doesn't sell an asset that has a capital gain, has nothing to distribute to the mutual fund owners so the mutual fund owners have no additional tax to pay.

The recording of capital gains and losses varies among fund managers. For example, value managers are essentially buy-and-hold investors, so they tend to minimize their capital gains distributions. On the other hand, aggressive managers with an active trading strategy will have high annual distributions; their funds will therefore generally have a lower after-tax value than those of value investors.

When you are pondering your asset allocation, don't forget to include your defined benefit plan at work. If you're a long-time employee with a good salary, chances are that you will have between $250,000 and $400,000 in pension assets. Since these assets are not available to you as a lump sum but instead guarantee a specific income in retirement, they should be calculated as a fixed-income asset around which you should structure the rest of your investments. If, for example, your other investments are all in fixed-income investments, or are half in fixed-income investments and half in equity, you should consider being much more aggressive in your personal investments. Your company pension will provide much of the "low-risk" portion you wish your portfolio to have.

As I've noted elsewhere, if you have sufficient funds to be investing both inside and outside an RRSP, your most tax-efficient strategy would be to invest in fixed-income investments inside your RRSP and dividend-earning and capital-gains-attracting assets outside the RRSP. (Remember, interest income is taxed at a top tax bracket of over 50%, while the top bracket for dividends is 36% and for capital gains 40%.) Obviously, if you can save only inside an RRSP, you need to consider your income level

in retirement. Are you middle income, and therefore in danger of having a higher tax rate in retirement than when you were working? Then you have to determine whether the potentially greater growth of equity investment will outweigh the fact that all the income will be taxed at full rates.

FIXED-INCOME STRATEGY

If you have a company defined benefit plan, you need only open the mail each month to get your income. If you are depending on your defined contribution or RRSP or personal savings outside your RRSP, you have to do a bit more work. Whether you invest inside or outside an RRSP, you need to decide what to do with the pool of investments when you reach age 69. Buying an annuity is the only option that gets you back to opening the mail to get your income. Your pool of funds will go to a life insurance company which will guarantee you an income for life. Your income will reflect the prevailing rate of interest (low right now, and if you buy an annuity now, low forever), and the contract is irrevocable.

Creating a bond "maturity ladder" is another way of ensuring a steady stream of low-risk income. A bond is made up of two parts: the principal, or face value of the bond, and the interest you earn for the period when you don't have the use of your money. The bond and the interest "coupon" (not long ago, people actually clipped the coupons off the bonds and presented them to the company or government agent for payment) can be split from each other and sold separately to investors with particular needs. A maturity ladder can be either the bonds (without the interest income stream) or the interest income stream (without that principal). You can see how they would appeal to investors with different investment goals. Some investors prefer not to receive any income other than their wages, because they have to pay tax on additional income. A stripped bond with a maturity date (i.e., when the principal has to be repaid) far in the future would be a good investment, because it can be bought

at a deep discount to its face value. Here are two examples. The sample strip bond ladder is appropriate for people who have not retired and do not want income now. It can be purchased inside or outside an RRSP.

TABLE 9–4 **Sample Strip Bond Ladder**

ISSUER	MATURITY DATE M/D/Y	MATURITY VALUE $	COST $	YIELD TO MATURITY %
Canada	02/01/2003	10,000	7,841	4.95
	03/01/2004	10,000	7,324	5.25
	03/01/2005	10,000	6,787	5.65
	03/01/2006	10,000	6,630	5.23
	03/01/2007	10,000	6,280	5.27
	03/01/2008	10,000	5,673	5.80
	03/01/2009	10,000	5,548	5.47
	03/012010	10,000	5,232	5.52
	03/012011	10,000	4,927	5.55

You can see that if you adopt this strategy years before you need the income, the amount you spend is a fraction of what you will get back.

TABLE 9–5 **Sample Strip Coupon Ladder**

YEAR	PURCHASE PRICE OF 5.5% INTEREST COUPONS OF A $5,000 BOND	ACCRUED ANNUAL INTEREST
2000	4,036.08	221.98
2001	4,258.06	234.20
2002	4,492.26	247.07
2003	4,739.33	260.67

This second ladder is appropriate for people who are already retired and who want to ensure a steady income stream. It is the other side of the strip bond ladder. Strip bond buyers buy the

bond without the income stream. Strip coupon buyers buy the income stream without the bond.

DO-IT-YOURSELF PORTFOLIO MANAGER

If you're one of the six million Canadians who own part of the $250 billion socked away in RRSPs, you have to think about more than the traditional options of rolling your portfolio into a RRIF or buying an annuity. The proposed Seniors' Benefit has been scrapped by the federal government, but for two years they maintained that there was nothing inequitable about raising tax rates to more than 60% for families with incomes in retirement of between $35,000 and $78,000. Although the government cancelled the "reformed" retirement plan, they entertained the idea of raising taxes on retirement income 10 to 20 percentage points above the top tax rate for earned income, and left many people suspicious that another "reform" package will hit the middle class hard.

This is not the first time the government has changed the rules for RRSPs. In 1995, it froze contributions of those without company pension plans, disadvantaging people who need to save for their retirement more than those with plans at work. In 1996, it limited RRSP contributions to the year in which the contributor turned 69, thus cutting off two years of tax-deferred RRSP savings. Then it announced the deeply flawed Seniors' Benefit but scrapped it before it became law. These gaffes have left many people rethinking their retirement strategy.

The rule of thumb used to be, use your non-RRSP money first as retirement income, because the RRSP money is growing tax deferred. With effective tax rates rising for the middle class, it makes as much sense to use your RRSP money first and before more "reforms" are imposed. At the moment, the jury is still out, but if you are middle class and between 55 and 65, consider using your RRSP proceeds as a bridge to retirement at 65. That way, the RRSP money is taxed at your highest rate, which may be 40% but no more than 52%. If you're close to retirement age,

you might want to think twice about contributing to your RRSP. It makes little sense to contribute now for a 50% deduction and take it out in four or five years and possibly pay a higher rate. Or, if you are a knowledgeable investor, you may want to borrow some money and invest it outside your RRSP to make more. The interest on your loan, as long as it's not for putting into an RRSP, is tax deductible.

A study by William M. Mercer Ltd. suggests that a one-income couple with an income of $75,000 can improve their after-tax income by about $10,000 simply by not being married. If you're a low-income couple with one or two incomes, your after-tax income rises by 20% if you're not married. Current Canadian tax law is a disincentive to marriage. If you want to increase your after-tax income, get divorced. (Or leave the country. When you give up your residence in Canada and de-register an RRSP, the highest tax rate is 25%. So you can get 75% of your accumulated wealth out of your RRSP to invest again somewhere else.)

PAY DOWN THE MORTGAGE OR PAY THE RRSP?

This has been a thorny question for more than a decade. The answer is becoming clearer. While Canadians support the concept of RRSPs, the government does not. For years it has maintained that RRSPs—a tax shelter of its own making—"cost" the government billions of dollars. It's difficult to understand how politicians and bureaucrats can equate a deferred tax that is collectible at age 69 with tax freedom, unless they are ideologically opposed to RRSP contributions. In view of this, ideally one would want to take advantage of the tax-deferred status of RRSPs but have the option of claiming the money before retirement if it is tax advantageous to do so.

There are a couple of considerations in choosing between your RRSP and the mortgage. Your tax bracket will make a difference, but the basic factors to look at are your mortgage rate and the return on your RRSP investments. If you're paying more in mortgage interest than your RRSP is earning, even tax-deferred,

it would be better to pay down the mortgage. If you're contributing to your RRSP with non-borrowed money, a good compromise is to use the tax refund to pay down the mortgage. If it's a choice between saving and paying down the mortgage, it will be important to save inside an RRSP *only if* the potential return is significantly higher than the mortgage rate being paid.

There are a couple of things to remember here. First, an owner-occupied home is still the greatest tax-free asset one can hold in Canada. It has been less of a target of greedy government than the RRSP (although, as they say in the mutual fund business, past performance is no guarantee of future performance). Second, if you still trust that RRSPs will not be taxed at a higher rate than they are currently, you might want to pay down the mortgage and "bank" your RRSP contribution room, which you can do indefinitely. So, unlike a few years ago, you don't lose the opportunity to contribute if you miss a year. What you do lose is the length of time to compound. Mind you, there's no guarantee of a continued indefinite carry-over. Before 1996, the carry-over was limited to seven years. Before that, there was no carry-over at all. I wouldn't be surprised to see another change in this rule, to prevent or limit your ability to carry forward unused contribution room. It's your choice, but my own preference would be for less reliance on government.

10

Tax
Planning

Even if you're on the right track,
you'll get run over if you just sit there.
—Will Rogers

FOR THE SEVENTH YEAR IN A row, Canadians are being subjected to an insidious tax grab. When inflation is below 3%, the rate at which the federal government adjusts tax brackets and amounts used to calculate personal tax credits, we get "bracket creep." The last time Ottawa made these adjustments was in 1992, when inflation was 5.8%. Ever since, Canadians have paid a hidden tax as the cost of living rises. Back in the bad old days of double-digit inflation, during the 1970s and '80s, John Turner, then federal Finance Minister, indexed personal income tax to the inflation rate, so that if you got a wage increase, you didn't lose the whole thing to inflation. Mike Wilson scrapped that in 1985 in favour of a system that adjusted tax brackets, credits and clawbacks on Old Age Security only when the consumer price index rose more than 3%. As that hasn't happened for seven years, we're all getting bumped into higher and higher tax brackets.

From the government's point of view, bracket creep is the perfect tax, as it's hardly noticed and doesn't require legislation or

parliamentary debate. According to KPMG, a tax and management consultant, each percentage point of non-indexing gives Ottawa $350 million in extra taxes. Since 1992, that cumulative tax take is approaching $20 billion. What it means for you is this: last year, had there been full indexing to inflation, you would have been bumped from the lowest to the next bracket when you had $35,941 of taxable income. As it is, you were bumped at $29,590. That means $6,351 of income that would have been taxed at 26% now gets taxed at 40%. That's an extra $1,210 in tax.

There was a time when paying tax was a privilege, when people not only knew what they were getting for the money they voluntarily gave to governments but were proud to do it. That time has passed. According to recent polls, more than half of Canadians are using the tax system to cut the taxes we pay. This doesn't mean that these people are cheating on their taxes; it means they are actively studying the tax system (or having someone do it for them) to be sure they are not paying a penny more than they have to. A sizable number are also evading taxes by bartering goods and services or paying cash to avoid the GST.

Most Canadians would probably like to pay no taxes, but that's not what they expect. After all, tax collectors vie with prostitutes as members of the oldest profession. Taxation began when some ruler somewhere, back before biblical times, decided to take a share of someone else's hard work for something he wanted to do—have a war, build a monument, whatever. People complied because they would rather pay up than lose hands, eyes, or daughters.

Almost everyone understands that there are some things, such as building roads and organizing rural postal delivery, that can't be done by individuals alone. Thus began the process of institutionalizing the community projects—that became governments. They used to help us, or at least we used to think they helped us. Now it's not as clear to Canadians that they're getting value for their money. The underground economy was "discovered" about 20 years ago in Canada, and estimated to average

10% of the value of all goods and services produced every year. Revenue Canada denies its size regularly, but since its discovery, the underground economy has never been seen to shrink from the previous calculation. With the increasing ease of doing commerce and moving money electronically, governments are spending more and more time trying to figure out how to collect the money they deny exists.

Coercion is difficult to reconcile with voluntarism, but in Canada they are the essence of the tax system. The Canadian tax system is voluntary, but if you don't pay, you're prosecuted, fined and possibly jailed.

The concept of "cheating" implies that there are rules for paying taxes (although many Finance and Revenue Canada employees seem to believe that any money any Canadian makes belongs to them). Justice and Revenue Canada do have rules for the tax game. Minimizing one's taxes while playing by the rules is called "tax avoidance" and is legal. Therefore, a good part of this chapter, like in dozens of other books, describes ways of avoiding taxes. These books are a growth industry, as there are a lot more people outside government dreaming up ways to avoid taxes than there are people inside government dreaming up new taxes.

There aren't many books on how to evade taxes, because such advice is illegal, but we can set out the rules. Minimizing your taxes in ways that Revenue Canada's rules don't allow, i.e., tax evasion, is defined thus: "the commission or omission of an act knowingly with the intent to deceive so that the tax reported by the taxpayer is less than the tax payable under the law, or a conspiracy to commit such an offense."

There are lots of reasons people don't want to pay taxes: an ideological belief that governments have no legitimate right to tax, an individual's desire for freedom from government interference, a religious or ethical objection to the way tax money is spent. The biggest objection, however, seems to be not the fact of taxes but the heft of them, and the fact that, except for the indirect protest of voting out the government every few years,

individuals have no effective way to say what they want their money spent on. Taxation has become the biggest growth industry in the country. For the last 25 years at least, taxes have not only outstripped the growth of income, they top every major spending category.

CHART 10–1 **Taxes and Basic Expenditures* of the Average Canadian Family, 1961–1998**

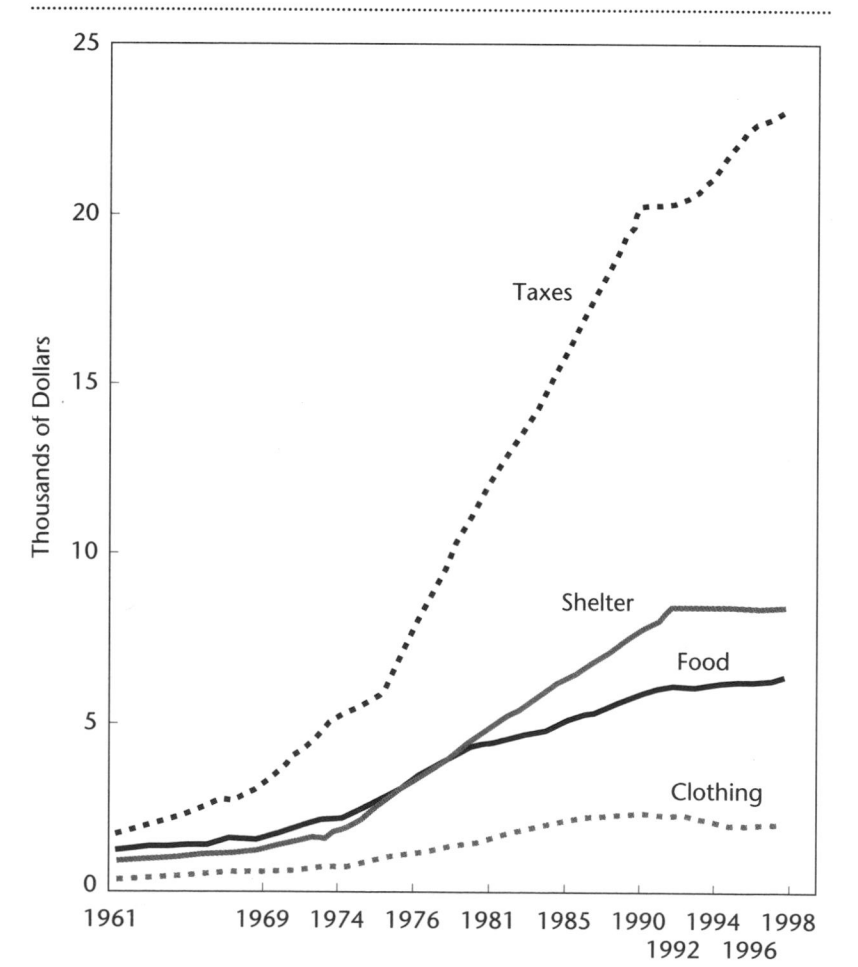

*All expenditure items include indirect taxes.

Source: Fraser Institute, Joel Emes and Michael Walker, authors, "Tax Facts 11," (1998)

CHART 10–2 **How the Consumer Tax Index Has Increased Relative to Other Indices, 1961–1998**

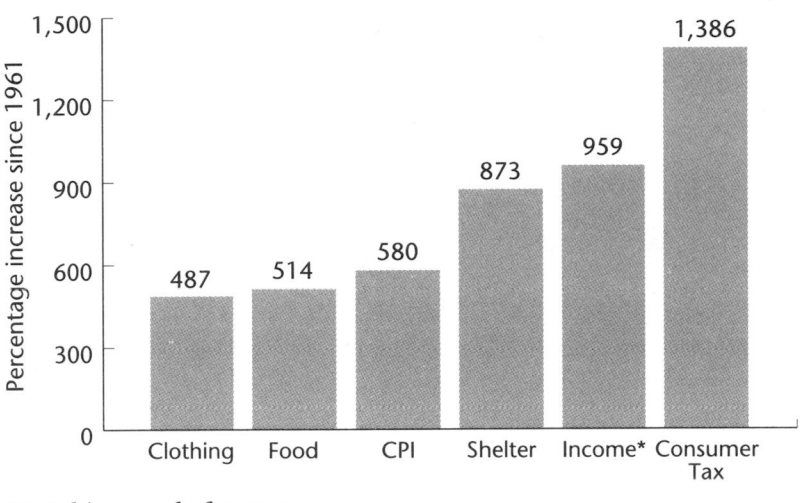

Total income before tax.

Source: Fraser Institute, Joel Emes and Michael Walker, authors, "Tax Facts 11," 1998

CHART 10–3 **Taxes and Expenditures of the Average Canadian Family as a Percentage of Income**

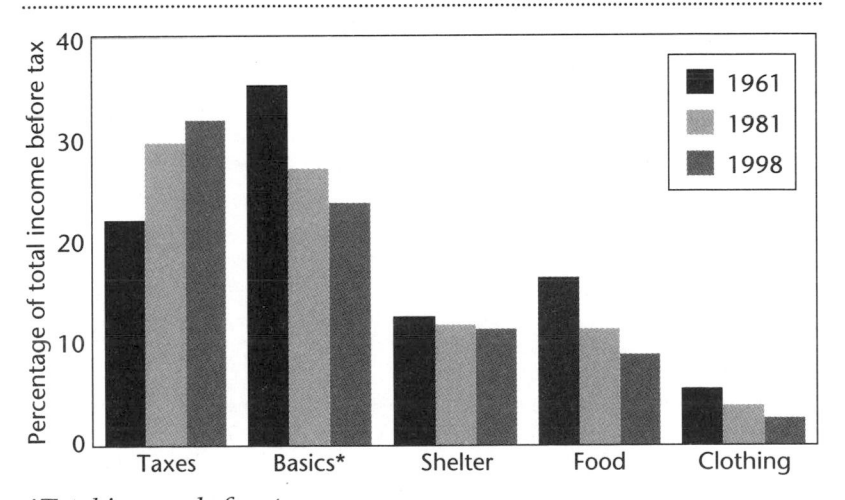

Total income before tax.

Source: Fraser Institute, Joel Emes and Michael Walker, authors, "Tax Facts 11," 1998

There are thousands of reasons for that: a groaningly large public service with a pension plan that other Canadians would kill for, and a 50-year-old mindset that Canadians could afford everything their governments dreamed up to buy their votes. Thirty years of such activity outstripped the growth of the economy; another 20 years was pursued with money borrowed from either the international community or future generations. In the 1990s, governments have reined in the most obvious excessive spending, but a $700-billion debt remains, on which interest has to be paid.

What also remains is a distorted tax system with dozens, maybe hundreds, of inconsistencies, which cost a lot of money and make little sense. Over the years, the Income Tax Act, a creation of Finance Canada, and its interpretation by Revenue Canada have grown more ponderous and puzzling. This in itself has created major problems, some internal to the workings of the departments that write and interpret the Income Tax Act, and some external, for the lawyers and accountants who advise taxpayers. It will take a monumental effort to sort this stuff out.

Everyone knows that they pay heavy taxes in Canada. Only if you earn less than $6,500 do you pay no income tax. If you make $30,000 a year, on average more than 25% goes to taxes. Of the next $30,000, $12,000 goes to tax. Half of anything over that goes to tax. (If you live in Alberta, the Northwest Territories or the Yukon it's slightly less; if you live anywhere else in Canada it's slightly more.) In British Columbia 54% of any income over $90,000 goes straight to the government.

But it's not just the wealthy who pay high taxes. Canadians also pay more at lower levels of income. Canada has one of the highest marginal tax rates on personal income (50%+) in the OECD, and it is applied at an extremely low level of income ($63,000). In contrast, the U.S. top rate is 47%, not applied until an individual earns $168,000.

CHART 10–4 **Marginal Tax Rates, Various Countries**

	TOP MARGINAL TAX RATE (%)	INCOME THRESHOLD (C$)
France	57	73,000
Germany	53	107,000
Canada	52	63,000
Italy	51	260,000
Japan	50	350,000
United States	47	168,000

Source: Calculated from OECD, Deloitte & Touche, and Business Council on National Issues data

If you're employed, there is almost no way you can escape, and the taxes and the complications to the system just keep coming. Sometimes they're called "premiums," as in the case of the Canada Pension Plan, but they're taxes all the same. With a $700-billion debt on the books, another $600-billion debt off the books (this is the liability in the Canada/Quebec Pension Plan, discussed in Chapter 4), some $40 billion of interest to pay every year, and only 15 million taxpayers to pay it all, it seems unlikely that governments are going to stop taxing so heavily any time soon.

Indeed, it seems more likely that the tax burden will get heavier, not withstanding periodic tax reductions when public pressure becomes unbearable. First, people who can afford to buy advice can legally save thousands in taxes. Second, people are thronging to the underground economy and working for cash. That's not legal, but it's reality. Third, in our global economy, it's getting easier for everyone to do what transnational business has done for some time: move the production and money to a more advantageous tax regime. It's not totally clear whether this is tax avoidance (legal) or tax evasion (illegal), and it will become more murky in the next decade, as electronic commerce blurs the production process so much that it will be impossible to determine in what jurisdiction value is being created. But what's clear is that governments are getting more anxious to

track every dollar, as they realize that tax collecting in a global world is more difficult than it was in an industrial one. So they're penalizing more, scrutinizing more, and taxing more.

A big part of retiring in style involves understanding what you have to pay, and not paying a penny more than that. It sounds simple, but just about every bean counter in the country will tell you that most people pay more taxes than they have to. Small wonder, with a tax system that's so complicated it takes thousands of pages to write down and uses a basic income tax form that has 451 lines to complete.

More than half of Canadian taxpayers are looking for legal ways to reduce the amount of tax they pay, according to a *Financial Post* survey, and this tax planning is the best way of finding it, short of a tax revolt.

CHART 10–5 **Canadians Actively Engaged in Tax Planning**

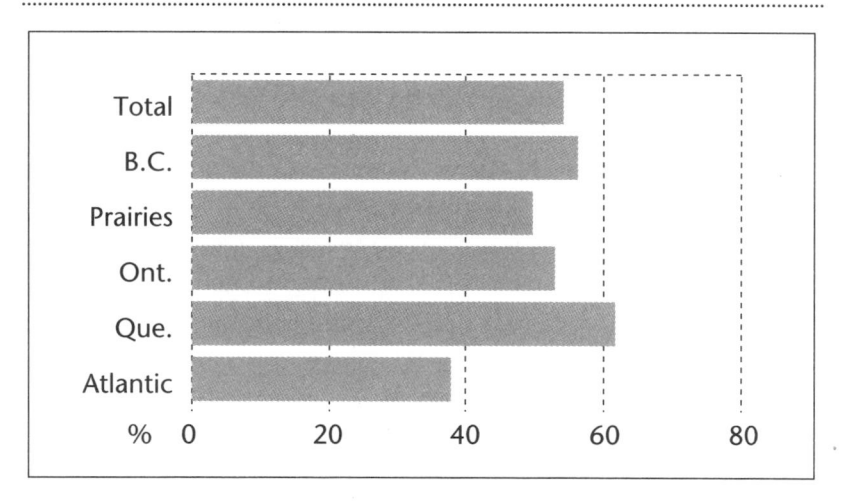

Source: Financial Post/COMPAS

A good place to start is with year-end tax strategies. These will frame your planning for the whole year. If you don't give this aspect of your life much attention until you complete your tax return in April, this overview will give you a head start.

DEDUCTIONS

Deductions are categories of expenses you can deduct from your income before you calculate how much tax you will pay. The more money you make, the more valuable the deduction becomes. If you make $35,000 a year, a $100 deduction saves you $39 in tax. If you make $100,000, a $100 deduction saves you $50. Certain deductions qualify only if they are paid before the end of the year. Make a list of things such as accounting fees, moving expenses, charitable donations, and medical and child care expenses. Make sure you pay them before the end of the year. Then, don't forget to take the deduction.

All eligible deductions save you money, but some are really big. Moving, for example. If you move 40 km closer to your job, whether it's a new job, a new business or a transfer, you can deduct just about everything associated with the move. If you sell your house, the real-estate commission is deductible. The same is true if you buy a house in your new location. Your storage costs, legal fees, and the costs associated with selling and buying, as well as your travelling costs, are all deductible from your taxable income. The only proviso is that an employer has not reimbursed you for your expenses. This deduction is also open to students moving to university or to a summer job.

Okay, not everyone moves, but the next biggest deduction is a Registered Retirement Savings Plan. As mentioned earlier, you're allowed to deduct 18% of your income, up to a maximum of $13,500, every year, if you put the money into an RRSP. This is a neat tax deduction, and also a neat way of using what would otherwise be taxes to invest and make money on. Just be sure you've reviewed my speculations in Chapter 9 about where to put your first savings—home mortgage or RRSP. Remember, too, to review the federal government's tax policies with regard to RRSP withdrawals every year. It may be a great savings strategy, but we have to be wary of government.

If you decide that having an RRSP is a good idea, open one as soon as you can. Get used to putting your money in early. You

have 14 months to put money in an RRSP in any given year, from January of that year until the end of February or beginning of March of the following year. The advertising frenzy that happens in January and February is aimed at last-minute contributions for the previous year. And, indeed, most people put their money in at the end of the allowable period, that is, January or February. However, if you put your money in your RRSP in January or February of the year in which it will be tax deferred, you'll get an extra 12 months of tax deferment and an extra 12 months of tax-deferred income growth.

Know how much you can put into your RRSP. It is based on your earned income in the year for which you're paying income tax. Recall that the maximum you can put in is $13,500; for that you need an earned income of $75,000. If you have some control over your income (for example, if you run a small business, or are a fee-based, independent, contract employee), arrange your income flow so that you can put the most possible into your plan. If you have more than the maximum contribution room because you've neglected to contribute for a few years, try to fill up your RRSP. When interest rates are low, it may pay to borrow your RRSP contribution, but only if your budget allows you to pay it off within the year.

There's another circumstance in which it may pay for you to borrow. One assumption of this book is that you pay cash for all your personal expenses, with the single exception of your home. But that credo does not apply to investments. Revenue Canada allows Canadians to claim a deduction for interest costs incurred to (1) earn business income, (2) earn income from property, and (3) earn investment income. However, you have to be careful about selling your investments; you can't use the money for personal expenses and still claim the interest deduction. For example, suppose you borrow $100,000 to invest, and your investment makes $40,000. You cash in $50,000 and buy a Lexus. Revenue Canada will disallow half the interest expense. Why? Because $50,000 represents half your original loan. If you sell any part of

the investment to use for personal expenses, Revenue Canada equates the sale to the original loan and assumes you could have repaid it. So it disallows the interest deduction. Use other money to pay personal expenses. If you have invested in something that gives you income (such as a bond or GIC), you may use the income from those investments for personal expenses and not risk an interest deductibility problem.

You don't have to take the tax deduction all in the same year if your tax planning indicates it would be more advantageous to hold some of it over to a future year.

CHILD CARE EXPENSES

Day care, babysitting, nursery school, and nanny and summer camp expenses are deductible if they allow you or your spouse either to earn a living or to get training to do so. The formula for calculating how much you can deduct is: the lesser of $7,000 for each child under seven and $4,000 for each child between seven and 14. In Quebec, either partner can claim the tax credit; in the rest of the county, the lower-income partner must claim.

CHILD SUPPORT EXPENSES

There are two sets of rules covering the payment of child support or spousal support. One rule is for people who had a written agreement before May 1, 1997. The other rule is for those who did not. If you had such an agreement, the one who makes the payments can deduct them from income and the one who receives the payments must add them to income. The rules also stipulate how and under what conditions the payments are to take place. For example, they cannot be a lump-sum payment, they must be a regular allowance determined in advance, either by the courts or in a legal, written agreement. The payments needn't be in the form of cash; they can be the regular payment of bills, such as rent, mortgage, or other expenditures, as long as it is in the written agreement. (And, by the way, former partners cannot live together.)

If you didn't have such an agreement before May 1, 1997, the child or spousal support payments have no relevance to income tax: they are neither deductible nor taxable.

To complicate matters, if you had an agreement before May 1, 1997, you can choose to continue with the agreement or you can sign a form from Revenue Canada saying you want the new rules to apply. But beware: if you want the old rules to apply, you cannot change your agreement; if you do, the new rules apply automatically.

HOME BUSINESS

If you have a business that you operate from home, you are entitled to some deductions, if you follow the rules. It doesn't have to be your principal occupation—you can have another job—but you can't have another office for the business you claim as a home business. Whether this is a full- or part-time thing, you have to convince Revenue Canada that your business has some reasonable expectation of making money at some time in the future. So you can't set up an office that does no business, just to claim the deduction; it has to be a legitimate business with business sales. (Otherwise, you'd have no income against which to claim the deductions.) If this fits your situation, you can deduct regular household expenses proportionate to the amount of space your home office occupies: rent or mortgage, property taxes, telephone, household insurance, and all your office supplies, including your computer, printer, printer paper, and so on.

If you have a business, you can hire family members. This is a good way to split income with them, thereby saving taxes as well as providing them with an earned income from which to contribute to an RRSP and CPP. However, if you do this, you won't be able to claim them as dependants, so make sure you figure out which is better for you. If you do have a business, consider buying capital equipment, such as a computer or furniture, near the end of the year. That way, you'll be able to claim half

the regular depreciation amount in the year in which you made the purchase.

TAX SAVINGS RELATED TO INVESTMENTS

Review your investment portfolio—for two reasons. First, if you have realized capital gains during the year, look at your portfolio to see if you have potential capital losses. If you do, consider your investment strategy: capital gains can be reduced by capital losses, but only if you've realized both. Keep in mind that capital gains are taxed less than some other kinds of investment income, but not inside your RRSP. Which brings me to the second reason for reviewing your portfolio. If your investment performance is not up to your expectations, now's the time to take action. Remember, capital gains and dividends are taxed preferentially, so ideally you should hold them outside your RRSP.

MAKING YOUR MORTGAGE TAX-DEDUCTIBLE

If you own a home outright or have paid off a considerable amount of the mortgage, or have other money somewhere, you may be able to rearrange your finances to create deductible interest. The Income Tax Act says you can deduct expenditures you make in the effort of making money. That means you can borrow money to invest, using the equity you have in your home, and the interest on that borrowed money (invested in pursuit of making money) is tax deductible.

TAX CREDITS: 17% IS THE MAGIC NUMBER

A tax credit is different from a tax deduction. Whereas a tax deduction is deducted from your income before you calculate the amount of tax you have to pay, a tax credit is deducted directly from the amount of tax you have to pay.

Everyone gets a basic credit of $1,098. That's why you don't pay tax on the first $6,456 of income. (The $1,098 equals the 17% tax rate on $6,456.) If you're over 65, you can claim another $592 if your income is below $26,000 a year. Between $26,000

and $49,000, you can claim some proportion of the old-age tax credit. At just over $49,000, it disappears.

If you have a partner, you can claim a credit of $915, provided your partner doesn't make more than $500 a year. Between $500 and $6,000, you can claim some proportion of the credit. At $6,000 of "spousal" earnings, it disappears. (Right now, your partner has to be of the opposite sex, although you don't have to have gone through a marriage ceremony to be considered spouses.) Right now, too, all tax credits are considered in relation to your personal income; it is possible that this will be changed to family, or household, income. Yet another reason to follow the tax rules and use a professional tax advisor.

If you're physically or mentally disabled, you can earn an additional $4,230 without paying tax on it. That's a tax credit of $720. In order to qualify for this, your medical professional has to complete a Revenue Canada form stating that your disability is long term (more than a year) and keeps you from normal daily activities.

If you support a child or another member of your family in your home, and haven't claimed the spousal tax credit, you can transfer that claim to the person you support. It's what's called the "equivalent to married" claim. The person you support has to be under 18 or physically or mentally disabled.

People who stay in school are entitled to tax credits equal to 17% of their eligible tuition. Of course, there are rules to qualify. The student has to be 16 or older. The courses taken have to cost more than $100. The institution has to be certified as an educational institution. The institution can be a post-secondary institution, a vocational school or an institution that teaches specialized skills such as painting or dancing. If the student has no income, making the tax credits worthless, they are transferable to a parent, partner or grandparent to a maximum of $850. If the courses are a full-time activity, the student can claim an additional $34 for each month he or she was in full-time enrollment.

If you have medical expenses that health care or your health benefits don't pay for, you can claim any receipted expenses that are over 3% of your income. Once again, the credit is equal to 17% of any amount over 3% of income. This tax credit extends to all members of your household whom you support. (Your tax professional can tell you what kinds of expenses qualify, but the list is very long and more inclusive than exclusive.)

If you give money to registered charities or to any political party, you can earn a tax credit to a maximum of 20% of your annual income.

ESTATE PLANNING AND TAXES

If you have a partner or children, the most tax-effective way of holding your assets, in all parts of Canada except Quebec, is to hold them "jointly," with the right of survivorship. That means the assets pass to the survivor automatically and directly, without becoming part of your estate, so probate taxes are avoided. This is perfectly straightforward if you buy an asset and register it jointly when you buy it. But what happens to many of us is that we accumulate assets over our lives, and then decide to re-register an asset to hold it jointly. This can be a tax trap for you to avoid. The trap is sprung if the re-registered asset has appreciated since you bought it. If you do nothing more than re-register it to own it jointly with, say, a child, Revenue Canada "deems" that you have disposed of half the asset and requires that you pay capital-gains tax on the appreciation of the half you have given to your child.

Here's an example. I have owned 2,000 Canadian Pacific shares for 10 years. I bought them when they were trading for $20 a share, and now they're trading for $40 a share. I decide to re-register them jointly with my daughter, with right of survivorship. I avoid probate taxes, because when I die the shares will pass directly to my daughter without having to go through my estate. But I immediately trigger a capital-gains tax on half the shares—1,000 shares, bought for $20,000 and now worth $40,000.

I therefore have to pay $7,500 in capital-gains tax now (75% of $20,000 at a tax rate of 50%).

But a little knowledge will help me avoid that trap. Section 54 of the Income Tax Act makes it clear that if you *legally* change the ownership of an asset without *beneficially* changing the ownership, you are not deemed to have disposed of it. So, along with the re-registration, I have to make an arrangement with my daughter that ensures I retain all future rights not only to any income generated by the shares but also to all the capital gains. This means that I will continue to pay taxes on the income from the dividends as I always have. To ensure that Revenue Canada will allow you to re-register assets for joint and last survivor rights with a legal but not beneficial change in ownership, get your lawyer to draw up such an agreement.

FAMILY TRUSTS

You can use a trust to put assets aside for children or other beneficiaries. A trust is a relationship between trustees, beneficiaries, and you, the settlor. You can transfer assets into a trust, thereby separating control of the assets from the beneficiaries. The Income Tax Act allows income and capital gains of a trust to be payable by the beneficiaries. If the beneficiaries have low marginal tax rates, taxes are minimized, and the income after taxes can be used to pay the expenses of the beneficiaries.

Here's an example from the *Financial Post*. Assume an investment portfolio earning 7% a year is transferred by a parent to a trust for the benefit of a child who is a minor. To avoid having to pay taxes on the income earned by the transferred asset to a child under 18, the trust issues a $200,000 promissory note to the parent, bearing interest at 5% (Revenue Canada's prescribed rate). So the parent earns 5% interest on the note, which the trust pays. The trust earns 7% on the portfolio, and the interest it paid to the parent is tax deductible as an expense of earning income. The trustee then uses the net 2%, in this case $4,000, for the benefit of the child. If the child has no other income, the annual basic

exemption of $6,400 would eliminate any taxes on the $4,000 net investment income. Such a trust can be maintained until a child is 21, provided the right to the income is vested with the child.

The benefits of the trust depend on two things: the size of the portfolio, and the spread between the loan rate dictated by the government and the rate of return on the portfolio. You'll need professional advice to set up a trust, but once it's up and running, it's easily maintained.

TAX-FREE RETIREMENT INCOME?

There is a way to generate tax-free retirement income, but it depends on your priorities. If you have a great desire to leave money behind, this might be for you. The key to the tax-minimization strategy is to borrow money from a bank when you retire; the loan is ultimately repaid with a tax-free death benefit. (This is also called "leveraged" life insurance, a concept that flies in the face of the cardinal rule not to borrow for personal expenses, especially after you've left your job.)

Here's how it works. Universal life insurance is a relatively new product that is life insurance plus a "cash-value" fund that is sheltered from taxes (much like an RRSP). The policy holder buys investments over several years inside the cash-value fund, and an annual premium is withdrawn from the fund to pay for the insurance coverage. When the policy holder wants to draw on the income in retirement, the accumulated capital in the cash-value fund is used as collateral for a series of bank loans—in effect, tax-free income. Interest is tacked on to the outstanding balance, and the loan isn't paid off until the policy holder dies. The loans are structured so that the sum of the loans plus interest never exceeds 75% of the accumulated investment account. If the package is designed properly, when the loan is paid off, there will be money left over to be distributed to the heirs.

People who sell these packages say they are of interest to affluent or middle-income earners who have at least 15 years before retirement, contribute the maximum annually to their RRSP and

have money left over (or who have decided they don't want an RRSP). Unlike RRSP contributions, this insurance retirement plan is not tax deductible, but its payouts are tax free, whereas withdrawals from an RRSP or RRIF are taxable. Moreover, these packages are not bound by the foreign-investment and withdrawal rules of RRSPs or RRIFs.

Here's an example, to show what happens to $10,000 a year in an RRSP for 35 years versus putting $6,000 towards a universal life policy for 35 years. (These amounts are the same in after-tax dollars.) The assumptions are that the investment return is 6%, the inflation rate is 2% and you are in a 40% tax bracket before retirement and a 50% tax bracket after retirement. The total death benefit when the universal policy is set up is $270,000. The accompanying chart shows that RRSP growth stops at 65 (the age of retirement) and begins to reverse after 69, when it becomes a RRIF.

CHART 10–6 **Universal Life vs. RRSP/RRIF**

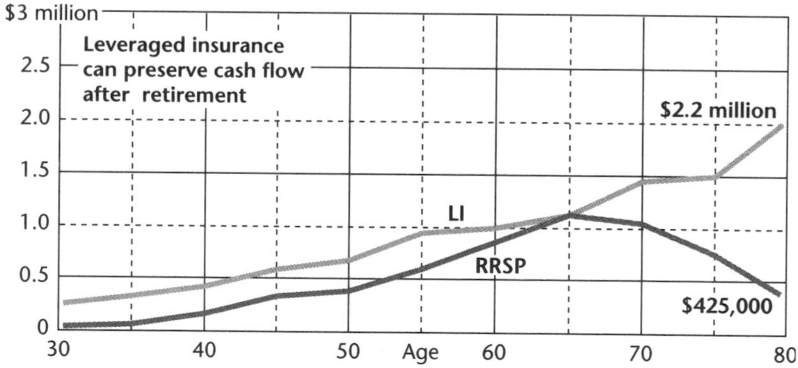

The universal policy is worth $736,000 at age 66 and is used to borrow $46,500 a year until you die, in this example at age 80. At that time, your estate will owe the bank $1.4 million, including interest on your loans. The cash value of the policy, $697,000 at age 65, has grown to $2.2 million at age 80.

Your estate pays off the bank, and has $822,000 left to

distribute to your heirs. Meanwhile, your RRIF assets are heading towards zero.

Clearly, there are some minimal risks. Interest rates will affect what you pay to the bank. Return on investments will affect the growth of your policy. But insurance companies are pretty conservative investors, and you can tie your investments to guaranteed returns. The biggest risk is, as usual, that the government will change the tax rules.

TO STAY OR TO GO

With Canada's high tax rates, a lot of people are pondering whether they'd be better off leaving the country, terminating their Canadian residency and paying the taxation rates in the country of destination. Alex Doulis, a former Canadian resident, has written two best-selling books, *Take the Money and Run* and *My Blue Haven*, that attest to the benefits of doing just that. Of course, terminating your Canadian residency also means terminating your provincial health care insurance, selling your home or renting it out at arm's length, which usually means to a stranger, and having your lawyer, accountant or financial planner check off the things you need to do to ensure that Revenue Canada has no claim on income earned abroad.

The hardest thing about terminating residency, aside from having to visit your native land, friends and family rather than being a couple of blocks or cities away, is that when you take your assets, you are deemed to have sold them at fair market value. This doesn't apply to real property, pension benefits or the right to receive payments from the CPP. It does apply to securities and other assets held outside an RRSP.

Your RRSPs don't have to be terminated when you leave the country. You can let them grow tax free, but you can't put any more money into them. If you do choose to collapse the RRSPs, all you'll pay is a 25% withholding tax. That's about the best deal going.

Most other countries have significantly lower income taxes

than Canada, but every country has social security taxes, some of which are high. You get to deduct mortgage interest if you buy a home in the U.S., but you have to contend with both estate taxes and medical costs. If this is a possibility that appeals to you, do the reading, talk to a consultant, and learn everything you should about the country you have your eye on.

Tax planning is a tedious bits-and-pieces kind of activity that appeals only to those who want to pay the taxman nothing more than his due. You need a "big picture" overview of the tax system as well as detailed information on specific areas when they apply to you. This chapter has supplied some of each, but you need to update your knowledge at least annually, because tax rules change. All the big accountancy firms in the country publish tax planning guides every year; they'd all be happy to send you one if you ask.

11

RRSP Maturity Options

IN THE YEAR YOU TURN 69, the government has a birthday present for you: you have to do something with your RRSP before December 31. If you don't, on the stroke of midnight, it turns into a pumpkin—half of it disappears into the tax coffers.

You don't have a whole lot of options, but you should know what they are so you can make tentative decisions in advance. I say tentative decisions because tax rules are written in sand, and although you might build a strategy for saving, it can be derailed by some politician with the stroke of a pen. But ignoring it all until the last minute will be no better for your financial health, unless you are in a very low income bracket.

THE OPTIONS

- Take the money and run.
- Give the money to an insurance company in exchange for an income for life—a life annuity.
- Give the money to a financial institution in exchange for an income for a specified period of time—a term-certain annuity.
- Transfer the funds to a Registered Retirement Income Fund.

You aren't limited to an "either-or" choice. You can have all or any of the options. You can also implement your decisions at any time, as long as it's before the age deadline. So if you're 55, for example, you can retire from your job and take out part of your RRSP each year until you're 60 or 65 or whenever your employer-sponsored pension plan begins. Or you can buy an annuity, to begin at whatever age you want. (The only person I know who knew nothing about investing came into $250,000 in 1981. He was 42 years old. He bought a life annuity. His $250,000 bought him an income of $40,000 a year for life. You should be so dumb. Of course, those were the days of 20% interest rates. Today, $250,000 would buy a 42-year-old male $20,000.)

Whatever options you choose, the income you take each year is fully taxed as ordinary income. The amount of money you take each year is added to whatever other taxable income you have and will be taxed at your highest marginal tax rate. All the money you leave in the tax shelter will accumulate tax free until it is taken as income.

If you are 65 or older, the regular payments you receive from RRIFs and annuities are considered qualified pension income for income tax purposes. They are therefore eligible for the $1,000 pension-tax credit.

If you choose to have a RRIF before you're 69, you can do that. And if you're still receiving what is defined as "earned income," you can also contribute to an RRSP.

After you've reached 69 years of age, you can no longer contribute to an RRSP even if you are still working. The only exception is if your spouse is younger than 69; then you can contribute to a spousal RRSP and take the tax deduction against your income.

In thinking about what options may be right for you, there are several factors to consider. First, of course, are your income requirements. Use the worksheets in Appendix 2 to work out whether your income needs will increase or decrease during retirement, and whether you will be in a higher or lower tax

bracket than when you were working. You will also have to figure out how much you want to live on and how much you want to leave as an inheritance. (My own preference is for giving money to your family or friends while you're alive, when you can see that it is surplus to your needs, given how long your retirement income has to last.)

THE PROS AND CONS OF EACH OPTION

Option 1: Take the Money and Run

Taking your RRSP in a lump sum will likely catapult you into the highest tax bracket if you stay in Canada. However, if you give up residence in Canada (you can still visit for 181 days a year), taking your RRSP assets in a lump sum is smart: the withholding tax rate is just 25%, one of the lowest in the Canadian system.

You might want to look at using your tax-sheltered assets before you have to collapse your RRSP if you can conclude that your pension from work is both secure and, with your non-RRSP savings, sufficient for your post-retirement needs. This will involve a decision to be less dependent on the government for your retirement income, and that your RRSP savings will be an adequate bridge to retirement.

Another reason for this would be if your medical professionals have given you less than two years to live and you have no dependants nor anyone you want to leave money to; you decide to take what's left over after taxes are paid, and have a gigantic blowout year.

Option 2: Life Annuities

The life-annuity option guarantees you a fixed amount of money each year or month for the rest of your life. The annuity payments are taxed as they are received. The amount of your annuity payments is determined by the value of your RRSP, your age, current interest rates, how long you want the payments guaranteed, and whether you want your surviving partner to receive payments for life.

A "plain vanilla" annuity guarantees that as long as you live, you'll have an income. That means that if you take your $100,000 RRSP, buy a life annuity and die two days later, the insurance company keeps your $100,000. This prospect makes a lot of people unhappy.

Insurance companies have therefore devised other annuity options. You can buy an annuity guaranteed to last as long as you live but also guaranteed to pay out for a set period, whether you live or not. The guaranteed period can range up to 15 years or even longer. If you have a partner, you can buy an annuity with a "joint and last survivor" clause so that your partner will receive monthly payments for life, even if you die.

Other life-annuity options include inflation protection—paying out an increasing amount over the years, to offset inflation—and a "poor-health" option to pay out higher amounts if you have a medical professional certify that you have an illness that will significantly shorten your life. All but the last option will reduce your basic annuity payments.

The best thing about a life annuity is that you never have to worry about outliving your money. The worst thing is that it is irrevocable. Once you've bought one, you can't change your mind. The other characteristic of life annuities can be either good or bad. The amount of income you can buy with your RRSP proceeds depends heavily on interest rates. If they're high, all other things being equal, you'll get more; if they're low, you'll get less.

Option 3: Term-Certain Annuities

A term-certain annuity provides a fixed income until age 90. This kind of annuity simply earns interest at the going rate and pays out a blended payment of interest and principal between the age of purchase and age 90. If you die before you are 90, your spouse will continue to receive payments until the end of the year in which you would have turned 90. Your spouse can also elect to receive a lump-sum cash payment. If you do not have a

TABLE 11–1 **Sample Annuity Payments**

Assumptions: 6.5% for the first 15 years, 6% thereafter. Calculations based on annuity beginning January 1, 1998, monthly payments.

Sample: $100,000 annuity purchase:

AGE WHEN BOUGHT	MALE: YEARS GUAR. 0	MALE: YEARS GUAR. 5	MALE YEARS GUAR. 10	FEMALE YEARS GUAR. 0	FEMALE: YEARS GUAR. 5	FEMALE: YEARS GUAR. 10
55	$699	$695	$685	$636	$634	$630
60	768	761	741	683	680	673
65	869	853	811	750	745	729
66	893	875	827	767	761	743
67	920	898	843	785	778	757
68	948	922	859	805	796	771
69	977	947	875	826	816	786

Source: Retire Web Annuity Calculator

Table 11–2 **Sample Joint and Last Survivor Annuity Payments**

Joint and Last Survivor (note pay-out to survivor is 66 and ⅔)

AGE WHEN BOUGHT	MALE: YEARS GUAR. 0	MALE: YEARS GUAR. 5	MALE YEARS GUAR. 10	FEMALE YEARS GUAR. 0	FEMALE: YEARS GUAR. 5	FEMALE: YEARS GUAR. 10
55	$629	$627	$624	$610	$609	$608
60	673	671	665	649	648	646
65	736	732	720	705	703	697
66	752	747	733	719	717	709
67	767	763	747	734	731	722
68	787	780	761	750	747	736
69	806	798	779	767	764	751

Source: Retire Web Annuity Calculator

spouse, the balance of the contract is paid to your estate as a lump sum.

It's hard to think of the best thing about a term-certain annuity. It seems to have the downsides of the life annuity without the guarantee of an income for life. Moreover, if your spouse is significantly younger than you, or has a much longer life expectancy, he or she will not be protected for life.

TABLE 11–3 **Sample Term-Certain Annuity Payments to Age 90**

Term certain to 90, monthly payments.

AGE WHEN BOUGHT	MALE	FEMALE
55	$747	$705
60	$799	$732
65	$885	$781
66	$907	$794
67	$936	$816
68	$966	$839
69	$999	$865

Source: Source: Retire Web Annuity Calculator www.retireweb.com

Option 4: Registered Retirement Income Funds

A RRIF is just like an RRSP except that it works in reverse. An RRSP allows you to accumulate assets tax free. A RRIF forces you to supplement your income after age 69 by withdrawing minimum amounts each year. You are not limited to the minimum withdrawals—you can withdraw as much as you want—but you need to be mindful that the money has to last at least as long as you do. You can have more than one RRIF, but if you do, you will have more difficulty seeing your portfolio as a whole when you want to make asset allocation decisions. You may also face higher management fees.

TABLE 11–4 **Minimum Annual RRIF Payments**

AGE AT JANUARY 1	RRIF PURCHASED BEFORE 1993 (%)	RRIF PURCHASED AFTER 1992 (%)
55	2.86	2.86
56	2.94	2.94
57	3.03	3.03
58	3.13	3.13
59	3.23	3.23
60	3.33	3.33
61	3.45	3.45
62	3.57	3.57
63	3.70	3.70
64	3.85	3.85
65	4.00	4.00
66	4.17	4.17
67	4.35	4.35
68	4.55	4.55
69	4.76	4.76
70	5.00	5.00
71	5.26	7.38
72	5.56	7.48
73	5.88	7.59
74	6.25	7.71
75	6.67	7.85
76	7.14	7.99
77	7.69	8.15
78	8.33	8.33
79	8.53	8.53
80	8.75	8.75
81	8.99	8.99
82	9.27	9.27
83	9.58	9.58
84	9.93	9.93
85	10.33	10.33
86	10.79	10.79

87	11.33	11.33
88	11.96	11.96
89	12.71	12.71
90	13.62	13.62
91	14.73	14.73
92	16.12	16.12
93	17.92	17.92
94	20	20
95	20	20
96	20	20
97	20	20
98	20	20
etc.	20	20

TABLE 11–5 **Sample $100,000 RRIF purchased after 1992**

Assume rate of return of 8% and minimum annual withdrawal.

AGE	RATE OF RETURN	VALUE OF RRIF	MINIMUM WITHDRAWAL	REMAINING VALUE OF RRIF
69	8%	$108,000		$108,000
70	8	116,640	$5,552	111,088
71	8	119,975	6,310	113,665
72	8	122,758	6,825	115,933
73	8	125,208	7,362	117,846
74	8	127,273	7,955	119,318
75	8	128,863	8,595	120,268
76	8	129,889	9,274	120,615
77	8	139,538	11,372	128,166
78	8	149,791	13,955	135,836
79	8	160,657	13,704	146,953
80	8	158,709	13,887	144,822
81	8	156,407	14,060	142,347
82	8	153,735	14,251	139,482
83	8	150,640	14,431	136,209
etc.				

If you decide to withdraw more than the minimum amount, the plan trustee will withhold a proportion of the tax that will be payable on April 30 of the following year.

TABLE 11–6 **Withholding Tax Rates**

EXCESS AMOUNT	WITHHOLDING TAX EX. QUEBEC	WITHHOLDING TAX, QUEBEC
Up to $5,000	10%	21%
$5,001–$15,000	20	30
More than $15,000	30	35

If you want to convert your RRSP to a RRIF before you are 69, the minimum payment is calculated as follows:

$$\frac{\text{RRIF value at beginning of year}}{90 - \text{Your or your spouse's age}} = \text{Minimum annual payment}$$

For example, if you decide to convert your $100,000 RRSP to a RRIF at age 63 and take an income the first year, your minimum annual payment will be

$$\frac{\$100,000}{(90 - 63)} = \$3,700$$

The best thing about a RRIF is that you get to decide on the investments, just as you did with your RRSP. Indeed, if this is your choice, you don't need to do anything to change your investments; you just roll them all into the RRIF. The investments you leave inside the RRIF continue to grow on a tax-deferred basis until you withdraw them. Thus, for as long as you live, which will be another 15 or 20 years, on average, you can continue to manage your wealth accumulation. At any time, you can use some of the accumulated funds to buy an annuity. The other good thing about a RRIF is that you aren't required to take the minimum income in the year you open the RRIF. So, as you can see

from the example in Table 11–4, your RRIF funds can accumulate for one extra year.

The downside of having a RRIF is that your investments may do less well than you expect. So before you make choices, get your financial advisor to run you a couple of schedules with different rates of return, so you can see what your income would be if the return was, say, only 6% or 4%. (You can also get a software program that will do it for you.)

If you choose to change your RRSP into a RRIF, you can make an additional maximum contribution. Here's how: Say you have to convert your RRSP by December 31, 2000. You've already made your contribution for 2000. If you make another contribution in December 2000, the government will assume this additional contribution is an "overcontribution," and will penalize you a modest amount—1% of the amount you overcontribute. As soon as it's January 2001, the extra contribution is no longer an over-contribution, because the new year brings new contribution room. You still have to convert your RRSP to a RRIF by the end of December 2000, but in exchange for a 1% penalty, which cannot be more than $135 (1% of $13,500), you will have the extra contribution, several thousand dollars, to deduct from your taxable income.

At your death, all that remains in your RRIF can be rolled over, tax free, to your partner. If you have no spouse, the money passes to your estate, to be taxed at your highest marginal tax rate as calculated by your executor on your final income tax return. The after-tax balance will be distributed to your beneficiaries. If you have a child or grandchild who is dependent on you or is mentally or physically disabled, there are several other options for the disposition of the RRIF. Depending on the age of the child, the RRIF income can be spread over a number of years, or even over the life of the child. The options depend on the circumstances, so professional financial advice is crucial.

On your death, your partner has several choices about receiving the money in your RRIF.

- The money can simply remain in the RRIF, and the partner continues to receive the income. If this option is chosen, and if the minimum payout of the RRIF was calculated on the basis of your age, the partner has the choice of continuing it that way or having the payouts recalculated using the *partner's* age.
- If the partner is under 69, the money can be rolled into the spouse's RRSP, irrespective of whether it is more than the partner's annual contribution limit, where it will continue to grow tax deferred.
- The money can be taken as cash and added to the partner's income for tax purposes.

"LOCKED IN" RRSPS AND "LOCKED IN" RETIREMENT ACCOUNTS

It used to be that people had one employer, and at retirement got a pocket watch and a pension. Nowadays, if you stay long enough for your pension to vest, whatever funds you have accumulated when you leave get "locked in" to a registered plan to prevent you from doing something with the money—like maybe starting your own business—before you need it for a retirement income. And that's the improved, 1990s-style disposition of pension funds. Before 1990, the only option you had was to buy a life annuity; but more employees shifted work and demanded more flexibility for their funds, so legislation was changed across the country.

You can't transfer this money to an ordinary RRSP or RRIF, which can be collapsed at any time, but you can transfer it to a locked-in RRSP or a locked-in Retirement Account. The rules governing locked-in accounts both before and after retirement are more stringent than those governing ordinary registered accounts. Nothing can be withdrawn from either a locked-in RRSP or a locked-in Retirement Account. The money stays and earns sheltered investment income until you are at least 55 (if you are retired) and no older than 69. At that time, the money can be transferred to one or a combination of:

- a life annuity
- a Life Income Fund (LIF)
- a Life Retirement Income Fund (LRIF) in Saskatchewan or Alberta

Since pensions are provincially regulated, you are allowed to transfer your commuted pension entitlements only to a locked-in plan that has the blessing of the registering province, even if you move somewhere else. In other words, if your former employer's pension plan was registered in, say, Quebec, you have to transfer the funds to a Quebec-approved plan, even if you choose to move to British Columbia. If your former employer had a federally regulated plan, you are restricted to other federally regulated plans.

LIFE INCOME FUNDS

A LIF is sort of like a RRIF, only more restrictive. With both types of funds, you are required to withdraw a minimum amount each year. However, while there is no maximum amount you can withdraw from a RRIF, there is with a LIF (see Table 11–7). With a RRIF, you never have to give up control of the investments in your plan until you die; with a LIF, you have to buy a life annuity in the year in which you turn 80. With a RRIF, there's no requirement to indicate a spousal survivor benefit; with a LIF, the life annuity you are compelled to buy must have a 60% spousal survivor benefit. With a RRIF, you can use your spouse's age to determine the minimum withdrawal—a big help if your spouse is younger than you and you want to take out only the minimum amount. With a LIF, you have to use your own age.

LIFE RETIREMENT INCOME FUNDS

If you leave a company that has a registered pension plan that is registered in Alberta or Saskatchewan, you have a third choice: transferring your locked-in funds to an LRIF. It differs from a LIF

in two ways: you don't have to buy a life annuity at 80, and the maximum amount you can withdraw in any year is calculated differently.

TABLE 11–7 **Minimum and Maximum LIF Withdrawals, 1997**

AGE ON JAN. 1	LIF MINIMUM %	6% LIF MAXIMUM*
55	2.8	6.45
56	2.9	6.51
57	3.03	6.57
58	3.13	6.63
59	3.22	6.70
60	3.33	6.77
61	3.45	6.85
62	3.57	6.94
63	3.70	7.04
64	3.85	7.14
65	4.00	7.25
66	4.17	7.38
67	4.35	7.52
68	4.54	7.67
69	4.76	7.83
70	5.00	8.02
71	7.38	8.225
72	7.48	8.44
73	7.59	8.71
74	7.71	9.00
75	7.85	9.33
76	7.99	9.71
77	8.15	10.15
78	8.33	10.66
79	8.53	11.25

*For the first 15 years of a LIF, the maximum may be higher than 6% if long-term bond rates are higher.

MAKING THE BEST CHOICES

Your age and your assets are the prime determinants of your choices. If you are nearing the end of your full-time job, you have fewer choices, so let's start there.

Depending on your assets, you may need to change the allocation of the assets in your RRIF. A number of studies and surveys by academics, accountants and financial planners are in categorical agreement that the risk of outliving your money grows as you age. (The first critical reader of this book thought I put that statement in as a joke: "Of course the older you are and the more you spend, the more likely it is that your money runs out," she said. Sure, it's obvious; and maybe it's the most important piece of information in the book. But the number of people who pay no attention to this possibility until it's too late, and so live out their lives in relative poverty, is far too high.) That means that if your assets are modest—namely under $600,000 at age 60—you need to consider shifting to an equity portfolio. With interest rates at single-digit levels, it takes around 15 years to double your money. Equity investments typically make three times the return of more conservative investments.

The only circumstance under which it is advisable to buy a life annuity is if you have decided to buy or already own life insurance of an equivalent amount. By buying a life annuity with no guaranteed period or last-survivor clauses, you ensure both the highest possible guaranteed annuity income and a tax-free estate, as life insurance is not taxable at death.

Making these choices can be complicated enough that you should consider consulting with a financial planner. Failing that, there are a number of software programs that will allow you to plug in your own numbers and make your own scenarios. Or try www.retireweb.com to begin. This is a website developed by an entrepreneurial Canadian software maker on a "shareware" basis (donations welcome). Its home page (reproduced on page 230) offers an accessible entry to retirement planning.

CHART 11–1 **RetireWeb Home Page**

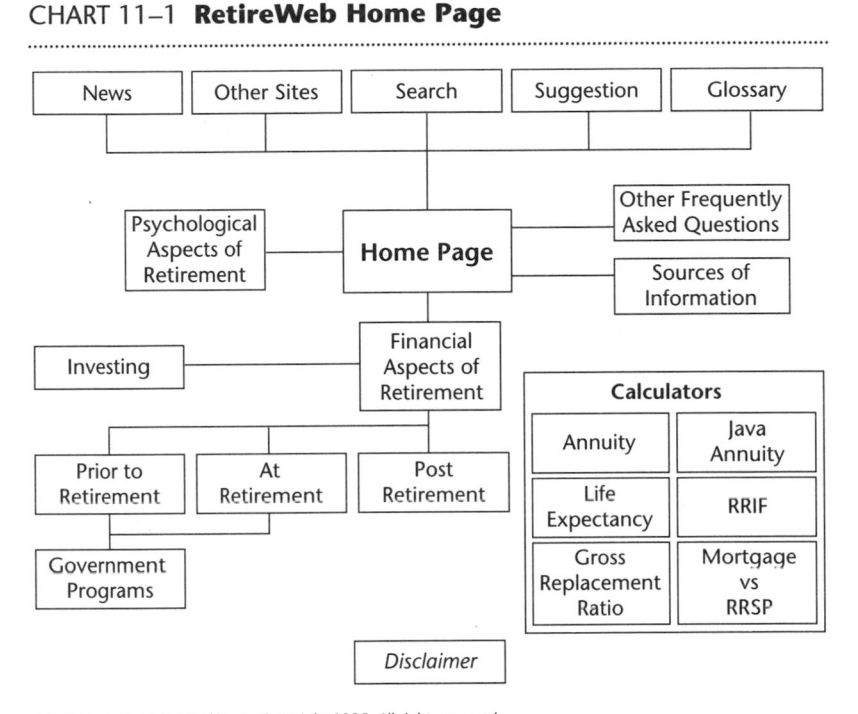

Site designed by Scott Parkinson. Copyright 1995. All rights reserved.

There are, as you well know, dozens of money management and retirement books available. What is less well known is the vast array of information available on the Internet. I am particularly enamoured of a book co-authored by Jim Carroll and Rick Broadhead called *Canadian Money Management Online*. If you're into the Net, the book is invaluable, as it leads you to suppliers of products, as well as calculators that allow you to plug in your own numbers for "what if" scenarios.

12

Estate
Planning

Not everything that can be counted counts,
and not everything that counts can be counted.
—Albert Einstein

WHEN YOU'RE RELATIVELY young and learning the rules of
the life game, planning the end doesn't have a high priority—
although game strategists tell us that visualizing the whole game
makes a difference to how you play it. (We explored some of
that long-term planning in Chapters 9 and 10.) Most of us think
estate planning is something you do in retirement, in your last
decades. But then, most of us don't plan much of anything
when we're young. If we plan at all, it's for the shorter term: a
vacation, education, family, etc. Besides, when we're young we
don't have many assets, and no dependants, and we can't visu-
alize ourselves as dependent. Yet even for young adults, estate
planning has relevance. By the time we're 20 or 25, most of us
have some notion of how we want to be cared for if we become
seriously ill, what quality of life we want, whether we want to
be resuscitated in the event of a catastrophic accident. And we
may have sufficient assets that we'd like them deployed in
particular ways.

If you're somewhat older, whether you're thinking about retirement or not, if you haven't spent some formal time dealing with your estate planning needs, you should, because you have to face the fact that you're going to die some day. Okay, even if you don't really believe that, consider the possibility that there will be a part of your life when you won't be working and may not be able to look after your own affairs. Having a plan for such an eventuality is part of estate planning.

You've spent a lifetime accumulating stuff. Estate planning can be as simple as deciding that your stuff has no value to anyone, and you don't care what happens to it after you go. But most of us are a little more attached to the stuff we've got, or concerned about the people in our lives. Or we're determined not to give the government any more than it has already got from us.

So one way or another, you're going to spend some time devising a plan for the "it" that you can't take with you. This chapter is intended to help you focus efficiently, and impress on you the importance of establishing an estate planning program.

BEFORE YOU GO

I find the question, "What happens if I can't manage my own affairs?" much harder to deal with than, "What happens after I die?" It's really hard to think of being unable to be in charge. This is even more difficult for young people, but the fact is that anyone, at any age, can be in an accident that mentally incapacitates them. Indeed, statistics show that in the prime of our lives, we're four times more likely to be disabled than to die.

If such an event happens to you, not your wife, husband or any other close relative or friend has the automatic legal right to direct your finances. They would have to go to court to get that right. They wouldn't even necessarily be able to deal with things they own jointly with you—for example, the home you own jointly that now has to be sold. Luckily, making a contingency plan for such a circumstance is not complicated. It involves creating three documents:

- a signed, up-to-date power of attorney for your financial affairs,
- a signed, up-to-date power of attorney for your personal care, and
- a "living will" that provides instructions about medical treatment in the event of a catastrophic illness or accident.

A financial power of attorney is simply a legal document that gives the person you name the right to manage your financial affairs if you aren't able to. It has a very limited life. As long as you are alive and in charge, the document has no authority. If you are temporarily or permanently unable to look after your financial affairs, the power of attorney gives that power to the person you have named. If you die, the power of attorney dies with you. Then the instructions you've written in your will take over.

You should discuss your power of attorney with the person you want to name, to be sure they are willing and able to act on your behalf, and you should review your decision once a year to be sure the person you've named is still the person you want and that they are still prepared to step in if necessary.

If you value the people closest to you as well as your financial assets, you need a financial power of attorney. If you don't have one, a government bureaucrat will take charge (and charge you for his services). And if you don't say the right things in the right language, the power of attorney can be invalid. As this is an area overseen by the province in which you live, you need a lawyer to make sure your financial power of attorney is properly done. It's not expensive, and the "do-it-yourself" kits available are chancy.

The important thing to understand in creating a power of attorney is that the person you select in case you become incapacitated will be able to do everything with your financial assets that you are able to do. You can limit the powers of your named "Second in Command," but you need to think through the possible repercussions of such a decision as carefully as about giving

full authority. Although this is a simple document, it requires serious thought. A legal professional will help you think through the various issues.

The second document you should consider creating is a "personal-care" power of attorney so that someone you trust (rather than a stranger from the government) can make decisions about how you'll be looked after if you become incapacitated. This document is not as essential as a financial power of attorney, if you are content to leave it to your family to make these personal decisions for you. Nevertheless, it provides the authority to whomever you name to speak for you when you can't speak for yourself. In provinces that have accepted "living wills," a power of attorney for personal care can be incorporated into the financial power of attorney. The provinces are in various states of acceptance of this type of document.

A "living will" is the third document you need to cover dealing with the possibility that you will be alive but unable to make your own decisions. A "living will" has nothing to do with your assets. It gives instructions as to *how* you are going to die. As long as you are alive and in command of your faculties, you can tell your doctors what treatments you want or don't want. However, if you are unconscious or mentally incapacitated, doctors assume you agree to any and all treatments and so-called heroic measures they have at their disposal. A "living will" is your statement of what treatment and how much you want. If you have created a personal-care power of attorney, the person you've named can put forward your desires regarding, for example, being kept alive on mechanical support systems or not. A living will can also document your desires regarding, for example, pain medications and organ donation. Not all provinces consider "living wills" to be legal documents, but even if you live in one that does not, such a document gives your family greater understanding of what treatment you would have accepted or refused had you been able to.

It goes without saying that you need to be as explicit and as clear as possible about your wishes, so it's a good idea not just to

ask the people you want to name whether they'll act for you should the need arise, but also to discuss with them your thoughts on the financial and personal-care aspects of your life. The more they know about how you feel, the better able they'll be to articulate your desires. And you need to point out that even though they love you and want to do all they can to keep you with them, they are being asked to speak for *you*, to tell others what *your* wishes are, not to articulate their own.

It also goes without saying that all these documents must be accessible when they're needed. Tell your nominees where to find the documents they will need. (I have left my powers of attorney with my lawyer, and have told my family to contact him immediately should anything bad happen to me.)

Finally, the documents should be reviewed once a year, partly to make sure that your desires haven't changed and partly to make sure the people you named are still willing and able—and suitable—to act for you.

AFTER YOU'VE GONE

The main reason you need a will is that if you don't leave a set of instructions about who gets what, the government rules decide, and it would be a miracle if the government rules corresponded with what you wanted. But there are also other reasons for having a valid will:

- it makes the life of those who have an interest in you and your estate easier;
- your assets can be distributed faster; and
- in all likelihood, your estate will pay less tax.

If you don't have a will, or nobody knows where it is, each province has an intestacy formula that dictates where your money will go. And don't think for a minute that it will all go to your spouse. If you're married with children, your spouse may or may not get a lump sum before the balance is paid out. If you

have children, they may share two-thirds of your estate; your spouse would get one-third. Check out the intestacy rules in your province. It's easy to do: any financial institution will have a pamphlet on the subject. Dying without writing down what you want done with your assets is not the best of goodbyes.

Most Canadians must be under the delusion that if they write a will, they will immediately thereafter die, as most of them don't have wills. Apparently, they like paying taxes and don't give a hoot what happens to their family and friends. What? That's not you? Then listen up. Making a will does not spell death. It has no validity while you're alive, so you can change it as often as you want. Even if you don't change it, you are not bound by it while you're alive. Neither does it have to be complicated or be written in complicated language. Get it? So do it.

True, a will is a formal document; so there are specific things that must be true of you, and it, for it to be valid. You must be mentally competent. You must be of legal age (usually 18); if you're a minor, you can still have a will if you're married or in the armed forces. The will has to specify:

- who is writing the will (the "testator"), and when, i.e., it has to be dated;
- that it is the *last* will, and supersedes any others you may have written;
- who will carry out the instructions in the will and do all the legal tidying up after you're gone (the "executor");
- instructions to pay any debts, taxes, and medical and funeral expenses before the estate is distributed, and
- who will get what (the "beneficiaries").

These are the bare essentials of all wills. You can have lots of other instructions and details, but they will depend on what your assets consist of, and who your beneficiaries are. For example, if you have young children, you may want to specify who you would like to look after them. (Make sure you've first checked

it out with the people you name, to be sure they're willing.) You may want to have part of your assets managed in trust for one or more of your beneficiaries. If you do, you have to state who the trustee is to be, and what powers he or she will have. The trusts may last until a specified age, or for the life of the beneficiaries.

There are a lot of things to think about when it comes to writing your will, so it's a good idea to start early and get some practice. This is one of the best exercises to get you thinking clearly about what you have and how you want it deployed, both during your life and after it.

There are several different ways to write a will. Not all of them require the services of a professional, but it's wise to seek advice to make sure you do it right. The simplest will is one you write by hand. It's called a "holographic" will. But if yours is much more complicated than "I leave everything I own to ____," go to a professional. It doesn't cost a lot, and it can save your beneficiaries a great deal of heartache. You can buy a "do-it-yourself" will, but the same cautions apply as with do-it-yourself powers of attorney. The last thing you want is for a badly drawn up will to be declared invalid, or to be contested by your beneficiaries. A lawyer or financial planner will suggest ways of getting what you want done efficiently and cost-effectively. Get advice even if you decide to make a holographic will.

A formal will other than a holographic one has to be dated, signed and witnessed by two people who are not beneficiaries of the will. A holographic will cannot have anything on it except the handwriting of the person making the will. Therefore, it should not be witnessed.

There are ways other than a will of ensuring that your assets are distributed according to your wishes. You can give them away before you die. Obviously, this is a strategy for people who are certain they have enough for their personal needs, and for people who are close to the end. As I've suggested throughout this book, there are good reasons to contemplate this strategy, among

them lower taxes and the advantage of making people happy while you can still appreciate their thank-yous. You need to get professional advice on the "attribution" rules that determine who will pay tax on the income earned from your gift. (The gift itself is tax free; only the increased value of the gift thereafter is taxable.) For example, if you give stocks or bonds to your spouse, or to children or grandchildren under 18, you will continue to be responsible for the taxes due on interest, dividends and capital gains. If you give such gifts to adult children or grandchildren, they are responsible for paying the tax. (Look back at Chapter 10 to see some tax planning suggestions related to giving assets and saving taxes.)

When you die, your will becomes a legal document. Make sure the people closest to you, including the executor, know where it is. Most wills need to be probated, that is, approved by the court for the transfer of ownership of the assets. The exceptions to probate are:

- if the estate is small, the instructions in the will are simple, and no third parties (such as financial institutions) have to be dealt with, or
- if the will is a "notarial" will, which is available only in Quebec, and if the deceased has no assets outside the province.

All other wills have to be probated. Probate is a fairly short process, usually proceeding within a couple of months. Probate fees (read taxes) vary. Most provinces have a sliding scale, depending of the size of the estate. With the exception of Alberta and Quebec, whose maximum fees vary from under $100 (Quebec) to $6,000 (Alberta), no province has a maximum fee. Thus, we can consider probate fees in most provinces to be a thinly disguised death tax. As accountant and author Tim Cestnick says, "What looks like a tax, acts like a tax, and hurts like a tax, is a tax."

There's no sign that any government in Canada is thinking of reimposing death taxes or succession duties any time soon. (Being unfair to taxpayers is not the motive; unless every province did it uniformly, people would move their assets to the province where they would be most lightly taxed.) However, any province could, at any time, increase the taxes to probate a will. British Columbia and Ontario recently raised the fees charged to have the courts certify that a will is valid. On even a modest estate, these fees, which go to the province, can be substantial. Suppose your estate adds up to $600,000. If you live in Ontario, you'll pay the government $250 on the first $50,000 and $15 per $1,000 on the balance. That comes to $8,500 over and above the capital-gains taxes your estate will owe on your death. If you live in British Columbia, your estate will pay $14 per $1,000, or $8,400. Go back to Chapter 10 to review a few of the ways of avoiding some of these probate taxes.

There are overt taxes as well. Yes, you remember correctly: estate taxes were abolished in Canada 25 years ago. Nevertheless, probate taxes are only one of your worries. Unless you are leaving everything to your spouse (wedded or common-law except in Quebec), your entire estate is subject to final, "terminal" tax, i.e., the last one ever filed on your behalf (see following).

YOUR EXECUTOR

Being an executor is a big job, even if you are dealing with a simple will and few assets. One of the duties of your executor is to file an income tax return to account for the income you earned up to the time of your death. This tax return is no different than any other you've filed. However, since this is the last one filed on your behalf, it is supposed to include all income on which taxes are owing, and is due on April 30 of the year following that in which you died. This tax return will include taxes due on your income to the date of death and the capital gains from the deemed sale of every asset you own. This doesn't mean your executor has to sell anything. Revenue Canada considers that all

your assets are sold at "fair market value" whether or not they have been sold. This is an important distinction.

All taxable assets are valued at their price on December 31, 1971 (when capital-gains tax in Canada began), or, if purchased after that date, the price for which they were bought. That value is subtracted from their value on the date of your death. The difference is taxable. The easiest way of figuring this out is to make a copy of the financial planning worksheets in Appendix 2. List the assets not left to your spouse, their cost base and their current market value. Then calculate the profits on which taxes will be due. If you have capital losses, subtract them before you estimate the taxes. Three quarters of all capital gains are taxable at ordinary tax rates. The other quarter is tax free. Your RRSP is treated as if you cashed it in just before you died, unless it is going to your spouse. And the money in it is taxed as ordinary income.

There may be some income coming in that takes your executor longer than the period between death and the due date of the next tax return. If that is the case, additional tax returns can be filed. Examples of such income are income from a business or trust that has a year-end other than the calendar year-end. (Tax planning for small business is dealt with below.)

WHAT'S NOT INCLUDED IN THE FINAL TAX RETURN

- Your principal residence, that is, the home in which you live, is not included. You can leave it to anyone you want, tax free. However, if you're married, your spouse is protected by law from being turned out of the house. If you don't designate a beneficiary for your home, it becomes part of your estate, and will attract capital-gains tax if its value increases between the date of your death and the date of the sale or transfer.
- Your RRSP is not included if it's left to your spouse. The difference between this and a home is that the tax is deferred on the savings vehicles only until your spouse dies.

If, however, the spouse remarries, the RRSP can again be rolled over to the surviving spouse of the new marriage. Tax is collected when the last spouse dies. (Also, if you have unused contributions to your RRSP at the time of your death, and you have a spouse, your executor can contribute to a spousal RRSP in order to create an additional deduction for the final income tax return.)

- Your RRIF is not included if you have a spouse. The spouse can continue to get the income from it, or it can be transferred to the spouse. If the spouse is under 69 and doesn't need the income, your RRIF can be converted back into an RRSP. That way, no income need be taken out: the whole thing is tax sheltered until the spouse converts it into a RRIF.
- If you don't have a spouse, but are supporting a dependent child or grandchild under 18, the proceeds from your RRSP or RRIF can be used to buy an annuity for that person.
- Eligible farm property can pass to the children, grandchildren or even great grandchildren without attracting capital-gains tax. If it is sold, it may qualify for a special $500,000 exemption from capital gains.
- Charitable donations create a non-refundable tax credit that would reduce or eliminate the taxes due on your terminal tax return.
- Life insurance is not included, but only if you've named a beneficiary other than your estate. If you have, it passes directly to the named people, tax free, and will not be included in your estate for probate-fee purposes.

WHAT IS A SPOUSE?

Generally speaking, a spouse is a person who is legally married to another person. In the Income Tax Act, the legally married spouse is the one who has the rights to the family home, the rollover rights to RRSPs and RRIFs, and the right to be supported by the proceeds of the estate before any other beneficiary benefits.

Since the trend towards common-law marriages has become so pronounced and permanent, the Income Tax Act also recognizes most of the same rights for common-law spouses. The exception is the right to property. Common-law rights do not at present extend to same-sex couples.

If you are in a common-law relationship, it is prudent to signify this in writing. There are a couple of ways of doing this. Naming each other as beneficiaries in each of your wills is one way to do it. Owning property jointly is another. Having a legal document stating your wishes with regard to property and support is a third.

If you are supporting a former spouse and/or children, make sure you know what's in your separation or divorce agreements, and make sure it corresponds to what is in your will. If your will says (implicitly or explicitly) that your former spouse is not a beneficiary, you may want (or have) to make other arrangements in order for the payments to continue. Buying insurance is the usual way of doing that.

USING LIFE INSURANCE FOR ESTATE PLANNING

Aside from the suggestion made above, life insurance has several uses in estate planning. It has always been an "instant estate" for people to leave to their heirs.

If you have a mortgage, the mortgage holder might suggest, or insist, that you have sufficient life insurance to pay it off should you die before it is retired. Even if the mortgage holder doesn't ask, you may want to consider it.

You may use life insurance to pay off your outstanding debts at death, or to pay the expenses associated with your death. These include the probating of your will, the cost of your funeral, the taxes that will be triggered at death, etc. If you have life insurance, none of your assets will have to be sold to pay these estate costs. Part of all good estate planning involves reviewing your assets and estimating your tax liability at death. Then you can decide whether you want to buy insurance, or whether your assets

will cover the taxes. The way to estimate that tax liability is simple. Use one of the worksheets in the appendices. List your assets. Remember that even if you have a spouse to leave assets to, any asset apart from your home, RRSP or RRIF will have a tax liability. This is one important reason to keep records, so you can easily subtract the price you paid for the asset, as the difference is subject to capital-gains tax. (You might want to leaf back to Chapter 10 to review the more complex strategy for making your estate tax free.)

WHAT KIND OF INSURANCE?

There are lots of different kinds of insurance, but all of them are variations on two basic kinds: the kind you rent and the kind you own. Insurance companies used to sell what they wanted to sell, until they smartened up and began offering people insurance that people understood and wanted to buy. Now you can buy life insurance that pays before you die as well as when you die.

Term insurance is rented. You contract for both a specific amount of money that will be paid on your death and for a specific term—one year, 10 years, to age 100, etc. It is the least expensive kind of life insurance you can buy, and is often bought by young people who have dependants and few assets. It is also commonly used to cover estate debts and tax liabilities. With all but the term-to-100 policies, the premium will increase each time you wish to renew it. That's because as you get older, the likelihood of you dying increases. So if you have a 10-year term, for example, the premiums will stay the same for 10 years, and then will rise sharply because you're 10 years older. If you are considering this type of policy, make sure that the insurance company guarantees that you will be able to renew it, even if your health has changed.

Here's an example of how term insurance might work to pay the taxes payable at death. Let's assume that you're a 65-year-old non-smoking woman whose RRSP is worth $300,000. It's growing at the rate of 8% a year (inflation = 3%), and you have decided

that you won't withdraw money until the year after you change to a RRIF, and then you'll withdraw the minimum.

TABLE 12–1 **Sample RRSP Earnings, Withdrawals and Tax Liability at Death**

AGE	ANNUAL WITHDRAWALS	RRSP/RRIF BALANCE	TAX LIABILITY AT DEATH
65	$0	$300,000	$150,000
70	19,000	361,000	180,500
75	25,000	360,000	168,500
80	41,000	435,000	217,500

A term policy for $200,000 that would cover most of the tax liability at death would cost this woman about $4,500 a year. (A similar policy for a man would cost about $6,000.) The rule of thumb is that such a policy costs 2%–3% of the cash paid out at death.

The kind of insurance you own is called "whole life." Not only is your life insured but you also get a savings component, available either as a loan or as a cash payment if you cancel the life insurance. This is great if you buy it when you're young and healthy, because you get the same premium for life.

There are several variations on these two basic types of insurance. Universal life, for example, combines the best features of both. You buy term insurance for a specific premium and pay an additional premium for an investment vehicle that will provide income in addition to the face value of the insurance you buy. The face value of the insurance is guaranteed; the amount of additional income will depend on the investment performance.

With some of these hybrid policies, the policy owner will be able to select the types of investments. With others, the insurance company will do the selection. Some of the hybrids allow the policy holder to change the face value of the insurance component, either increasing or decreasing it as circumstances change. One estate planning technique (described more fully in Chapter

10) is to buy one of these policies, accumulate significant cash in the investment component, and then take the policy to the bank as collateral to borrow up to 75% of the balance in the investment account, with an agreement stating that the bank gets its loan repaid from the proceeds of the death benefit. If you consider such a policy, ask about flexible terms for paying the premium. Obviously, you can pay the premium for life, or to age 100, but you can also opt for a schedule that allows you to pay larger premiums for six or 10 years, at which time your policy will be fully paid for.

So, for example, if you're 50 and plan to retire at 60, you may buy a policy and pay premiums for as long as you are working, at premium levels large enough that thereafter, the policy is completely paid up and remains in force until you die, without you having to pay premiums out of your fixed retirement income.

Joint and last-to-die insurance is also available to partners (usually married) who have assets they want to pass on to the next generation. These insurance policies don't pay out until the second partner dies.

In addition, a relatively new insurance vehicle has been developed for Canadians. I say "relatively new" although this type of policy has long been available to citizens of countries without universal health and medical care. Now that more Canadians worry that the health care system won't be there when they need it, the insurance industry has come up with "critical illness" or "dread disease" insurance. You can now insure yourself against a few dozen medical conditions: if you survive 30 days after diagnosis, the policy pays its face value in a lump sum. This may be worth considering, as the money is paid directly to the policy holder.

IF YOU HAVE A BUSINESS

If you are the owner of a small business or partnership, or a family business, you have to do estate planning for the business as well as for your family. If you are the key asset of the business, you

have two choices. One is to buy "key person" insurance, which would provide money to hire someone to replace you. The other choice is to sell the business while it is still a going concern and you are around to offer advice for continuity.

If yours is a family business, you have to deal with such difficult questions as, do you leave it to your family equally, or to a particular person? There are no "right" answers, but recent Canadian history is filled with family strife—and the demise of family businesses—because no estate or succession planning was done.

Insurance is often used to protect small-business partners. For example, partners can buy joint insurance that will pay out when the first partner dies. The purpose of this is to give the surviving partner sufficient funds to buy out the deceased partner's share of the business.

An increasingly common estate planning and retirement technique when a business is involved is estate "freezing." This technique consists of "freezing" the value of an asset in your hands, even while the value is appreciating, for example, by exchanging the common shares in your business for voting preferred shares. The preferred shares have a fixed redemption price and pay sufficient dividends that you are ensured an adequate income when you retire. As the shares are voting shares, you keep control of the business. The beneficiaries, or a trust, acquire new common shares. The value of all future growth will accrue to these shares.

A properly executed freeze will accomplish several desirable outcomes: avoiding immediate tax consequences, keeping control of the business, ensuring retirement income, and timing the transfer of the business to your successors. In all cases, ensuring the continuity of a business will likely require the services of one or several professionals. The important thing, as with all estate planning, is to do it.

13

Making It Work: Future Tense

The road to success is always under construction.

THIS BOOK HAS NOT BEEN AN easy read. I've often wished my chosen subject was more entertaining, if not downright comedy. If you've worked through every chapter, you've come a long way. You'll understand that I wrote it because the world has changed so much that you can't rely on standard advice alone if you want to have a comfortable retirement. (In fact, the world is changing so rapidly, you can't predict what will happen next.) But you have the map to know with some degree of certainty where you want to go and what it will take to get there.

Before concluding, however, I want to leave you with a key piece of advice: the future hasn't happened yet. Over time *anything* can happen. So let me give you some rules of thumb for handling uncertainty. Call this Cohen's Guide to Political Risk.

Political risk arises from what governments do or don't do. If a policy change can harm your investment, then it is at political risk. But don't despair: political risk can be estimated, and these estimates factored into your investment decisions.

Let's take an example: How smooth is the globalization process?

There are lots of books about preparing for the next millennium. Most look at the demographics, and the globalization process, and the consensus is that this process is irreversible. Maybe it is. But before the Great Depression there were those who thought the prosperity of the 1920s would ensure that the world could sort out its imbalances and move forward, too.

In fact, there are arguments that progress might be blocked. And there are certainly some good reasons for thinking the process will be less than smooth even if it does go forward. For instance, about half the world's population still doesn't participate in the global economy. When the Soviet Union broke up, it looked as though hundreds of millions more people would be able to share in the opportunities available to market-oriented economies; it didn't happen. As well, Russia is in a state of economic anarchy from which rapid recovery seems impossible. In the wake of the "Asian financial contagion," the number of people not participating is again rising. Moreover, capital does not yet circulate freely in China, and Indonesia is in a tailspin under the tough-love treatment of the IMF. Latin America is teetering on a knife-edge. Japan is mired in a long-lasting slump. Sub-Saharan Africa is more or less out of globalism; local warfare is increasing.

So far, Western Europe and the U.S. have seemed inoculated against these problems. But each region has its Achilles heel: Russia, desperate for foreign exchange, and a major producer of the industrial world's most needed commodities, from nickel to natural gas, is keeping commodity prices low by flooding the industrial world with supply.

Any number of events have the potential of tipping equity markets into deflation: war in the Balkans, civil war in Russia, a problem with the introduction of the euro or a change in the policies of the German central bank (perhaps to head off rising anti-democratic forces in former East Germany), all could affect European markets. A market meltdown in Brazil or Argentina could tip the U.S. equity market into deflation.

So what to do about these all too possible situations? When

considering risk, we need to remember a little high school math of probabilities. As I write, financial analysts give about a 25% chance of further negative impact on the market from events in the world's troubled regions. That means one chance in four. All else being equal, you can protect your investment against this risk in three ways:

1. Stay out of any investment that could be seriously affected by these situations. (The advice to "stay out of all equities" may seem a little excessive, as you might lose profitable opportunities.)
2. Invest only if the investment offers a 25% or higher return above the average market return; and/or
3. Invest 25% less in the equities market and put that 25% in a risk-free investment that pays close to average market return discounted by 25%. So, if the stock paying no dividend would be expected to increase in value by 15% over the year without the impact of global problems, then an equivalent risk-free financial instrument (such as a GIC, U.S. bond or strip, for example) would pay around 10% in real returns. To whatever degree it pays less (current yields are around 5.25%), you absorb that proportion of the risk. Still, a 4% risk is a lot better than a 25% risk.

Of course, if any one event could occur once in four, what are the chances of any two occurring? If the events are unconnected, there is one chance in 16 of any two occurring together. (Multiply the probabilities of each single event [1/4 x 1/4] to get the probability of both events occurring.)

Unfortunately, it's a bit more complicated, as we know that all these events may be connected. Short-term capital flows can operate like a hot potato: "hot" (i.e., speculative) money melts out of one economy by surging into others, bidding up the price of the receiving country's money. The inflow raises domestic prices and lowers interest rates, effectively inflating values until

there are no more gains to be had. Moreover, as the country continues to import, it develops substantial deficits on its trading account. In reaction to this, speculators sell the inflated currency, forcing down its value, bringing shakily regulated banks to their knees, destroying ordinary people's savings, driving up interest rates and generally trashing the economy. As the highest profits are the first to leave the economy, the "hot" money melts away as traders act like a crowd leaving a burning dance hall, to begin the cycle in the next small-country currency. (The IMF then comes in, offering debt relief to foreign bankers caught in the rush and, by imposing stern deflationary measures on the domestic economy, ensures that small savers never recover.)

So far, this depressing story has limited itself to just a few countries. The hot potato scenario has turned out to be inaccurate in its latest incarnation. Instead of "hot" money cascading from one small currency to the next, trouble provokes an immediate flight to quality. Rather than continued speculation, the "hot" money heads for the huge pools of reserve currencies like the U.S. dollar, the German mark and the Swiss franc. The massive scale of U.S. and European capital markets has been enough to absorb the shocks from the turbulence in smaller economies. Nevertheless, continued chaos and depression and the flooding of world commodity markets certainly can, if they continue, tip other currencies and countries into the whirlpool. That's why many investors fear Latin America could be next.

Let's play out a couple of "what if" scenarios. Suppose a bad event in one place makes another bad event twice as likely to occur. For example, suppose there's one chance in four that the economic meltdown in Indonesia will adversely impact the market. Suppose further that if it occurs, there is one chance in two that the market will also be impacted by meltdown in Thailand (and vice versa). The probability of the two events occurring together doubles from one chance in 16 to two in 16 (i.e. from [1/4 x 1/4] to [1/4 x 2/4]). You can see that when events are connected, the market gets progressively riskier than if the events

were independent. If you suppose that the occurrence of those two events raises the probability of a third event (say, the negative impact from a meltdown in Malaysia) to three in four, then the total risk from the three combined events jumps from one in 64 (1/4 x 1/4 x 1/4) to six in 64 (1/4 x 2/4 x 3/4), i.e., between 9% and 10%, making the market very much riskier than if those events were independent of one another. However, the cascade of bad events remains about 2.5 times less likely than the initial trigger event. Therefore, the key risk remains that first triggering occurrence: if you can protect yourself against that, then for practical purposes you can ignore the possibility of the cascade.

So let's accept that at present there's a 25% chance that markets will be severely impacted by future events in Asia. Is this the end of globalization?

That would be very unlikely. Remember, in my view, four sea changes have already occurred and can't be undone:

CHANGE #1

National economies that were once relatively closed have now become relatively open. Even if the process stays static with respect to middle-income countries, I think it's bound to continue among the more advanced countries because of technology. This new openness has already changed the way national economies work, in the sense that there are very few feedback loops that happen nationally anymore. Prices are set by international supply and demand. Just-in-time manufacturing means that inventories don't accumulate much anymore. Firms now generally concentrate on their "core competencies" and make alliances for the complementary goods or services they need for a complete value chain. These alliances are international so that their networks can flow around obstacles in order to generate high returns.

Moreover, money itself has achieved an existence beyond the control of governments, although coordinated government policies can, to some extent, affect the direction of

flows according to real rates of return. Thus, investment security is no longer so much a matter of rules and regulations as it is of individual investment strategies. Although obviously the strength and capability of a nation's financial supervisory system is fundamental, the idea that governments can impose security through taxes and barriers is simply untrue. For example, when "hot" money destabilizes a country, the government will try to limit the flow of short-term capital into and out of the country. (An economist, James Tobin, suggested some years ago that a tax on capital flows might be enough to discourage speculators, and that idea has its followers. Governments may succeed in imposing a "Tobin tax," but that will simply raise the cost of capital and thereby make investment, entrepreneurship and job creation more difficult in areas that have the tax.)

The more fundamental point is that economic activity is shifting from individual countries to three identifiable regions: the Western Hemisphere, Western Europe and its hinterland, and Asia-Pacific. Effective economic policy instruments will have to have regional dimensions as well. This has been explicitly acknowledged in Europe for some time, but not in Asia and the Americas. Instead of an overarching commission as in Europe, the Western Hemisphere countries are controlled by the dominant U.S. market. We are all a kind of 13th federal reserve district and we hang on the reports of the Federal Open Market Committee and the Congressional testimony of the Chairman to see what the economic weather will be.

Growing international regionalism has enormous implications for small countries like Canada. It means that inevitably Canada's ability to make domestic policy will migrate to regional and multilateral institutions. Public policy will be less and less national and more and more that of groups with alphabet-soup names: OECD, G8, etc. Currencies will come under regional control. Even if the Canadian dollar does not disappear, its supply will be linked to money stocks in the U.S. and offshore. (Indeed, the market already makes these connections.) Policy is likely to

strengthen those links and make them more explicit. In other areas as well, such as telecommunications, civil aviation, and the so-called cultural industries, Canadian insistence on "exceptions" to the rules will disappear, or else economic dynamism will simply bypass these sectors.

This has important implications for your retirement planning, as it suggests that the best values are to be had in companies that have already successfully globalized or that have the potential for successful globalization. This will likely diversify your portfolio from the domestic requirement for your RRSP that 80% of its value be in "Canadian" stocks. This trend also puts a long-term question mark over the viability of Canada's investment industry, given the restrictions on investing abroad and the 15% withholding tax that operates on all cross-border assets. (However, these artificial barriers to the free flow of capital will give way, sooner or later, to greater global openness.)

There will also likely emerge a North America–wide small-payments system for e-commerce. This already exists for credit- and debit-card payments. The problem is that while you can make deposits in U.S. financial institutions, there is major inconvenience in cashing cheques drawn on Canadian banks in the U.S. The banks themselves probably will not fix this problem, but on-line financial services will, especially intermediaries specializing in electronic cash. Indeed, these are already with us, but play a very minor role. With the development of on-line commerce, such remaining distortions will inevitably disappear.

CHANGE #2

Another established trend has become a new rule of the game, even if many policy makers are still in denial about it. It is this: innovation is the universal solvent and technology is its widest application. The Japanese manufacturing revolution underlined the arrival of this reality 20 years ago. Having no space for inventory storage, the Japanese auto companies created just-in-

time delivery in the assembly process. Having no sources of cheap energy, Japanese products were designed to be energy efficient. (Thus, when energy prices took off in the early '80s, Japan had a major advantage.)

Another example is software. Consider the next wave in computing. As Microsoft owns the desktop, any innovator must work around that fact. Along comes Java, which moved in to take over the links, thereby undercutting the desktop's importance.

There are many examples in banking. For instance, look how electronic banking through your computer bypasses (and undercuts the investment the banks have made in) automatic teller machines and specialized networks like Interac, which was set up by the Big Six Canadian banks 10 years ago so they could back away from branching. Imagine what banking would be like today if Microsoft and Quicken (then the world's largest financial management software company) had been allowed to merge. Every desktop could have been linked via the Microsoft network, to the accounts payable and accounts receivable of virtually every small business in North America: real-time accounts settlement North America–wide. (To understand the dimensions of the savings involved, add up your own bank and accounting charges and multiply them by the number of consumers on the network.) So, innovation is the key to economic growth and today's information- and bio-technologies make commercially successful innovation easier than ever before. It is unlikely the slump in equities will change this. Declines in equity prices will simply make debt easier to get—and debt is the preferred vehicle for entrepreneurs. So innovation will continue.

What has this got to do with retirement planning? First, it might change your idea of retirement. Experienced people with capital can participate in this process as "angels" to new inventors. Keeping some assets liquid and working with knowledgeable intermediaries can enable you to help some wonderful innovation come to life. But even if you choose not to participate in the development of innovation, your retirement will nevertheless be

vastly improved by innovation; for innovation will change the way we live. Which brings us to—

CHANGE #3

Increasingly, the Internet will be the computer. Being connected is increasing, and getting easier. It will continue to change the ways we work and what we do with our leisure time. Perhaps the most interesting thing about this development is that it is a bottom-up, consumer-driven change, at least in North America. In Europe, the opposite trend seems to be occurring, but the North American approach is much more efficient and much less costly.

The major implications here are for health care delivery and education. Health care and education, along with debt service, are now the major expenses of government. More and more medical expertise is being turned into information and sent out across networks. This makes possible greater preventive care and less expensive monitoring of patients at risk. Education is becoming much more personal and flexible, with many more choices open to individuals. Change will not come easily—particularly not in Canada, where the provincial and federal bureaucracies have such a tight lock on the system—but a continent-wide system rooted in information technology, pharmaceutical therapy and disease prevention will substantially change the current picture.

CHANGE #4

The other big change is the "dematerialization" of the economy: more and more "stuff" is being replaced by information. For instance, the huge quantities of chemical dyes and pesticides now in use are being substantially reduced by pest-resistant crops and fibres, such as cotton that can be grown to particular colour specifications. Biotechnologists are already working on products that can be "manufactured" in plant "factories" powered by sunlight. How about a plant that makes a plastic-like

substance that biodegrades? And there are others that produce specific pharmaceuticals. One implication is that small farmers will be able to manufacture for large companies, as it will take only a few acres of these new crops to produce the entire world supply of say, a new drug.

Decreased materializing and increased informationalizing is driving businesses to foster relationships with their employees as well as their customers. Businesses (finally!) want to have a long-term relationship with you, because they know that employees who walk out the door take their knowledge with them; unless a business satisfies its customers, they, too, will walk—right into the arms of myriad competitors. Business is also beginning to take responsibility for the whole product cycle. Instead of selling you a carpet, say, and letting you worry about disposing of it when it wears out, carpet companies will let you "lease" the carpet and offer you timely replacements, rather like the on-line relationship you are beginning to have with your software vendor. And businesses don't have to be big to have these relationships: buyer-seller confidence will become a huge advantage to smaller firms.

If we apply the rule—that innovation is the way change flows around resistance—to governments, are the gigantic revenue streams governments have counted on since World War II going to be there years from now? Electronic networks moving money around will drastically reduce governments' ability to force people to pay taxes. Local taxes will be easier to collect because people are inclined to pay for local services; sales and property taxes will be the most effective taxes left.

But how will this affect the income tax? Some governments will become very repressive and trash civil liberties in order to keep the money coming. But innovation will route economic energies around them. Eventually, you may be able to negotiate your income tax, and maybe other taxes, based on how much money you spend within a given region. Most of this will be truly voluntary, enforced the way that contracts are enforced now.

Most people will want to pay something to maintain the roads, bridges and other infrastructure. (Although, as with the PBS broadcasting system, there will be some free riders.) But governments will be unable to take more than a small proportion (maybe 25%) of GDP, except for specific, voter-subscriber programs.

This will be a shocking change for the public sector. Once they understand how the emerging forms of business are putting them in mortal danger, they will react, sometimes viciously. To enable these changes to become global, the institutions we have become used to will have to change profoundly, so here's another reality that will have to be acknowledged: the Southern, less developed countries will increasingly seek to use their power in international and regional forums to pry additional resources from the Northern, developed world. The North in turn will demand better guarantees, including strengthened institutions and more respect for human rights.

What are the implications for retirement investment? Simply this: the international arena is going to be very different 10 years from now, so thinking that what we see today is also the future is a risky strategy. Yet I think we are better prepared than ever before to make the changes that will be necessary. Things that may seem alarming because they are unexpected may really only be shaking up our preconceptions. So hang on for an interesting ride.

Historically, the international world is like a barroom brawl, with shifting alliances around the biggest sluggers. The real sluggers are those whose weapons are "cost-effective at the margin." The defining question is, "What does it cost to take out one of your opponents' weapons compared to its replacement cost?" Let's apply that question to our increasingly wired world. What is the cost for a hacker's army to attack your cybersystems? No more than the educational budget of a small town. What is the cost of its potential damage? Trillions of dollars, as traffic lights fail, bank-payment systems are compromised, and airline traffic control gets disrupted.

As well, the increasing importance of multilateral institutions has handed these developing countries a hammerlock on Western progress. Current international rules on the intellectual property of plants and the transborder shipment of genetically modified organisms essentially gives developing countries the right to shut down biotechnology—unless they get access to some of its benefits as owners rather than aid recipients.

These issues will inevitably get larger because, as Jeffrey Sachs argues, the West is trying to get globalization for nothing. Many southern-tier countries, which have not developed the institutions they need to participate fully in the modern world and are incapable of doing so without much more help than they are currently getting, now have a way of getting it.

And how does all this affect your retirement? Well, first think about the future of Canada. If these trends remain powerful, Canada looks more impressive as a region within North America —like Texas or California—than it does on its own. (Already we're more dependent on the U.S. market than those two states, each of which outweighs us in terms of GDP.)

Probably we will hang together as a diplomatic entity, but the Canadian dollar will disappear in reality if not formally. The Canadian dollar will become an acknowledged part of a North American money supply managed by the U.S. Federal Reserve Open Market Committee as a single money stock. The concept of "national unity" will be mainly folkloric. Instead, Ontario and British Columbia will anchor super-regions across relevant borderlands.

I don't foresee Canada being absorbed by the U.S. because we have a poison pill defence: Canada's unaffordable social programs and enfeebled regions (Quebec eastward). Canada will likely remain a great place to live and even retire in, but young people will seek more opportunity in the south, and the centre of NAFTA gravity will shift to the southwest. Over the next 10–20 years, Mexico will likely replace Canada as the U.S.'s largest trading partner. It's possible, therefore, that Canada's best days

as a country lie behind us; I'd like to be wrong on this.

Whatever happens, the future is going to be different. You can't do much about these changes but you can help armour-plate your investments against the downside. How? It's what most professional investors do every day: it's called "hedging." The essence of hedging is to find things to invest in that move in opposite directions: stocks vs. bonds, for example. Classically, when stocks go up, bond prices go down. This pulls interest rates up, which then moves stocks down.

Occasionally, the two move together. When that happens, money flows out of the exchanges to cash or to gold, or into the market from cash or gold. Gold is really a crummy investment: it's a bet against civilization. Gold serves no useful purpose, earns no interest, and has to be stored carefully under lock and key. Its only use for investors is that when civilization is breaking down, the price of gold shoots up and it's instantly convertible internationally. (In these circumstances, the price of other things, like toilet paper and cigarettes, goes up, too; but gold is easier to conceal on your person and won't disintegrate in bad weather.) Every retirement portfolio therefore should have some gold.

Basic hedging will safeguard your portfolio better than government guarantees of particular payouts. Government rule-making can only make hedging easier; it can't make your investments safe.

The hedging that professional traders do is a calculated counterweight to their original investment, designed to offset measurable risk. The kind of hedging I'm suggesting you do is similar, but because the future is really unpredictable, the amount of hedging you do is a judgment call. The basic idea, drawn from economist Thomas Schelling's law of market conservation, is that every sale has a buyer. If you diversify your holdings so that you own both sides of a transaction, you will have hedged your future well. In other words, your portfolio should have in it representation of the places money flows to as well as from. A four-way hedge to keep you solvent would include stocks and bonds,

reserve currency instruments (i.e., US$ vs. the euro)—and some gold, just in case. Safety lies in diversity. (When hedge funds collapse, it's because they didn't hedge.)

So there it is. The new world of retirement is more complicated than the old world, but it's also a lot more interesting.

APPENDIX 1

Your Family and
Financial Documents
Worksheets

Your Family Documents

PERSONAL DATA

Family name _____

Address _____

Phone_____ Fax _____

Internet _____

	FIRST NAME	DATE OF BIRTH	S.I.N.	MEDICARE
1.	_____	_____	_____	_____
2.	_____	_____	_____	_____
3.	_____	_____	_____	_____
4.	_____	_____	_____	_____
5.	_____	_____	_____	_____
6.	_____	_____	_____	_____

LOCATION OF:

Birth certificates _____

Citizenship papers _____

Marriage certificate _____

Divorce papers _____

Education records _____

DRIVER'S LICENCE NUMBERS

1. _____

2. _____

3. _____

REAL ESTATE

Home is in the name of _____

Mortgage is held by _____

Contact person _____

Address _____ Phone _____

Location of deed of sale _____

Renewal date _____

Mortgage will be paid off on _____

Property tax bills located _____

Home owner's insurance policy number _____

Location of policy _____

Amount of coverage _____

Contact person _____

Address _____

Phone _____ Fax _____

Property #2

Property is in the name of _____

Mortgage is held by _____

Contact person _____

Address _____

Phone _____ Fax _____

Location of deed of sale _____

Renewal date _____

Property tax bills located _____

Homeowner's insurance policy number _____

Location of policy _____

Amount of coverage _____

Contact person _____

Address _____

Phone _____ Fax _____

FINANCIAL RECORDS

Primary financial institution _____

Address _____

Account number _____ Type _____

Account in name of _____

Contact person _____

Phone _____ Fax _____

Safe deposit number _____   Key number _____

Names of persons with access to box _____

Contents _____

Account #2

Financial institution _____

Address _____

Account number _____   Type _____

Account in name of _____

Contact person _____

Phone _____   Fax _____

Safe deposit number _____   Key number _____

Names of persons with access to box _____

Contents _____

Account #3

Financial institution _____

Address _____

Account number _____   Type _____

Account in name of _____

Contact person _____

Phone _____   Fax _____

Safe deposit number _____   Key number _____

Names of persons with access to box _____

Contents _____

INSURANCE (life, health, disability, other)

Company _____

Policy number _____   Type _____

In name of _____

Broker/agent name _____

Phone _____   Fax _____

Address _____

Plan/coverage _____

Location of policy _____

Company _____

Policy number _____ Type _____

In name of _____

Broker/agent name _____

Phone _____ Fax _____

Address _____

Plan/coverage _____

Location of policy _____

Company _____

Policy number _____ Type _____

In name of _____

Broker/agent name _____

Phone _____ Fax _____

Address _____

Plan/coverage _____

Location of policy _____

Company _____

Policy number _____ Type _____

In name of _____

Broker/agent name _____

Phone _____ Fax _____

Address _____

Plan/coverage _____

Location of policy _____

AUTOMOBILES

Car #1

Owner _____

Model, year _____

Registration number _____ Location _____

Insurance policy number _____

In name of _____

Company _____ Coverage _____

Address _____

Contact person _____

Phone _____   Fax _____

Car #2

Owner _____

Model, year _____

Registration number _____   Location _____

Insurance policy number _____

In name of _____

Company _____   Coverage _____

Address _____

Contact person _____

Phone _____   Fax _____

CREDIT CARDS (BANK, STORE, ETC.)

Name _____

Card in name of _____

Account number _____

Phone no. of company _____

Name _____

Card in name of _____

Account number _____

Phone no. of company _____

Name _____

Card in name of _____

Account number _____

Phone no. of company _____

Name _____

Card in name of _____

Account number _____

Phone no. of company _____

Name _____

Card in name of _____

Account number _____

Phone no. of company _____

Name _____

Card in name of _____

Account number _____

Phone no. of company _____

Name _____

Card in name of _____

Account number _____

Phone no. of company _____

Name _____

Card in name of _____

Account number _____

Phone no. of company _____

Name _____

Card in name of _____

Account number _____

Phone no. of company _____

Name _____

Card in name of _____

Account number _____

Phone no. of company _____

INCOME TAX RECORDS

Tax preparer's/accountant's name _____

Address _____

Phone _____

Location of tax records (cancelled cheques, receipts, etc.)

_____

Location of copies of previous tax returns _____

WILLS

Will in the name of _____

Date of will _____ Drawn up by _____

Address _____

Phone _____

Location of original will _____

Location of 2nd copy _____

Will in the name of _____

Date of will _____ Drawn up by _____

Address _____

Phone _____

Location of original will _____

Location of 2nd copy _____

RETIREMENT RECORDS

Name _____

Employer plan _____

Address _____

Contact person _____ Phone _____

RRSP—institution _____ Account # _____

Address _____

Contact person _____ Phone _____

RRIF—institution _____ Account # _____

Address _____

Contact person _____ Phone _____

Brokerage account—institution _

Account # _____

Address _____

Contact person _____ Phone _____

Name _____

Employer plan _____

Address _____

Contact person _____ Phone _____

RRSP—institution _____

Account # _____

Address _____

Contact person _____   Phone _____

RRIF—institution _____   Account # _____

Address _____

Contact person _____   Phone _____

Brokerage account—institution _

Account # _____

Address _____

Contact person _____   Phone _____

INVESTMENTS

Stocks

Location _____

Broker's name _____

Address _____

Phone _____

Stock listings

Name _____   Date purchased _____

Quantity _____   Purchase price _____

Estimated value _____

Name _____   Date purchased _____

Quantity _____   Purchase price _____

Estimated value _____

Name _____   Date purchased _____

Quantity _____   Purchase price _____

Estimated value _____

Name _____   Date purchased _____

Quantity _____   Purchase price _____

Estimated value _____

Name _____   Date purchased _____
Quantity _____   Purchase price _____
Estimated value _____

Name _____   Date purchased _____
Quantity _____   Purchase price _____
Estimated value _____

Name _____   Date purchased _____
Quantity _____   Purchase price _____
Estimated value _____

Name _____   Date purchased _____
Quantity _____   Purchase price _____
Estimated value _____

Name _____   Date purchased _____
Quantity _____   Purchase price _____
Estimated value _____

MUTUAL FUNDS

Location _____
Broker's name _____
Address _____
Phone _____

Mutual fund listings

Name _____   Date purchased _____
Quantity _____   Purchase price _____
Estimated value _____

Name _____   Date purchased _____
Quantity _____   Purchase price _____
Estimated value _____

Name _____   Date purchased _____
Quantity _____   Purchase price _____
Estimated value _____

Name _____ Date purchased _____

Quantity _____ Purchase price _____

Estimated value _____

Name _____ Date purchased _____

Quantity _____ Purchase price _____

Estimated value _____

Name _____ Date purchased _____

Quantity _____ Purchase price _____

Estimated value _____

Name _____ Date purchased _____

Quantity _____ Purchase price _____

Estimated value _____

Name _____ Date purchased _____

Quantity _____ Purchase price _____

Estimated value _____

Name _____ Date purchased _____

Quantity _____ Purchase price _____

Estimated value _____

BONDS

Location _____

Broker's name _____

Address _____

Phone _____

Bond listings

Name _____ Date purchased _____

Amount _____ Purchase price _____

Maturity value _____ Date of maturity _____

Name _____ Date purchased _____

Amount _____ Purchase price _____

Maturity value _____ Date of maturity _____

Name _____   Date purchased _____

Amount _____   Purchase price _____

Maturity value _____   Date of maturity _____

Name _____   Date purchased _____

Amount _____   Purchase price _____

Maturity value _____   Date of maturity _____

Name _____   Date purchased _____

Amount _____   Purchase price _____

Maturity value _____   Date of maturity _____

OTHER INVESTMENTS

List by type of investment along with any pertinent data:

_____

_____

_____

_____

_____

_____

_____

_____

_____

_____

Your Retirement
Planning
Worksheets

WORKSHEET 1 Your Financial Documents

Personal income statement   *for the year ended* _____

Revenue:		MINUS	
Salary	$ _____	**Expenses:**	
Wages	$ _____	Mortgage/rent	$ _____
Commission	$ _____	Property taxes	$ _____
Dividends	$ _____	Utilities (heat, light,	
Interest	$ _____	phone, cable)	$ _____
Gifts	$ _____	Maintenance	$ _____
Fees	$ _____	Property insurance	$ _____
Sub Total	$ _____	Food	$ _____
	_____	Clothing	$ _____
	_____	Personal	$ _____
	_____	Car registration,	
	_____	licence	$ _____
	_____	Car payments	$ _____
	_____	Car operating costs	$ _____
	_____	Car insurance	$ _____
	_____	Public transit costs	$ _____
	_____	Life insurance	$ _____
	_____	Disability insurance	$ _____
	_____	Loan payments	$ _____
	_____	Credit card payments	$ _____
	_____	Education	$ _____
	_____	Medical, dental	$ _____
	_____	Gifts	$ _____
	_____	Entertainment	$ _____
	_____	Vacation travel	$ _____
	_____	Income taxes	$ _____
	_____	Savings	$ _____
	_____	Alimony, child	
	_____	support	$ _____
	_____	Other	$ _____
		Sub Total	$ _____
		EQUALS	
		Net income:	$ _____

Statement of retained earnings   *for the year ended* _____

Net worth balance . . . . $ _____

Add profit for the year (net income from
     personal income statement) . . . . $ _____

Subtract losses . . . . $ _____

Retained earnings balance . . . . $ _____

WORSHEET 2 Your Financial Documents

Monthly Budget

Revenue:

Salary	$ _____
Wages	$ _____
Commission	$ _____
Dividends	$ _____
Interest	$ _____
Gifts	$ _____
Fees	$ _____
Total	$ _____

Expenses:

Mortgage/rent	$ _____
Property taxes	$ _____
Utilities (heat, light, phone, cable)	$ _____
Maintenance	$ _____
Property insurance	$ _____
Food	$ _____
Clothing	$ _____
Personal	$ _____
Car registration, licence	$ _____
Car payments	$ _____
Car operating costs	$ _____
Car insurance	$ _____
Public transit costs	$ _____
Life insurance	$ _____
Disability insurance	$ _____
Loan payments	$ _____
Credit card payments	$ _____
Education	$ _____
Medical, dental	$ _____
Gifts	$ _____
Entertainment	$ _____
Vacation travel	$ _____
Income taxes	$ _____
Savings	$ _____
Alimony, child support	$ _____
Other	$ _____
Total	$ _____

WORKSHEET 3 Your Financial Documents

Personal balance sheet

Date: _____

Assets		Liabilities	
Cash on hand	$ _____	**Current bills outstanding**	
Chequing account	$ _____	Dentist	$ _____
Amounts owing to you	$ _____	Utility	$ _____
Car	$ _____	Credit cards	$ _____
House	$ _____	Charge accounts	$ _____
Vacation property	$ _____	Personal loans	$ _____
Jewellery	$ _____	Car payment	$ _____
Art/antiques	$ _____	Other loans	$ _____
Furniture	$ _____	Income tax	$ _____
Savings accounts	$ _____	Property tax	$ _____
Real estate	$ _____	Mortgage debt home	$ _____
Bonds	$ _____	other	$ _____
Stocks	$ _____	Other: _____	$ _____
Mutual funds	$ _____		
Company pension plan	$ _____	**Total liabilities**	$ _____
RRSP	$ _____		
RRIF	$ _____	**Net worth:**	
Other: _____	$ _____	**assets minus liabilities =**	$ _____
_____			
Total assets	$ _____		

WORKSHEET 4 Pre-Retirement Planning

CURRENT EXPENSES	WORKING	ESTIMATED AT RETIREMENT
Mortgage/rent		
Property taxes		
Utilities—heat, light, phone, cable		
Maintenance		
Property insurance		
Food		
Clothing		
Personal (hair, dry cleaning, etc.)		
Car registration, licence		
Car payments		
Car operating costs		
Car insurance		
Public transit costs		
Life insurance		
Disability insurance		
Loan payments		
Credit card payments		
Education		
Medical, dental		
Gifts—birthday, Christmas, etc.		
Contributions to charity, political parties, etc.		
Entertainment/recreation		
Vacation travel		
Income taxes		
Savings		
Alimony, child support		
Other		
Lump-sum payments for vacation home, etc.		
Financial assistance to others		
Inheritance		
Total		

CHART 8–2 **Number of Years in Retirement**

1. Your present age   _____
2. Your retirement age   _____
3. Years to retirement   _____   (#2 minus #1)
4. Life expectancy (Table 8–1) _____
5. Years in retirement   _____   (#4 minus #3)

WORKSHEET 5 Future Value of Retirement Expenses

Estimated expenses in retirement (from
   Worksheet 4)   _____

Multiplied by inflation factor (from Table 8–3,
   Inflation Factors)   _____

Equals the future value of your retirement expenses _____

WORKSHEET 6 Sources of Retirement Income

SOURCE	AMOUNT	GROWTH RATE	AMOUNT AT RETIREMENT
OAS		CPI index	
GIS		CPI index	
C/QPP		CPI index	
Pension from work		Estimate from work	
RRSP			
Other savings			
Earnings from work			
Total			
Assets			
Gifts/inheritances			
Home			

WORKSHEET 7 Retirement Balance Sheet

Estimated future value of retirement expenses
    (from Worksheet 5)   _____
OAS/GIS/C/QPP (from Worksheet 6)   – _____
Employment pension payments (annual)   – _____
Amount needed from savings each year   _____

WORKSHEET 8 Checklist

THINGS TO DO	WHEN BEGUN	REVISION #1	REVISION #2
Make a budget	_____	_____	_____
Think "after tax"	_____	_____	_____
Develop a savings goal	_____	_____	_____
Pay cash	_____	_____	_____
Establish a credit rating	_____	_____	_____
Have an emergency fund	_____	_____	_____
Start regular reading about the economy	_____	_____	_____
Organize your receipts	_____	_____	_____
Reevaluate your budget and financial plan once a year	_____	_____	_____
Get a good tax preparer	_____	_____	_____
Buy a home	_____	_____	_____
Buy insurance as needed	_____	_____	_____
Learn about investment choices	_____	_____	_____
Understand the equity market	_____	_____	_____
Invest for the long term	_____	_____	_____
Start serious tax planning	_____	_____	_____
Check the pension plans outside your control–defined benefit, C/QPP	_____	_____	_____
Make a will	_____	_____	_____
Review all financial aspects of your life once a year	_____	_____	_____

Tables

TABLE A3–1 **Annual Investment Needed to Equal $100,000**

	RATE OF RETURN				
AFTER YEAR	6%	8%	10%	12%	15%
5	$16,735	$15,785	$14,890	$14,055	$12,900
10	7,160	6,390	5,705	5,090	4,285
15	4,055	3,410	2,860	2,395	1,830
20	2,565	2,025	1,590	1,240	850
25	1,720	1,265	925	670	410

TABLE A3–2 **Growth of $10,000 Lump Sum Investment**

	RATE OF RETURN				
AFTER YEAR	6%	8%	10%	12%	15%
5	$13,380	$14,690	$16,105	$17,625	$20,115
10	17,910	21,590	25,935	31,060	40,455
15	23,965	31,720	41,770	54,735	81,370
20	32,070	46,610	67,275	96,460	163,665
25	42,915	68,485	108,345	170,000	329,190

TABLE A3–3 **Future Value of $1,200 Invested Annually**

	RATE OF RETURN				
AFTER YEAR	6%	8%	10%	12%	15%
5	$6,765	$7,040	$7,325	$7,625	$8,090
10	15,815	17,385	19,125	21,055	24,365
15	27,930	32,580	38,125	44,735	57,095
20	44,145	54,915	68,730	86,463	122,932
25	65,835	87,725	118,015	160,000	255,350

TABLE A5–4 **Future Value of $1 Lump Sum Investment**

$1 compounding annually

AFTER YEAR	1%	2%	3%	4%	5%	6%	7%	8%	9%	10%	12%	15%
1	1.01	1.02	1.03	1.04	1.05	1.06	1.07	1.08	1.09	1.10	1.12	1.15
2	1.02	1.04	1.06	1.08	1.10	1.12	1.14	1.17	1.19	1.21	1.25	1.32
3	1.03	1.06	1.09	1.12	1.16	1.19	1.23	1.26	1.30	1.33	1.40	1.52
4.	1.04	1.08	1.13	1.17	1.22	1.26	1.31	1.36	1.41	1.46	1.57	1.75
5	1.05	1.10	1.16	1.22	1.28	1.33	1.40	1.47	1.54	1.61	1.76	2.01
6	1.06	1.13	1.19	1.27	1.34	1.42	1.50	1.59	1.68	1.78	1.97	2.31
7	1.07	1.15	1.23	1.32	1.41	1.50	1.61	1.71	1.83	1.95	2.21	2.66
8	1.08	1.17	1.27	1.37	1.48	1.59	1.72	1.85	1.99	2.14	2.48	3.06
9	1.09	1.20	1.30	1.42	1.55	1.69	1.84	2.00	2.17	2.36	2.77	3.52
10	1.10	1.22	1.34	1.48	1.63	1.79	1.97	2.16	2.37	2.59	3.10	4.05
15	1.16	1.35	1.56	1.80	2.08	2.40	2.76	3.17	3.64	4.18	5.47	8.14
20	1.22	1.49	1.81	2.19	2.65	3.21	3.87	4.66	5.60	6.73	9.65	16.37
25	1.28	1.64	2.09	2.67	3.39	4.29	5.43	6.85	8.62	10.84	17.00	32.92

Example: $100 invested now at 8% compounded annually for 30 years would accumulate to (10.06) ($100) = $1,006.

TABLE A3–5 **Future Value of $1 Invested Annually**

	RATE OF RETURN				
YEAR	6%	8%	10%	12%	15%
1	$1.00	1.00	1.00	1.00	1.00
2	2.06	2.08	2.10	2.12	2.15
3	3.18	3.24	3.31	3.37	3.47
4	4.37	4.51	4.54	4.78	4.99
5	5.64	5.86	6.10	6.36	6.74
6	5.97	7.33	7.71	8.11	8.75
7	8.39	8.92	9.49	10.09	11.07
8	9.69	10.64	11.43	12.29	13.73
9	11.49	12.48	13.58	14.77	16.78
10	13.16	14.48	15.93	17.55	20.30
15	23.27	27.15	31.77	37.28	47.58
20	36.78	45.76	57.27	72.05	102.44
25	54.86	73.10	98.34	133.33	212.79

TABLE A3–6 **Individual Income Tax Rates for 1998**

Federal

TAXABLE INCOME	TAX	MARGINAL RATE ON EXCESS
$1	$0	17.0%
29,590	5,030	26.0
59,180	12,724	29.0

These rates exclude the federal surtax of 3% of federal tax and the high income surtax of 5% of federal tax in excess of $12,500.

For 1998, the 3% general surtax is reduced by an amount equal to the lesser of 50% of the 3% federal surtax before the reduction and the amount by which $125 exceeds 3% of the federal tax over $8,333.

Provincial

RESIDENT OF	% OF BASIC FEDERAL TAX	
Alberta	44.0%	(a)
British Columbia	50.5	(b)
Manitoba	51.0	(c)
New Brunswick	61.0	(d)
Newfoundland	69.0	(e)
Northwest Territories	45.0	
Nova Scotia	57.5	(f)
Ontario	42.7	(g)
Prince Edward Island	59.5	(h)
Saskatchewan	49.0	(i)
Yukon	50.0	(j)
Non-residents	52.0	(k)

(a) Alberta imposes an 8% surtax on Alberta tax payable over $3,500, plus a flat tax of 0.5% of taxable income.

(b) British Columbia imposes a high income surtax of 30% of British Columbia tax over $5,300, plus 26% of British Columbia tax over $8,600.

(c) Manitoba charges a 2% tax on net income, plus a 2% surtax if net income exceeds $30,000.

(d) New Brunswick imposes a high income surtax of 8% of New Brunswick tax payable over $13,500.

(e) Newfoundland imposes a high income surtax of 10% of provincial tax over $7,900.

(f) Nova Scotia imposes a high income surtax of 10% of provincial tax over $10,000.

(g) Ontario levies a surtax of 20% of Ontario tax over $4,057.50, plus 33% of Ontario tax over $5,217.50.

(h) Prince Edward Island imposes a high income surtax of 10% of Prince Edward Island tax over $5,200.

(i) Saskatchewan imposes a flat tax of 2% of net income, and a 10% surtax on Saskatchewan tax payable (including the flat tax). In addition, a high income surtax of 15% is levied on

Saskatchewan tax payable (including the flat tax) in excess of $4,000.

(j) The Yukon imposes a surtax of 5% of territorial tax over $6,000.

(k) Non-residents are subject to an additional federal tax in lieu of provincial tax where provincial tax is not applicable.

QUEBEC TAXABLE INCOME	TAX	MARGINAL RATE ON EXCESS
$1	$0	20%
25,000	5,000	23
50,000	10,750	26

Residents (as of December 31) of provinces other than Quebec must pay provincial tax at the indicated rate upon their basic federal tax.

Residents of Quebec receive an abatement of 16.5% of basic federal tax (after deducting personal and dividend tax credits), but must pay Quebec income tax at the indicated rates.

A 0.3% anti-poverty surtax is also payable for 1997 and subsequent taxation years.

TABLE A3–7 **Federal Individual Tax Credits for 1998**

Non-refundable personal tax credits

	AMOUNT	17% CREDIT
Basic	$6,456	$1,098
Supplementary personal	$500/$1,000 (a)	$85/$170
Age 65	$3,482 (b)	$592
Disability	$4,233	$720
Married or equivalent-to-married	$5,380	$915
Net income threshold	$538	
Disabled dependants over 18	$2,353	$400
Caregiver		$400 (c)
Net income threshold	$11,500	

(a) For single persons and married persons who are the sole income earners in their families, the supplementary personal credit is reduced at a rate of 4% of income over $6,956. For a married person whose spouse has income, the credit is further reduced by the lesser of $85 and 17% of the spouse's income over $6,956. For 1998, the credit is 50% of the amount otherwise determined.

(b) Eroded by 15% of 1998 net income over $25,921; credit is unavailable once 1998 net income exceeds $49,134.

(c) The caregiver tax credit is reduced by 17% of the dependant's income for the year over $11,500.

APPENDIX 4

Glossary

Annuity An agreement or contract issued by an insurance company that pays a specified amount of money for a specified time in exchange for a lump-sum payment on issuance of the contract. Most often used in retirement to ensure an income for life or for a shorter period.

Arbitrage The simultaneous purchase and sale of a commodity, security or basket of securities in two different markets in order to profit from price discrepancies.

Arm's-length transaction Any transaction presumed to be conducted by two parties who are independent of each other. For example, the purchase of widgets by Company A, a retail store in Canada, from Company B, a separate and distinct firm in Germany.

Asset allocation The process of deciding what proportion of an individual's or an institution's assets will be held in various categories such as stocks, bonds, real estate, commodities, etc.

Attribution rules Provisions in the Income Tax Act that discourage income splitting. The rules have the effect of attributing the income earned by a gift back to the original owner, so that it is taxed in the original owner's hands, even though the income was not received.

Beneficiary A person who benefits from something. For example, a person named in a will to receive the benefits of the distribution of assets of the deceased person.

Bond An interest-bearing certificate of public or private indebtedness.

Bracket creep The process whereby a taxpayer is moved into a higher tax bracket, not because his or her income has increased but because the government does not compensate for inflation below 3%. Since 1992, this practice has transferred about $20 billion from Canadian taxpayers to government.

Canada Health and Social Transfer Act (CHST) Part of the federal-provincial Fiscal Arrangements Act legislated in 1996 to replace the Established Program Financing Act (which covered not only health, but post-secondary education as well) and the Canada Assistance Plan (federal transfers for social assistance). Funding is provided in the form of cash transfers and tax point transfers (a reduction of federal tax rates allowing provinces to raise additional revenues without increasing the overall tax burden on Canadians).

Capital gains or losses The difference between the cost of an asset and the proceeds when it's sold. If the sale price is higher than the cost, a capital gain is made; if the sale price is lower than the cost, a capital loss is made.

Capital markets Securities markets trading in equities and fixed-income assets.

Clawback The process of taxing back government benefits at a specified income level in order to maintain the appearance of the universality of the government programs.

Contribution holiday A circumstance in which a pension plan sponsor has actuarial assurance that the pension fund has surplus to the promise to members; the sponsor can then apply to the regulators to stop making contributions to the fund.

Contribution room The amount of money you are permitted to invest in your RRSP in a given tax year. Since 1990, you are allowed to carry over from previous years any money you were entitled to contribute to an RRSP but did not. Your contribution room is stated on the back page of the "notice of assessment" form you get from the government after they have reviewed your past year's income tax return. You can phone Revenue Canada's TIPS line, listed in your phone book, to get your up-to-date contribution room.

CPP (Canada Pension Plan) A compulsory, earnings-related federal pension plan, legislated in 1966, that covers all employed members of the labour force between the ages of 18 and 65. It is payable at age 65, and is interchangeable with the Quebec Pension Plan, legislated in Quebec in 1965 for residents of Quebec. A partial pension is available at age 60, as are disability and death benefits. The CPP and QPP are pay-as-you-go plans in which current payments are made out of current revenues.

Critical illness insurance An insurance policy that pays the face value directly to policy holders who survive 30 days after diagnosis of one of several medical conditions. Sometimes called "dread disease" insurance.

Deficit spending Spending, usually by a government, in excess of income.

Defined benefit plan A pension plan providing a pension whose amount is guided by a defined benefit formula, usually related to the years of employment and the salary attained.

Defined contribution plan A pension plan providing a pension whose amount is guided by the contributions of the employee and employer and by the income those invested funds have earned. Sometimes called a money-purchase plan, it operates like a group RRSP.

Deflation A fall in the general level of prices in an economy.

De-listing The process of removing from a specific list the name of someone or something previously on it. For example, a company can be de-listed from a stock exchange on which it was trading if it breaks the rules of the exchange; a pharmaceutical drug can be de-listed from a provincial formulary that pays for named prescription drugs.

Demand-side economics A view of economics, widely attributed to John Maynard Keynes, that focuses on total spending in the economy (called aggregate demand) and its effects on output and inflation. A primary tenet of demand-side economics is government intervention in the economy through the use of tax and interest rates. *See also* Keynes, John Maynard.

Devaluation A central bank-decreed decrease in the exchange value of a currency.

Discretionary income Income that remains after taxes and all essential spending on food, clothing and shelter have been accounted for.

Disinflation A reduction in the rate of inflation. *See also* inflation, deflation.

Dissaving Spending on consumable goods and services in excess of disposable income.

Employer-sponsored pension plan A pension plan offered by an employer, registered (RPP), and most often administered by the employer.

English form will The most common form of will, based on the laws of England. *See also* Holographic will, Notarial will.

Equity Shares of ownership that permit the owner to share in the fortunes of the company or property.

Estate freezing A legal way to freeze the value of your assets at a specific date and shift all future growth of the assets to your children or others younger than yourself. A tax-planning device to minimize taxes at death.

Estate planning The process of arranging your financial affairs so that at death your assets are distributed according to your wishes. The process is usually undertaken to minimize taxes at death.

Executor A person or company named in a will to carry out the instructions of the deceased person and administer the estate until the deceased's wishes are carried out.

Fair market value A disposition, for tax purposes, which may or may not have actually taken place. For example, at death, assets in an estate are valued according to what they could bring if they were sold in the marketplace. That is the value on which tax is calculated. The assets do not have to be sold.

Financial power of attorney A legal document that gives a named person the right to manage the financial affairs of the person who signed the power of attorney. It has a very limited life. As long as you are alive and in charge, the document has no authority. If you are temporarily or permanently unable to look after your financial affairs, the power of attorney gives that power to the person you named. If you die, the power of attorney dies with you. *See also* will.

Fixed exchange rate A rate of exchange of a currency that is allowed to fluctuate only according to fixed government rules.

Fixed-income investment An investment that yields a fixed amount of money. Typically, an investor buys an asset, such as a bond, whose characteristic is that it is a promise to pay the fixed income for the period during which the investor's money is unavailable to him, and then to repay the investor's capital.

Floating exchange rate A rate of exchange of a currency that is determined by the supply of and demand for the currency, rising and falling without government intervention.

Foreign direct investment (FDI) Investment by non-residents to establish or control an enterprise. FDI is distinguished from portfolio investment, which involves buying stocks and bonds.

Futures contracts A standard agreement that commits a party to buy or sell specified goods at a specified price, for delivery at a specified time in the future.

Futures market A clearing house that stands between the buyers and sellers of futures contracts and guarantees that both get what they contracted for. For example, a farmer who sells a futures contract may commit to deliver wheat in six or nine months. He does not have to find a bread company that wants to buy wheat; he and the bread maker will independently sell and buy on the futures market. In a world of volatile prices, both the buyer and seller of futures contracts do so to "lock in" their price for the product. Futures market speculators buy and sell contracts based on their belief that prices will rise or fall in the future.

GATT (General Agreement on Tariffs and Trade) A trade agreement reached in 1947 by 23 nations (including Canada), in which each agreed to reduce tariffs through multilateral negotiations, eliminate import quotas, and generally not discriminate against other countries' goods. The GATT has been superseded by the World Trade Organization, to which almost 100 nations now belong. *See also* WTO.

GIS (Guaranteed Income Supplement) An amendment to the Old Age Security Act that provides for an additional income for pensioners with little or no other income.

Globalization The combined effect of three simultaneous revolutions: the economic integration after WW II as multinationals invested worldwide; the technology revolution, especially the development of computer chips and modems; and the supply-side revolution in public finance.

Hedging Protecting a position in the market against adverse price fluctuations. This can be accomplished by buying or selling contracts in the underlying asset (a stock, a currency, a commodity, a portfolio) in the futures or options market.

Holographic will A handwritten will, signed and dated by the testator and witnessed by no one. Some provinces do not recognize the validity of a holographic will.

Intestacy rules Provincial laws that dictate how an estate is divided when no will is found.

Investment house *See* Securities Firm.

Investment style The basic investing philosophy of a mutual fund or asset manager.

Keynes, John Maynard English economist (1883–1946). So influential was Keynes between 1915 and 1946 that a whole school of economic thought bears his name. His criticism of the Treaty of Versailles (which laid out the penalties Germany had to pay after World War I) foretold of WW II. During the Great Depression, Keynes revolutionized economic thinking by urging governments to spend money to keep demand high; this was the creation of "deficit spending." After WW II Keynes was one of the architects of the postwar system of fixed exchange rates.

Key person insurance Insurance purchased by a firm on the key person in the organization, to cover the costs of replacing that person should he or she die or be incapacitated.

Life annuity A contract issued by an insurance company in exchange for a lump-sum payment that guarantees a monthly income for the life of the annuitant.

Life income fund (LIF) A more restrictive RRIF, but one you have to use if you have a "locked in" retirement account. There are both minimum and maximum amounts to withdraw. Whereas with a RRIF you never have to give up control of the investments in your plan until you die, with a LIF you have to buy a life annuity in the year in which you turn 80. *See also* Registered retirement income fund.

Life retirement income fund (LRIF) Available only in Saskatchewan and Alberta. *See* Locked-in retirement account.

Liquidity The ease with which an asset can be converted into cash.

Living will A document that gives instructions as to how you are going to die. As long as you are alive and in command of your faculties, you can tell your doctors what treatments you want or don't want. However, if you are unconscious or mentally incapacitated, doctors assume you agree to any and all treatments and so-called heroic measures they have at their disposal. A living will is your statement of what treatment and how much you want. If you have created a personal-care power of attorney, the person you've named can put forward your desires regarding, for example, being kept alive on mechanical support systems or not. It can also document your desires regarding, for example, pain

medications and organ donation. Not all provinces consider living wills to be legal documents, but even if you live in one that does not, such a document gives your family greater understanding of what treatment you would have accepted or refused had you been able to.

Locked-in retirement account A company's retirement account in which your pension benefits are "locked in" until you are 55. The money cannot be transferred to an ordinary RRSP or RRIF, which can be collapsed at any time; however, it can be transferred to a locked-in RRSP or a locked-in retirement account. The rules governing locked-in accounts both before and after retirement are more stringent than those governing ordinary registered accounts.

Maturity ladder An investment strategy that involves buying a series of assets with varying payout dates in order to create a steady income stream; can be purchased at a deep discount to its face value.

Medicare Health care paid for out of pooled tax revenues.

Money market fund A mutual fund whose portfolio holds not stocks but money market instruments: Treasury bills, certificates of deposits, commercial paper, bankers' acceptances—all low-risk, highly liquid debt of government and businesses with relatively short maturity dates.

Money-purchase plan *See* defined contribution plan.

Mutual fund A pool of money put together by a money manager and invested in a specified type of asset: equities, mortgages, bonds, etc. Purchasers of the mutual fund receive "units" of the fund (not unlike shares of a company), which have a net asset value (not unlike the price of a share). Open-end funds are continually issuing units to anyone who wants to buy them; closed-end funds reach a certain size and cease selling more units.

NAFTA North American Free Trade Agreement Pact signed in 1992 that will gradually eliminate most tariffs and other trade barriers on products and services passing between Canada, U.S. and Mexico.

National accounts The product of a social accounting measurement system that purports to measure the overall production performance of the economy. Widely criticized by several groups, mostly on the basis that it is outdated (it doesn't include environmental costs, or non-arm's-length transactions, etc.).

Networked enterprise A firm whose organization and production processes are integrated through the use of strategic alliances, joint ventures, cross-licensing and other, less formal agreements with other firms or even divisions of competing firms.

Networking Using networks to achieve competitive advantage. Networking has two properties firms and markets don't have. One is the increasing benefit to the whole membership from additional individual members. The other is simultaneous transmission: knowledge attained anywhere in the system is available to everyone in the system.

Non-tariff barrier A regulation designed to keep foreign goods out of a country. Examples include licensing requirements, unreasonable standards for product quality and safety, and red tape in customs procedures.

Notarial will A will, available only in Quebec, that is probated in advance of death, by a notary of the court. Many other provinces do not recognize the validity of a notarial will.

OAS (Old Age Security) A federal, taxpayer-funded pension plan payable to all Canadians who have lived in Canada a total of 40 years after their 18th birthday. In recent years, it has been subject to tax at progressively higher rates. For an income of about $85,000, OAS is taxed at a rate of 100%. (*See also* clawback).

OECD (Organization for Economic Co-operation and Development) An organization created in 1960 to supersede the Organization for European Economic Co-operation. The OEEC focused its activities from 1948 to 1960 on the reconstruction of the war-damaged economies of Western Europe. In 1960, the 24 member countries, including Canada, constituted a "club" of the world's most highly developed and richer countries, conducting research and making recommendations on common approaches to economic and trade policy issues.

OPEC (Organization of Petroleum Exporting Countries) A cartel formed between Venezuela, Iran, Kuwait, Iraq and Saudi Arabia in 1960 to obtain higher oil prices. In 1974, joined by seven other nations, it was responsible for reducing production sufficiently to raise oil prices from under US$10 a barrel to over US$25 a barrel. Since then, the colluding countries, of which Saudi Arabia is the largest producer, have had only sporadic success in raising the price of oil.

Open market operations The effect that central banks have on the supply of money in circulation by buying or selling government securities. For example, if the Bank of Canada sells $500 million of government securities, it puts that money in the chartered banks. The banks keep a small percentage as mandated "reserves" and lend out the rest. The central bank's injection of cash is thus multiplied many times over.

Outsourcing The process of contracting with another firm to provide a good or service that was previously provided inside the organization. Outsourcing can by anything that the firm believes can be provided cheaper or better than it can do itself, from accounting services to subcomponents to distribution services.

Participation rate The number of a given set of people in the labour force as a percentage of the number in that set available to work. For example, the participation rate of women in the work force is 58%.

Pay-as-you-go pension plan A pension plan, such as the Canada and Quebec Pension Plans, that depends on the contributions of working members to pay the pensions of the retirees.

Pension adjustment An adjustment to the amount individuals who contribute to a pension plan at work can contribute to an RRSP, by deducting the amount contributed at work from the amount allowed by government. The formula has, for many years, penalized people who have contributory pension plans at work.

Pension adjustment reversal A recalculation of a pension adjustment by an employer, on the termination of an employee of a contributory plan, to allow the employee to belatedly contribute more to his or her RRSP. Introduced by the federal government in 1998.

Personal-care power of attorney A relatively new type of document that empowers someone you trust (rather than a stranger from the government) to make decisions about how you'll be looked after if you become incapacitated. In provinces that have accepted "living wills," a power of attorney for personal care can be incorporated into the financial power of attorney. The provinces are in various states of acceptance of this type of document.

Power of Attorney *See* financial power of attorney.

Probate The process of proving to the court that a document such as a will is authentic. *See also* will.

QPP *See* CPP.

Reverse mortgage A contract in which a financial institution will make regular payments to a retired home owner based on the value of the home. Typically the institution will advance about 40% of the value of the home and add mortgage payments to the loan, and upon the death of the owner, have the loan repaid with the proceeds from the sale of the property.

Right of survivorship An arrangement under which two people, typically parent and child or marriage partners, jointly own an asset such that, when one of the pair dies, the other automatically becomes the sole owner.

Risk-reward The trade-off between buying higher-risk assets and earning higher rates of return.

Securities firm An organization created to deal in securities, by either underwriting new issues of securities or acting as an intermediary between buyers and sellers of stocks and bonds.

Securitization The process of packaging a basket of debt instruments and selling pieces of them in the equity market. For example, a portfolio of mortgages can be bundled together, divided into smaller units and then sold to smaller investors, thus freeing money to the original mortgage holder.

Settlor A person who creates a trust.

Stock-index futures A financial instrument that creates an obligation to buy or sell an underlying asset, in this case, the index of a basket of stocks. The Standard & Poor's 500 Index, the Value Line Index and the New York Stock Exchange Composite Index are all traded in the futures markets. They are used primarily by investors who are hedging their positions in the stock market and by speculators who believe that futures indexes lead market turns. *See also* hedging, liquidity.

Subsidy A transfer of funds by a government, firm or individual to defray the costs incurred by the recipient. For example, the federal government provides floor prices to farmers for many of their commodities

to stabilize their incomes, and provides non-commercial financing to exporters to enable them to develop export markets. Payments to domestic producers that reduce the prices of their products so they can compete internationally also cost money and weaken a country's capacity to earn money abroad.

Supply-side economics A view of economics that emphasizes the impact of tax rates on the incentives for people to produce and use goods efficiently. Supply-side proponents believe that lower tax rates reduce tax avoidance and evasion and enlarge the tax base. There is widespread acceptance of the view that tax rates in excess of 40% are a destructive influence on the incentive of people to work and use resources wisely. During the 1980s and early '90s, dozens of countries reduced personal tax rates. *See also* demand-side economics.

Tax avoidance The legal act of minimizing taxes payable; the purpose of tax planning.

Tax bracket A given taxable income level and corresponding tax rate. As your taxable income increases, so does the percentage of tax you pay. Tax brackets are also called marginal tax brackets because the higher tax rate applies to the additional income at the margin of the higher bracket.

Tax credit An amount subtracted from your tax payable. It differs from a tax deduction in that it is not part of the calculation of your taxable income. For example, eligible persons are entitled to claim a refundable tax credit equal to $500 or 25% of eligible expenses, whichever is less.

Tax deduction An amount the tax laws allow you to deduct from your taxable income. For example, if you have a home office out of which you run a business, the expenses associated with running the office can be deducted from your taxable income.

Tax-deferred investment An investment on which the tax laws allow you to defer paying tax. The longer you can defer tax on an asset, the longer you can use the tax money for investing.

Tax evasion The commission or omission of an act knowingly with the intent to deceive so that the tax reported by the taxpayer is less than the tax payable under the law, or a conspiracy to commit such an offence.

Tax-exempt investment An investment, such as (in Canada) your principal residence, that the tax laws have exempted from taxes.

Tax liability The amount of tax you owe. Specifically referred to in tax and estate planning to estimate the amount of tax your estate will owe at your death. Often, term insurance is purchased to pay the tax so that your assets will not have to be sold.

Tax-preferred investment An investment, such as one that yields interest income, that is taxed less heavily than ordinary income.

Tax shelter An investment that is encouraged by government and therefore treated preferentially under certain tax-law incentives that maximize deductions and minimize taxable income.

Taylorism An economic theory named for Frederick Taylor, who studied the addition to productivity of precise timing and movement. Taylorism led to "efficiency experts," the world's first management consultants, and set the pattern for precise job descriptions.

T-bill (Treasury bill) A short-term (up to 364 days) obligation of the government. T-bills are typically sold at a discount to their face value. The difference between their cost and face value is their yield.

Term certain annuity A type of contract issued by an insurance company that agrees to pay an income for a specified term (for example, to age 90) in exchange for a lump-sum payment.

Term insurance Life insurance that is rented for a specified term, after which it can be renewed or else terminates. Typically used by young families with dependents and few assets, because the premium is lower than permanent or "whole life" insurance, and by older people in estate planning mode to secure the cash to cover their tax liability at death. *See also* whole life insurance.

Testator The author of a will.

Trust The instruction that places legal control of assets with a trustee who administers them on behalf of the beneficiary.

Trustee The person who administers assets in a trust for another person. Trustees can be named by the person who set up the trust or by the court.

Underground economy The sum of activities conducted by people who barter goods and services or pay cash in order to evade taxes. The size of the underground economy is difficult to measure accurately because

of the covert activities of as varied a group as average citizens who pay their house cleaners in cash to drug dealers and organized criminals.

Unfunded liability The total amount of money a pension plan needs but does not have in hand to pay the members of the plan the promise of the pension.

Universal life insurance A hybrid life insurance policy that combines life insurance with a savings component. The savings component can include investments selected by the policy holder or by the insurance company.

Whole life insurance Insurance that has a permanent life-insured component and a savings component. The premiums stay the same for the life of the contract. The savings component accumulates and eventually has a cash value to the owner if the policy is cancelled.

Will The legally enforceable declaration of a person's wishes for the distribution of their assets at death.

Withholding tax A sum of money, usually a percentage of the total value of an asset, that is withheld by a trustee acting as an agent of the government. For example, when an RRSP is collapsed and the money withdrawn, the trustee of the RRSP withholds a percentage of the proceeds to remit to government. When the RRSP owner completes his or her income tax return, the amount withheld is subtracted from the total tax owed.

WTO The World Trade Organization. An international organization designed to supervise and liberalize world trade. Signed in 1995 by almost 100 nations, the WTO is the successor to the GATT.

Index